"Excellent presentation skills are
continuous change. This book is
presentation skills and for enhan
effectiveness."

—William R. Sigmund, II, M
Worldwide Medical, Pfizer, Inc.

"You'd think that there would be nothing new to say about public speaking, but in every chapter, Dorothy Leeds has new ideas on how to be a better presenter. She takes you to new heights."

—Les Brown, author of *Live Your Dreams* and *It's Not Over 'Til You Win*

"Whether you're a corporate executive, stock broker, teacher, salesperson—or are trying to figure out what it is you are meant to do—this book will add to your success."

—Terrie M. Williams, Founder & President of The Stay Strong Foundation, and author of *A Plentiful Harvest: Creating Balance & Harmony Through the Seven Living Virtues*

"What a great book! In a concise, easy-to-read format, Dorothy Leeds gives us a tremendously useful work on an all-important topic. Anyone interested in personal and professional growth can benefit immensely from this book."

—Nido R. Qubein, author of *Stairway to Success* and *How to Be a Great Communicator*

"PowerSpeak is the most useful, most comprehensive, and best book on public speaking that I have ever read. It's packed with invaluable advice for everyone from the novice to the polished platform professional, and it's written by someone who practices what she preaches to perfection. What a terrific book!""

—Michael LeBoeuf, Ph.D., author of *How to Win Customers and Keep Them for Life* and *The Perfect Business*

"PowerSpeak is a 'must-read' for anyone seeking to improve or fine tune his/her presentation skills. From everyday communications to business presentations, the tools and tips included in the book allow individuals to be at the top of their game to engage and impress their audiences."

—Theresa M. Moore, Director ESPN/ABC Sports Customer Marketing and Sales

POWER SPEAK

Engage, Inspire, and Stimulate Your Audience

DOROTHY LEEDS

Tata McGraw-Hill Publishing Company Limited
NEW DELHI

McGraw-Hill Offices

New Delhi New York St Louis San Francisco Auckland Bogotá Caracas
Kuala Lumpur Lisbon London Madrid Mexico City Milan Montreal
San Juan Santiago Singapore Sydney Tokyo Toronto

Tata McGraw-Hill Edition 2004

RZDYCRAIRXCYQ

Reprinted in India by arrangement with The Career Press.

Sales territories: India, Pakistan, Nepal, Bangladesh, Sri Lanka and Bhutan

Library of Congress Cataloging-in-Publication Data

Leeds. Dorothy
PowerSpeak : engage, inspire, and stimulate your audience / by Dorothy Leeds.
p. cm.
Includes bibliographical references and index.
ISBN 1-56414-684-7 (paper)
1.Public speaking. I. Title.
PN4129.15.L44 2003
808.5'1—dc21 2003046059

ISBN 0-07-058860-0

Published by Tata McGraw-Hill Publishing Company Limited, 7 West Patel Nagar, New Delhi 110 008, and printed at Krishna Offset, Delhi 110 032

The McGraw·Hill Companies

To my very special,
supportive, funny, loyal, devoted husband,
Arnold Weinstock.
And to my exceptional, talented children,
Laura Julie Weinstock and Ian Jeremy Weinstock.
They are always engaging, stimulating, and inspiring
and are a constant source of joy and love.

Special thanks and deep appreciation to:

PJ Dempsey, my very special editor and friend, who was the first one to realize the power of PowerSpeak.

Eve Collyer, the greatest speech teacher of them all.

Bob Shook, for his ongoing advice and support.

Nancy Lauterbach, for her belief and sharing her amazing contacts.

Sharyn Kolberg, for her constructive and encouraging editorial help.

Liza Lentini, who not only is a brilliant playwright and teacher, but a super speech coach too.

Michael LeBoeuf, for his constant advice, warm friendship, and funny jokes.

Angie Howard, for her initial belief in my ability to teach public speaking.

Jane Dystal and Michael Bourret, for their hard work, support, and encouragement.

And the staff at Career Press for believing in this book.

To all the associations, corporations, and universities who graciously provide me a platform upon which to practice the PowerSpeak system.

To all my friends and colleagues who so kindly endorse and practice the PowerSpeak concepts.

Contents

Part III: Conquer the Trouble Spots: The Basics—Openings, Transitions, Conclusions, Questions and Answers, and Visual Aids, 103

Part IV: Master the Fine Points of Powerful Speaking, 165

Part V: Special Speaking Situations, 209

Part VI: Success Is Turning Knowledge Into Positive Action. Keep Growing!, 253

Preface

When I first wrote this book, I asked myself, "Why another book on public speaking?" As a teacher of public speaking, I looked at the books available on this subject, and I found that not one book answered all my questions. I would have needed at least four different texts, so I decided to include all the necessary material in one book for myself, my students, and the companies and associations for whom I work. This is more than a book on public speaking: This is a book to help people who *communicate* learn how to make those *communications* more engaging, more stimulating, and more inspiring. After all, my motto is NEVER BE BORING.

So why revise the book now? Has speaking changed since 1988? Yes and no. People are still making the same major speaking faults and bumping up against the same trouble spots. True, there is a lot of new technology out there to make presentations jazzier, but speakers are still not much better at communicating their ideas than they were 15 years ago. Many books on the subject have been published since then, but I still found them lacking. So I decided to update *PowerSpeak* for the same reasons I wrote it in the first place.

The title *PowerSpeak* refers to adding power to all your speaking—being persuasive whether you are serving customers, talking to subordinates, or hoping to talk your boss into a raise. Many of the chapters in this book (that is, those on power language and body language) refer to topics that can be used in all types of everyday communication, not just platform speaking.

PowerSpeak is not only for people who make formal presentations. It is for teachers, for salespeople, and for anyone who conducts or participates in meetings. It is a book to make us all aware of the accessible and wonderful tools at our disposal. With persuasive speaking becoming so important and valued a skill, this book fills the need for a simple but complete text.

Through my years as an actress, an executive, and a speaker, I searched for easy ways to get information across to others and to help others use the value of speaking as I used it to help myself. Through words and a strong delivery—although I am only 5' 1"—I am able to command an audience.

If you don't have the attention of the other person or persons, you are not communicating. No matter how good your idea, if it doesn't get through or doesn't get sold, you are not communicating. To be an effective speaker, you must be persuasive. You must be a salesperson with words, and with ideas. This is the basic concept strongly and uniquely addressed by the PowerSpeak system.

Introduction

What You Need to Know Before You Read *PowerSpeak*

Make thyself a craftsman in speech, for thereby thou shalt gain the upper hand.

—Inscription found in a 3,000-year-old Egyptian tomb

If you can't tell a book by its cover, at least the title should make clear what you are getting for your money. *PowerSpeak: Engage, Inspire, and Stimulate Your Audience* promises—and delivers—a lot.

I have designed this book to be an all-encompassing aid for *anyone* who has to speak in public, whether that means a meeting with your boss, an important phone call, or a formal presentation to a hundred people. You can follow the chapters in order as in a course text, or you can study them one at a time, as you need them. If you do all the projects, follow the self-evaluations, and practice the exercises included, I guarantee you will become a Power Speaker.

PowerSpeak addresses a problem that almost everyone in the business world today faces: how to increase your personal and professional "power" in order to make more sales, to move up to a better position, or to be more effective in your present position. The way you speak greatly affects how you are perceived in meetings, during phone conversations, and in all your daily one-on-one relationships.

Everyone wants to be considered strong, confident, dynamic, and convincing. The "power" in the title comes from how people perceive you: Effective communicators are *perceived* as more powerful than their less verbal counterparts. Getting this power to work for you involves two steps:

recognizing how crucial public speaking is and then improving your own abilities. This book is designed to sharpen those abilities in a way different from that of any other book on the market.

Not Just a Book—A Complete Course

I have designed this book to answer all the questions that have come up during my years of teaching and to provide practical and professional techniques to be a complete guide to public-speaking success. The book is divided into the following six sections:

1. *Getting ready.* Why speaking adds to your power, how to banish fear, and how to prepare a presentation thoroughly.
2. *The six major speaking faults.* What they are and how to avoid them. This fault system works because people learn more quickly if they focus on what to *avoid,* rather than study a long list of the things they need to do right.
3. *The trouble spots.* An in-depth look at the mechanics of openings, transitions, conclusions, questions and answers, and visual aids.
4. *The fine points.* These chapters are filled with expert tips on power words and language, handling humor, stage managing, improving body language, and more.
5. *Special speaking situations.* Handling the media, audio- and video-conferencing, reading a speech, and moderating and facilitating meetings.
6. *How to keep improving.* Be your own coach and develop, polish, and celebrate your own unique style.

Each chapter covers an area that, once mastered, adds to your power as a speaker. To help you learn and put techniques to work immediately, the chapters also include practice exercises and projects that highlight the most important concepts. Where appropriate, I have also included handy checklists and questionnaires that will help you evaluate other speakers, track your own progress, and be prepared for all speaking situations.

This interactive format makes PowerSpeak a veritable course in public speaking and presenting; if you take the time to take advantage of this format, you will learn not just by reading but by *doing—before* you have to give your next presentation.

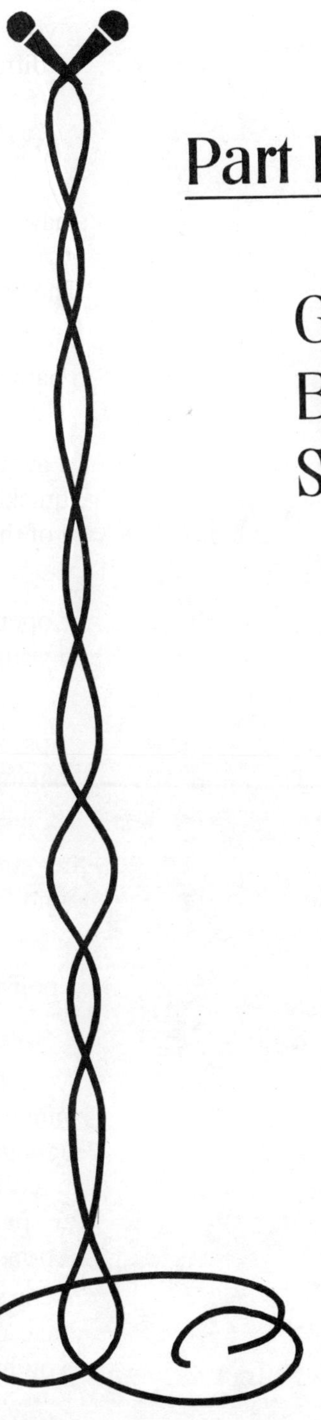

Part I

Getting Ready to Be a Powerful Speaker

Chapter 1

How Public Speaking Adds to Your Power

If all my talents and powers were to be taken from me by some unscrutable Providence, and I had my choice of keeping but one, I would unhesitatingly ask to be allowed to keep the Power of Speaking, for through it I would quickly recover all the rest.

—Daniel Webster

What do the words *public speaking* bring to mind? Large halls and after-dinner ramblings? Executive seminars where you listen to a speaker expert in some key area of business? Politicians at election time? Presenters using complex PowerPoint slides? These answers are all correct, but big events and big names are just the tip of the public-speaking iceberg. Public speaking embraces not only the formal settings for speeches but also myriad events in any businessperson's day.

Public speaking affects every aspect of communication. It refers to your ability to get ideas across and to inform and persuade your audience. Even though most people admit to disliking it, everyone has to rely on his or her speaking abilities in meetings, on the phone, when asking for a raise, or when explaining procedures to a new employee. There are two varieties of business communication: written and spoken. And while many professionals, managers, and executives complain about the number of memos and e-mails they have to write, they communicate verbally much more often.

Yet many people persist in divorcing lectern-style public speaking from the speaking required in a one-on-one meeting with the boss. They think the former is a very formal event requiring preparation, while the latter can be done off-the-cuff. It can be done this way, but the results won't distinguish you. In the business, powerful people know how to put the power of speaking to work for them *whenever* they are communicating verbally. Those who don't think of themselves as public speakers within their companies, organizations, or associations probably aren't perceived as good speakers by others either, and they lose the aura that goes along with being known as an effective communicator. Or worse, they have a reputation for being dull, unsure of themselves, and weak.

The Not-So-Hidden Benefits of Powerful Speaking

Powerful speaking is not a new phenomenon. In his 1880 book, *History of England: Volume I,* Thomas Macauley wrote about William Pitt the Younger, who became Prime Minister of England at the age of 24: "Parliamentary government is government by speaking. In such a government, the power of speaking is the most highly prized of all the qualities which a politician can possess; and that power may exist, in the highest degree, without judgment, without fortitude...without any skill in diplomacy or in the administration of war." That is why Pitt, who was lauded for his remarkable talent for making speeches, was a successful politician despite his lack of experience and political savvy.

I have seen what a newfound speaking ability can do for a person. Being a good presenter makes you *visible,* and in corporations, money, resources, and power flow to the visible high achiever. The visibility that speaking abilities give you becomes part of your overall professional growth. A colleague of mine at a large *Fortune* 500 company moved through the ranks with startling speed and ease. Many of his peers were just as competent, but he was a very good public speaker; his presentations were effective, persuasive events. He had an undeniable edge.

I also watched the careers of two executives at a large manufacturing firm. She was a highly persuasive speaker who had studied public speaking and ran dynamic meetings. She really knew how to inform *and* persuade. He, on the other hand, was a dull speaker. After five years, she was vice president of their division, and he was still a manager. Needless to say, the executives may well have been equally competent. If you don't use public speaking to your advantage, someone else will use it to his or hers.

There is just so much spotlight to go around, and it's a given that speakers occupy it regularly. Presenting in public is advertising with subtlety: You are displaying your abilities without touting them. As the old rhyme reminds us:

The codfish lays ten thousand eggs, the homely hen lays one.
The codfish never cackles to tell us what she's done;
and so we scorn the codfish while the homely hen we prize.
It only goes to show you that it pays to advertise.

That's why you should use every speaking opportunity possible. When someone needs a speaker, volunteer! If someone else is speaking, volunteer to introduce them! Get yourself in front of other people as often as you can. The more you do, the more you will be perceived as the confident, take-charge kind of person you truly are.

The 6 Major Speaking Faults

I have listened to *hundreds* of speeches. I have 22 years' experience with teaching and consulting with professionals. I have given hundreds of workshops and trained more than 10 thousand executives. The more I listened to people's presentations and speeches, the more I recognized a "pattern" of flaws that led to ineffective communication. And I discovered that in all these hundreds of speeches there were *six major speaking faults* that occured over and over again, even among experienced speakers.

The more I teach public speaking, the more convinced I become about the power of the six speaking faults, and the importance of a speaker recognizing these faults in him or herself. In a February 2001 Gallup Poll, the following question was posed to a representative sample of 1,016 Americans: "Which would help you be more successful in life: knowing what your weaknesses are and attempting to improve them or knowing what your strengths are and attempting to build on them?" Of all those surveyed, 52 percent believed that the secret to success lies in knowing their weaknesses.

If any one of these speaking faults is present—even if you are doing everything else right—your talk loses most of its effectiveness. Here are the six major speaking faults:

1. *An unclear purpose.* You want to motivate your audience in a certain way, but they would never know it from your meandering presentation.

2. *Lack of clear organization and leadership.* Your speech isn't structured and doesn't flow logically from one point to another.

3. *Too much information.* You overload your audience with details, some of them technical and most of them unnecessary.

4. *Not enough support for your ideas, concepts, and information.* You have compelling arguments to make, but you don't back your ideas up with colorful, memorable stories and examples.
5. *Monotonous voice and sloppy speech.* You believe in your subject and are excited by it, but your voice and manner of speech don't express what you're feeling.
6. *Not meeting the real needs of your audience.* You focus on what interests you, rather than on what your audience is interested in hearing.

These faults are closely linked; improve in one area and you almost automatically improve in the next. Of course, it takes patience and practice to truly hone your speaking abilities, but recognizing and eliminating these six major speaking faults will give you a competitive edge and improve your speaking abilities 100 percent!

The Trouble Spots

In addition to the six major speaking faults, there are five trouble spots speakers consistently run into. These are times that are hardest for the speaker and easiest to lose the audience. The trouble spots are:

- *Openings:* How to get and keep attention while making a strong, confident connection to your audience.
- *Closings:* How to avoid fading away at the end, and the techniques used to leave people on a high.
- *Transitions:* This often makes the difference between an average presentation and a great one (and also helps reduce the "uh's").
- *Questions and Answers:* How to stay in control and remain the expert, no matter who asks the question.
- *Visual Aids:* Visual aids used badly are not aids; they cost you 90 percent of the audience's attention. Used well, you gain 90 percent of their attention.

The Cardinal Rule: Never Be Boring

At a dinner party several years ago, the witty playwright Noel Coward and the Hungarian actress Eva Gabor were having a conversation.

"Noel, Dahling," said Eva. "Have you heard the news about poor Bahnaby? He vass terribly gored in Spain."

"He was what!?" cried Coward in alarm.

"He vass gored."

"Thank heavens," said Coward, "I though you said he was bored."

This book is imbued with a rule central to any speaker's success: Never be boring. An audience will forgive almost anything if you don't bore them to death. As a speaker your first job is to be interesting; that's where you generate power: *You* are effective to the degree you capture your *audience.* If you are interesting, entertaining, and memorable, then people will think of you as a powerful speaker.

The PowerSpeak system is a strategic shortcut gleaned from years of listening to and training speakers; chapters, exercises, and checklists that cover all the fine points of presenting; and a belief that power will stem from speeches that work hard to keep audiences entertained and interested. These elements make up an effective whole, as I'm sure you will see as you put the PowerSpeak system to work for you. This book was written with these three key words—*never be boring*—as the secret weapon that should be in the back of every speaker's mind.

What Do We Mean by Engage, Inspire, and Stimulate?

You engage your audience by drawing them in, by being interesting, by never being boring. You inspire your audience to take action by reaching their emotions—to get them to see things and feel things. People never take actions for intellectual reasons, there is always an emotional benefit or fear that spurs them on. As a speaker you want to stimulate people to think and to be open enough to consider your ideas.

Gain the Public-Speaking Edge

Confidence and speaking ability go hand in hand. The more speaking you do, the more confident you become—not only of your ability to present but also of your overall corporate skills. When you overcome your fears more easily, you have the ability to truly *persuade* superiors, peers, or customers.

Your confidence grows with every speech you give, and every new thing you try—I know. Several years ago, I decided to become an "out of the box" speaker. Audiences needed more and more stimulation to stay involved with me and with all speakers of all persuasions. Because my goal is always to encourage maximum attention, I created "infotainment"—a unique way to combine information with entertainment. I also wanted to find a way to use my theatrical background to make my message entertaining as well as informative. So I created the Theater for Learning program—I added songs, props, and costumes to my workshops. As you can imagine, I was very nervous the first time I tried out this idea, especially because the first audience to view my new program was an auditorium full of straight-laced executives from IBM, one of the most conservative corporate cultures around.

To my relief, they liked it! They really liked it! That gave me the confidence to go on and to develop my program even further. Not everything I tried was a success, but most things were. Simply by trial and error, I came up with a program that is informative and fun at the same time.

Nothing builds confidence more than trying something new and daring in front of an audience. Every step you take in a new direction is a step towards building your confidence as well.

Confidence is not the only benefit of public speaking. During my seminars and workshops, I ask participants to come up with a list of things they can gain by becoming a more persuasive speaker—all beginning with the letter *C*. Here are just a few of the answers I get:

Credibility	Charisma
Comfort	Career advantage
Character	Creativity
Contracts	Contacts
Clarity	Clout
Customers	Connections
Continuity	Courage
	CA$H

So how do you gain the public-speaking edge? By treating every speaking opportunity as just that—a valuable chance to inform and persuade effectively and, thus, shape the way you are perceived. This book will teach you how to bring to any meeting or conversation the tools of a powerful speaker's trade: preparation, organization, focus, relevance, enough support for your ideas, and attention to the needs of your audience, whatever the size.

This careful approach to public speaking is tactical; it is designed for you to control your public-speaking situations, rather than vice versa. Effective public speaking is a true boost to self-esteem. People who control the effectiveness of spoken communication don't just exhibit confidence, they become more confident. People perceive persuasive speakers as leaders. The ability to speak and present clearly, persuasively, and memorably is a skill that will pay off for years to come.

So read on, and start to look at your workday differently—not as a series of random conversations but as myriad chances to polish your skills as a powerful public speaker. The first thing to tackle is fear of public speaking, which the next chapter covers in depth. With fear behind you, you will be free to reap the benefits enjoyed by commanding speakers.

Chapter 2

Break Through the Fear Barrier

The only thing we have to fear is fear itself.

—Franklin Delano Roosevelt

The mind is a wonderful thing—it starts working the minute you're born and never stops until you get up to speak in public.

—Roscoe Drummond

At a personal and professional growth clinic I once ran, I worked closely with the meeting planners to determine the interests and needs of my audience. My group was concerned about increasing their power within their organizations, but they also indicated that they did *not* want me to spend a lot of time on public speaking. I held a discussion on it anyway and had the participants deliver presentations. At the end of the clinic, the evaluations indicated that public speaking was the most valuable segment of all. Some participants confessed the reason they didn't want to see it covered was fear—of public speaking.

According to *The Book of Lists,* public speaking—not bugs, heights, deep water, or even death—is the foremost fear in the world.

What are we so afraid of? What can a room full of people sitting quietly in their chairs—presumably unarmed—do to a speaker? Understanding why facing an audience inspires such fear is the first step toward controlling it.

The Origins of Public-Speaking Panic

It's Lonely in the Spotlight

As a speaker, you're a person apart from the crowd. People are more comfortable in groups than leading them; that way, no one is on the spot, and others can carry the conversation if you run out of ideas. Speaking isolates you; it removes you from your peers and designates you as different from everyone else—you're the one who has something worthwhile to say. Some people relish this attention; others, understandably, find the sudden spotlight daunting. The trick is to accept being singled out; it's temporary, and it's probably an honor, too. So try to see it as an honor, because your perception of the event will be crucial to your success.

It also helps if you don't let the spotlight become a barrier. Many novice speakers blow up their isolation in their own mind, until it takes on exaggerated importance. Think less about yourself and more about your audience. As you perceive yourself not as isolated but as part of the group you're addressing—a group that *wants* to hear what you have to say—some of the fear will leave

How Am I Doing? (It's Hard to Tell)

Except for optional question-and-answer sessions, speaking is a one-way street. You don't get the direct feedback conversation provides. You're not sure if people are really following you. You can see their eyes—though not very well—but you don't know what they're thinking. A person may leave the room, and you feel personally rejected, even though he is only stepping outside to make a phone call. A joke you've told many times with great success may not get a laugh.

What's missing is swift feedback and knowledge of where you stand, and the absence of this throws you off. Everyone, not just speakers, needs feedback. To prove this point, a man in a pub took bets from people in the pub and challenged one of England's champion dart throwers that he could make the expert falter in less than four throws, without interfering with the throw itself. The challenger held up a piece of paper in front of the champion just after he released the dart—so the champion could not see how he did—and then removed the dart before the next throw. Sure enough, the champion's game went to pieces in three throws. Without seeing—instantly—the results of each throw, he missed the next shot.

People do get reactions to their speeches—afterward. Knowing that during the speech you will plunge ahead like the dart thrower, without feedback, accounts for much of the nervousness speakers feel. But forewarned is indeed forearmed. *Expect* the pauses, the small silences, and they won't seem strange. Different audiences will also react differently; don't expect the same noises from both a general audience and one with a very technical bent. Ask any actor in a long-running show why they don't get bored doing the same show night after night and you always get the same answer: "The show may be the same, but the audience is different every night." And don't misread reactions out of sheer nervousness. Silence can indicate deep thought and agreement as much as it can alert you to boredom.

I once saw a speaker address a small group in a classroom seating arrangement. At the back of the room, a man seemed to be paying no attention; he spent the entire speech scribbling and gazing into space. During the break, other people in the audience asked the speaker how he could tolerate the noticeably rude man. The speaker was relaxed; he said he just focused on the rest of the seemingly more interested audience. But after the session was over, the scribbler came up to the speaker, identified himself as a reporter, said he was particularly fascinated by the presentation and would be writing an article on it, and thanked the speaker. Moral: Don't guess at what your audience's reactions mean. It detracts from your effectiveness to worry about those who don't seem to be listening, because they may be listening the hardest.

As one of the characters I use in my infotaining presentations, "Dr. Friend," would say, it's amazing how we get stuck on thinking about the negatives instead of the positives. If 99 out of the 100 people listening liked a speech, and one person was less than complimentary, we tend to focus on that one person's negative comment. If one person out of 100 isn't paying attention, that's where our attention naturally goes. But, as the above story demonstrates, you never know what's going on in the listener's head. And one person's opinion is just that—an opinion, not a fact. The more you speak, the more you learn to accept the compliments and laugh off the negativity.

I Don't Have the Gift

When I tell someone he or she can learn to be a commanding speaker, I usually get a swift, standard protest: "But you can't learn it; public speaking is a talent you are either born with or not." Not so. Public speaking is not an innate skill; good speakers are *made—not* born—through hard work and practice. As with any learned skill, some people are better than others, but everyone can work at it successfully.

If someone had told me 20 years ago that I, with my wispy voice and fear of crowds, would really enjoy public speaking, I would not have believed a word. But it's true; and one of the most important kinds of power that speaking brings you is the power to change your perceptions of yourself—not to mention other people's perceptions of you.

Giving a speech is not a natural, ordinary event. Speakers who expect to feel at ease are kidding themselves. It may seem hard to believe that even the most polished, experienced speakers get nervous, but they do. So don't expect, or long for, relaxation; expect the nervous excitement and energy that come from the task at hand. In other words, use fear to your advantage; charisma and adrenaline are closely linked.

Make Fear Work for You

Fear is nature's way of helping you protect yourself. New or dangerous situations trigger the "fight or flight" response: Your pulse quickens, your muscles tense, and the resulting rush of adrenaline equips you for any extra effort you might need. Whether you face real or imaginary fear, physical danger, or emotional stress, the reaction is the same. And speakers benefit: The adrenaline becomes energy; their minds seem more alert; new thoughts, facts, and ideas arise. In fact, some of my best ad libs come to me in front of my toughest audiences; it's yet another gift from the adrenaline.

Nervousness can give your speech the edge—and the passion—all good speeches need. It has always been so; 2,000 years ago Cicero said that all public speaking of real merit was characterized by nervousness. But how can you draw the line between nervousness that boosts and fear that debilitates? By understanding and tackling the four fears shared by all speakers:

- Fear of performing poorly.
- Fear of the audience.
- Fear of embarrassment.
- Fear your material is not good enough.

Tame the 4 Fears of Public Speaking

Fear of Performing Poorly

You are not alone. Worrying about your performance comes with the territory. It haunts novice and experienced performers alike: Even after 50 years of acting, Helen Hayes worried she would forget her opening lines. Red Skelton was always a nervous wreck before performances. Barbra Streisand's stage fright is notorious; it kept her from singing in concert for many years.

Even the most practiced public speakers do battle with nerves; it's a sign you're a true speaker. One night at a convention, a woman entered a room and saw the evening's keynote speaker pacing frantically. She asked him why he was so nervous. "What do you mean? Who's nervous?" he demanded. "If you're not nervous," she replied, "What are you doing in the ladies' room?"

- **The Power of Privacy.** Speaking before a group may seem like the most public act possible, but you still have privacy on your side. You don't have to reveal your nervousness; you can keep it to yourself. You gain nothing by letting others know you're worried; if you act confident, you begin to feel that way, too. People rarely *look* very nervous, no matter how jittery they feel.

  In my public-speaking classes, 95 percent of the people are amazed when they see videotapes of themselves giving a speech. They don't see on the screen the nervousness they felt. But they have to believe the camera and believe in an audience's positive response. Letting go of the fear means realizing it doesn't matter if you feel nervous; the audience doesn't know how nervous you are and won't be able to see it either.

  Keep in mind the example of the frightened boy walking past the cemetery on a dark night. As long as he walked casually and whistled gaily, he was fine. When he decided to walk faster, he could not resist the temptation to run; and when he ran, terror took over. It's the same with public speaking: Don't take that first fast step. Don't give in, don't show fear, and don't talk about your fear.

- **Tap Into Creative Visualization.** Expectations have a way of fulfilling themselves. If you assume your audience is hostile, you will adopt a defensive and abrupt manner, which is sure to alienate some people. Instead, form a mental image of how you want to look: *Creative visualization* is a technique that works for many public speakers and performers. Close your eyes and remember the positive points and audience rapport from your last speech. Imagine an audience of friendly, accepting people. Substitute that vision as the reality in your mind's eye and keep it there. Visualization is also a good way to try out new jokes or openings you are afraid to use. Imagine a positive audience reaction, and you're halfway to getting just that.

  Greg Louganis, the great Olympic diver, always visualized a perfect dive, even if he didn't take off from the board's "sweet spot," the area on a board that gives a diver an advantage if he hits it when he dives. Louganis took what he got and made it perfect nonetheless. Gold medals were the result. The key to a good speech is *envisioning* that you are hitting a sweet spot, even if everything isn't going perfectly, and even if you are nervous. When I speak, I envision myself *totally* in control—a gracious, charming, warm, and enthusiastic presenter. The key to visualization is controlling the mental image of yourself; don't let what you think the audience is thinking affect your image of yourself.

Envision the role you want to play and act the part. Don't worry about seeming phony—we all have many sides to our characters. You want to show your confident side; it is there for you to tap. With practice, confidence becomes natural and comfortable, and visualization is a powerful tool for gaining that confidence.

➤ **Work With Your Body.** Just as visualization works as a mental aid for speakers, these three exercises help you feel better physically:

1. *Proper breathing.* Concentrate on deep nasal breathing using your diaphragm. Breathe through your nose so you don't make your mouth dry.
2. *Progressive relaxation.* Working up from your feet, tense different parts of your body and then relax them. You'll lose much of that clamminess and nervousness.
3. *Easing neck strain.* Roll your head in a circle from shoulder to shoulder, as if you were a limp rag doll. This relaxes your throat and vocal cords.

You can do most of these exercises right on the dais (at least the first two). No need to resort to bathroom pacing.

➤ **Practice the 5 *Ps*:**

1. *Prana:* Prana is an Indian term meaning breath. One of the reasons that breathing through your nose helps relieve fear is that the nasal passages are connected to the limbic system, the part of the brain that controls emotions. Deep breaths calm your emotions and help get nervousness under control.
2. *Perception:* It's not what happens to us that counts—it's how we perceive what happens to us. Two people can have the same experience at the same time, yet one will see it as a creative opportunity, and the other will perceive it to be extremely frightening.

Public speaking is a perceptive experience. The more judgmental you perceive the audience to be, the more nervous you will be. Most audiences are not there to judge—they are there to learn something or to be entertained. They want you to be good. They are pulling for you. Focus on what you have to say to them instead of what you *think* they may be thinking about you.

3. *Psyche yourself up:* Imagine yourself not as you think you are, but the way you want to be. Hear the applause at the end of your speech, even before you give it. Use your creative visualization in your spare moments—not only prior to a presentation, but every time you have a few spare moments to daydream.
4. *Preparation:* Preparation is so important that the entire next chapter is devoted to the subject. Just remember this: There is nothing as frightening as the unknown. You're prepared when you know your subject matter like you know your best friend's telephone number; you're prepared when you've made a checklist of all the props, visual aids, etc., you need for your presentation (and checked the list twice); you're prepared when you familiarize yourself with the space before you get up to speak.
5. *Practice:* The more you practice, the more control you have over the entire speaking experience—and the less nervous you are. You don't practice so that you will be absolutely perfect (although that would be nice). You practice so that you will be comfortable in front of the audience, and so that they can be comfortable with you.

- **"Confidence Cards."** Aptly named, these notecards help speakers by organizing information, including all the points the speaker wants to make. They bring a sense of control to what often seems like an unwieldy situation. Chapter 24 ("Delivering With Style") will detail how to add to your comfort level and assurance by using "confidence cards" (which don't have to be cards—it can be a clipboard or anything that helps you remember what comes next and prompts you, should you lose your place or forget).

Fear of the Audience

Audiences are not out to get you. In fact, your listeners are probably thrilled that it's you up there and not them. They want to put themselves in your hands, listen, and learn. And they listen best when you appear confident and in control. Great speakers convince the audience they are completely in control, no matter how nervous they may really be. It's difficult for an audience to relax if the speaker appears uncomfortable; appear confident and you're already winning the audience's appreciation.

I attended a standing-room-only conference on stage fright where Frederick Zlotkin, first cellist for the New York City Ballet Orchestra, pointed out that how we perceive the audience affects our degree of fear and nervousness. He divides those perceptions into three kinds of anxiety: low range, medium range, and high range. Low-range speakers are slightly nervous but perceive the audience as basically neutral. Medium-range speakers assume negative thoughts on the part of the audience and consequently block out their listeners. They hide behind their lecterns and avoid eye contact. High-range speakers extend this mistake further and actually experience the audience as hostile and waiting for them to make a mistake.

➤ **Identify With Your Listeners.** In each of the above cases, the audience is the same and the differences are in the speaker's mind. One way to avoid this me-versus-them trap is to think about your audience instead of yourself. The more you know about your listeners, the more you will see them as friends and the less nervous you will be. What are their backgrounds, interests, needs? How will they benefit by hearing you? They want to enjoy listening to you; how can you make that happen?

➤ **Give Passion a Place.** My daughter Laura is not a public speaker, but she talks with total confidence to groups of 300 people about the importance of self-defense. She says she's so excited about her subject and about helping her audience learn to defend itself that she doesn't even think about being nervous.

➤ **Communicate Your Excitement.** Focus on *wanting* to tell your listeners something—something you feel is really worth your time and theirs. That kind of excitement is contagious; your audience can't help but catch it. And concentrating on teaching your audience something vital gets you thinking more about it than about yourself—the perfect antidote to fear.

➤ **Remember Who the Expert Is.** A final note on audience fear: Remember the facts. You were invited to speak. You're supposed to know more about your subject than the audience; you are there because you are more capable of covering the subject than most people. Believe it.

As Broadway star Ethel Merman used to say, "If the audience could perform better than I can, *they'd* be up here on stage singing."

Fear of Embarrassment

Many people are afraid to get up and speak because they think they'll do something foolish—they'll stumble over words, trip and fall, forget to include their most important point. The thing is, they're right! Embarrassing things do happen. It comes with the territory.

The good news is that audiences understand that we all make mistakes. What they want to know is how well you can handle them.

For instance, men often told me that their greatest fear was that they would standing up in front of an audience without realizing that their flies were open. "Well," I thought, "at least that's one thing I don't have to worry about!"

Two months later, I was on stage, doing a presentation, wearing slacks. About one hour into my speech, a man in the audience held up a sign that said, "Dorothy, your fly is open." My face turned as red as a New Jersey tomato, and I didn't know what to do. Then I spied the flip-chart in the corner. I slipped behind it, zipped up my fly, returned to center stage, spread my arms out wide, and said, "Ta da!" The audience loved it. As long as I was able to make light of the moment, they could too—and they knew they could trust me to handle anything else that might happen as well. And the audience wants to trust you, because for the time that you are standing up in front of them, you are their leader. They want you to take care of them. They'll understand if you fall down, but they don't want their leader to let them down.

Fear that Your Material Is Not Good Enough

This is the easiest fear to overcome because you are in control of preparation and content. You won't be on the spot if you know your subject thoroughly.

- **Construct Your Speech With Care.** Do your homework. Research. Prepare. The more thorough your preparations, the more you will be convinced the material *is* good enough. Work and rework your speech until you know it is interesting, worthwhile, and meaningful to the audience. Then edit it. All good writers will tell you there is no such thing as good writing—only rewriting.

Other chapters in this book will cover the organization and preparation of your speech. But planning is only half the battle; practicing your delivery is the other.

- **Fear of New Material.** Experienced speakers are often afraid to try something new: to change an opening that has always worked, to add new material that hasn't been tested. As scary as public speaking may seem, it's important to take risks. The first time I had to give physical directions to an audience, I was very nervous; my presentation required that at one point I ask everyone to move to the sides of the room. I panicked. What if no one moved? But I went ahead and there were no problems. Don't let fear keep you from trying something new to improve your presentations.

- **Practice Can Make Perfect.** Arthur Rubinstein, the great pianist, used to say, "If I don't practice for one day, I know it; if I don't practice for two days, my critics know it; and if I miss three days—the audience knows it."

  Practice until you are 100-percent confident. One hour for every minute of your speech is a good rule of thumb. Practice in different settings, at different times, testing different presentation techniques. Practice in front of a mirror, into a tape recorder, for a group of friends—anyone who will take the time to listen to you.

  Even with all your practicing, keep the speech or presentation fresh. After two thousand performances of *Othello,* Sir Laurence Olivier forgot his lines. He felt it was God's way of keeping him anxious. Every speech, no matter how many times you deliver it, should sound fresh.

  Of course, the best kind of practice is public speaking itself; the more you do, the better you become. But don't be misled by unrealistically high expectations. Public speaking is an art that only improves with time. Keep at it. You may still be nervous, but you'll also be better.

Mind Over Fear

Fear may not be welcome, but it is normal. Every successful speaker has his or her own tricks to *psych out* fear. Winston Churchill liked to imagine that each member of the audience was naked. Franklin Roosevelt pretended that the members all had holes in their socks. Carol Burnett thinks of them sitting on the commode. The point is, even though your mind seems to work overtime before a speech, filling you with dread, you can counter with tricks of the imagination that make you feel confident and in control.

The Best Tip of Them All: Confidence

Fear has its good side: The perception of public speaking as difficult and demanding adds to a confident speaker's power, because people are perceived as more knowledgeable and confident simply because of their ability to conquer the dreaded task of public speaking. That confidence comes from within; once you believe you have the ability to be a confident speaker, it's a lot easier to be just that.

The best way to bolster your confidence before a speech or presentation is to *think positively.* Saturate your mind with positive thoughts. Repeat to yourself any positive catch phrase that appeals: "I am poised, prepared, persuasive, positive, and powerful. I also feel composed, confident, convincing, commanding, and compelling."

Keys to Breaking Through the Fear Barrier

- Admit your fear; understand its sources.
- Tap the energy that fear produces.
- Recognize that fear is normal for public speakers.
- Realize your fear doesn't have to show.
- Visualize yourself as a powerful speaker.
- See the audience as your ally; focus on its needs.
- Speak about something you care about.
- Combine preparation with practice.
- Devise tricks to psych out your fear.
- Think positively about yourself.

By keeping these steps in mind, you can put fear in its place and get on with the career-enhancing opportunities that await you by becoming an excellent and persuasive public speaker.

Professional Projects: Work on Your Fear

1. Decide on your personal action plan for controlling your fear. For example: If your voice shakes when you give a presentation, tell yourself that you are going to practice deep breathing the next time you have to begin speaking. Write it on an index card and study it before each presentation.
2. Never avoid a chance to present. List three opportunities where you could volunteer to speak and when and how you will arrange to be the speaker. Commit to speak up at least once in every meeting you attend.
3. Decide on which visualization technique works best for you and then practice it conscientiously.

Chapter 3

Preparation: The Source of a Speaker's Power

The will to win is nothing, unless you have the will to prepare.

—Anonymous

Of all the ways to banish fear—and the previous chapter revealed a whole host of them—one stands out: simple, thorough preparation. For the unprepared speaker, the terror is real; it's a feeling all too close to everyone's classic nightmare in which it's exam time and you didn't go to class all term....

But the prepared speaker knows no such terror. He or she realizes preparation is the foundation, the blueprint, for a successful speech. There is an old saying that a speech well prepared is nine-tenths delivered. That's a statistic that really puts fear in its place and leaves you ready to deliver a polished performance.

In one of my past careers, I was a Broadway actress. The first job I got was in *Stop the World, I Want to Get Off*. The show was in Washington, D.C., in its post-Broadway tour, and I was a replacement for someone who suddenly left the show. I had one week of rehearsal in New York—with no other people, no sets, no props, no costumes—and before I knew what was happening, I was on stage performing, being gently "guided" around by the other actors so I would know where to go. That night was a total blur, and needless to say, I wasn't very good. How could I be, when I had had no time to prepare?

Lack of preparation would make anybody nervous. If I had had more rehearsal, I would still have had butterflies, but they wouldn't have been dancing quite so strenuously.

Audiences Sense and Appreciate Preparation

Preparation ensures that your audience will never be in doubt about what you are trying to say—and neither will you. Careful preparation sharpens your perceptions and gives you great confidence. The more homework you do, the more spontaneous, confident, and relaxed you are when you deliver the speech.

Preparation as Process

How do you prepare? The traditional answer—taking notes and memorizing them—is just a small part of it. Real preparation means digging something out of yourself; it means gathering and arranging your thoughts, nurturing your ideas, and finding a unique way to express them. A speech needs time to grow; don't try to manufacture one in a hurry. Select your topic as soon as you can but don't rush to write down your speech. Start a speech file as soon as you know you will be speaking and put everything that comes to mind in this file: thoughts, quotations, and topics. Let the thinking process go on for a long time—at least two or three weeks—depending on your subject and the length of the speech. Sleep on it; dream about it. Let your ideas sink into your subconscious.

Then bring your evolving speech out of hiding. Make it a topic of conversation at the dinner table. Ask yourself questions about your topic. Write down your thoughts and the examples that come to you. Once you have the pot cooking, keep stirring it and adding new ideas and illustrations. Examples will pop into your head at random times—jot down as many of these inspirations as you can.

Brood With the Best of Them

As you brood, you will be in good historical company. Abraham Lincoln was known to brood on a speech for days or weeks. He carried little notes to himself in his hat. Eventually he arranged these jottings in order, wrote, revised, and shaped his speeches. But up until that last moment, he pondered and polished. On the Sunday before he was to deliver the speech dedicating the Gettysburg cemetery, he told a friend that the speech wasn't exactly finished. "I have written it over two or three times," he said, "and I shall have to give it another lick before I am satisfied."

The night before, he closeted himself away from the crowds and practiced his speech. He worked on it all night and was still absorbed in thought as he rode to the cemetery. When the moment came, he delivered the nation's most celebrated 266 words in less than five minutes.

After you've applied the Lincoln method and let your topic simmer in your mind, your next step is to actually prepare your talk, step by step. The order of the steps is also important, because it addresses your concerns in the order they arise. By themselves, the steps are easy to tackle. They take the daunting task of doing a speech from scratch and make it manageable, even fun.

The 14 Easy Steps to Preparation

1. **Think About the Purpose of the Speech.** Is the purpose of your talk to inform, to entertain, to persuade, or to call your audience to action? Every speech must have its own topic and reason for being.

2. **Analyze the Audience.** A gossip is one who talks to you about others; a bore is one who talks to you about himself; and a brilliant conversationalist is one who talks to you about yourself. Speak *to* your audience; know its members and understand their interests, attitudes, goals, and fears. Speak to what they know and care about, and you are on your way to a memorable speech. Chapter 9 goes into this crucial step in detail.

3. **Gather Enough Material.** What do you already know and believe about this topic as it relates to this audience? What additional research can/should you do? This has become so much easier with all that data within instant access on the Internet. Start by collecting all your thoughts and notes. After you have exhausted your thinking on your topic, go to the library, ask colleagues, and research. Imitate the great journalists—they never use most of their research, but doing research gives them a reserve they can draw on. It makes them more expert in their topics than before they began.

   Take advantage of trade publications and associations—two excellent sources of industry-specific information. I once gave a speech to the members of the American Lung Association. I researched the association and its concerns so thoroughly that people listening to the speech thought I was on the staff of the association. That's the fun of preparation—learning enough so that you really communicate with your audience, while adding to your own knowledge as well.

Then be ready and willing to discard the unnecessary facts. Select only information relevant to your audience and to this particular speech. Your task is not to elaborate but to simplify and reinforce.

4. **Compose One Concise Sentence That Clearly States Your Purpose.** This will become your focus—or even your title—and, as you put the rest of your speech together, you will constantly refer back to this one line that will keep you on target.
5. **Construct an Outline.** Would you build a building without a foundation? You couldn't; and you also can't build your speech until you lay its foundation, which is the outline. In the outline you will reduce your ideas to three or four main sentences or key phrases and arrange them in the most convincing order. Chapter 5 will give you outlining ideas.
6. **Add Support.** Now you will fill out the outline by adding explanations, support, facts, anecdotes, and stories to give depth and meaning to your main points. As a rule of thumb, you can spend 5 percent of your time defining the purpose and mood of your speech, 10 percent of your time outlining, another 10 percent on visuals, and 25 percent practicing.

   That leaves 50 percent of your time to spend on working on the support that colors your speech and brings it to life. Your mood could be serious, jovial, or closely tied with concerns facing the audience. Whatever the mood, the support you choose must reinforce the mood you have chosen and ensure that your speech is never boring. Although it's easy to gather facts, they don't make an interesting speech by themselves.
7. **Prepare All Visual Aids.** If your speech needs visual aids, fine; if you don't need them, or your material does not lend itself to them, then don't try to fit them in.

   If used properly, visual aids can be effective. People remember 40 percent more when they hear *and* see something simultaneously. But remember that visual aids can be simple: I remember a salesman giving a speech suddenly holding up a shoe with a large hole for the audience to see. He made his point about the necessity of pounding the pavement—and memorably, too. Visual aids are covered in detail in Chapter 14.

8. **Devise an Opening With Impact.** It may be humorous, surprising, informative, challenging—an opening can be anything original that works for your particular speech. You make your first impression in the introduction; it can cloud all that follows or assure people that what follows is worth listening closely to.

   In business presentations, it's important to tell your audience what's coming up. But you have to do this without losing its attention. Refrain from sentences that start out, "I'm Jane Jones, VP of marketing. Today I'll be covering…." It's dull.

   It's much better to get your audience's attention first and *then* explain your purpose. Jane Jones could start her talk on the benefits of exercise by saying, "Good morning, I'm Jane Jones and I'll be talking to you today about why exercise is important for executives, no matter how busy you are." Or she could grab her audience, "Did you know that 20 minutes of exercise three times a week can add 10 years to your life? Good morning, I'm Jane Jones, and after my talk you'll be able to walk out of here ready to begin a sound exercise program."

   Refrain from saving major surprises for the end, and grab people with the facts—and your focus—early on.

9. **Craft Your Conclusion.** Build up to it, even if you are ending by summarizing your main points. Then end the speech with a strong, dynamic challenge that tells the members of the audience what you expect them to do with the information you've given them. Conclusions, like openings, must be memorable.

10. **Write Your Speech, Polish It, and Edit It.** Put it aside for a day or two, then go back and rewrite any parts you think need it. Remember Lincoln and his need to tinker. One way to achieve his admirable conciseness is to edit—ruthlessly. Don't be afraid to cut one-third—or even one-half—of your prose; this will leave you with a text that is stronger, leaner, and clearer. Technical presenters, in particular, are prone to excess words. Distill your speech down to the essentials, especially if it is technical, so it will be easier for your audience to follow. Don't be afraid of being brief and clear—too few speakers are.

    Effective written communication is different from its oral counterpart. A speech is a temporary event—words float in the air and are gone. Your words will have a better chance of staying with your audience if you take advantage of oral communication's greater informality: Use short sentences and words, colorful language, sentence fragments, contractions, repetition, and questions. All of these work to make your words lively and memorable.

And finally, once you are satisfied, practice your delivery.

11. **Have Your Confidence Cards Prepared and Ready.** Are they legibly numbered so that if you drop them, you can get them back in order?

12. **Get Your Timing Down.** Part of practicing your delivery is timing your speech. We speak approximately 150 words a minute, so three double-spaced typewritten pages take five minutes to deliver, depending on how quickly you speak.

    Even though you can never time a speech to the precise second, there is no substitute for recording your speech and estimating the time. If you have a lot of jokes, stories, and audience questions, you'll have to allow extra time for them.

    When it comes time to deliver the speech, keep a digital clock or a watch on the lectern where you can see it easily, or have somebody in the audience signal you when you have five minutes left. As you approach these final five minutes, you'll know you have just enough time left to finish an important point before going into your closing statement or before asking for questions.

13. **Make a Last-minute Checklist.** A key aspect of preparation is controlling and preparing your speaking environment. Avoid last-minute problems by making sure you take care of all the little details—such as arranging chairs in a small gathering and clearing away empty cups—before the speech. Other details to attend to before you speak can include:

    - ☑ Deciding what you're going to wear.
    - ☑ Making two copies of your text or notes.
    - ☑ Bringing your glasses.
    - ☑ Knowing if you'll have a podium.
    - ☑ Preparing visual-aid equipment and lighting.

    Lists compiled by truly prepared speakers are exhaustive and call attention to another crucial aspect of preparation: stage managing—overseeing all the details of your speech that don't have to do with your words. Chapter 18 will give you all the information you need on the key tasks that make up stage managing.

14. Have I orchestrated the question and answer period? (You may need to read Chapter 13, Professional Secrets of Question-and-Answer Sessions, before you can answer that question.)

Preparation Knows No Shortcuts

These 14 steps constitute the ultimate outline for a person giving a speech. Sure, you can skip one, or cut a few corners, but the audience will notice. Every *minute* of your presentation should be supported by an *hour* of preparation time. It's also important to prepare for your general communications: talking to your boss about a raise or presenting something to a client. Even a telephone call requires preplanning: You should know what you plan to cover and what your objectives are.

Without preparing sufficiently, the odds are you will commit one of the six major speaking faults, which are explained in depth in the next six chapters. Tackle each step in order and you will have the foundation for a memorable speech.

Here's a summary in the form of questions you can ask yourself:

- ☑ In one concise sentence, what is the purpose behind this speech?
- ☑ Who is the audience, and what is its main interest in this topic?
- ☑ What do I already know and believe about this topic as it relates to this audience? What additional research can I do?
- ☑ What are the main points of my outline?
- ☑ What supporting information and stories can I use to support each of these main points?
- ☑ What visual aids—if any—do I need?
- ☑ Do I have an arresting opening?
- ☑ In my final summary, have I explained what I expect the audience to do with this information?
- ☑ Have I polished and practiced the language of the speech to the best of my ability?

☑ Have I written a concise introduction for myself?

☑ Have I taken care of all the little details that will help me speak confidently?

With fear put into perspective and with the foundation of preparation under you, you're ready to start eliminating the six major faults that get in the way of powerful speeches, and the next six chapters will show you how.

Professional Projects: Build Confidence Through Preparation

1. Go through the preceding questions. Note first your strengths in preparation and then the aspects of issues you tend to avoid. What are you going to do about them? Create a realistic action plan for yourself.
2. Make note of how you feel when someone is not prepared. Do you want your listeners to feel the same?

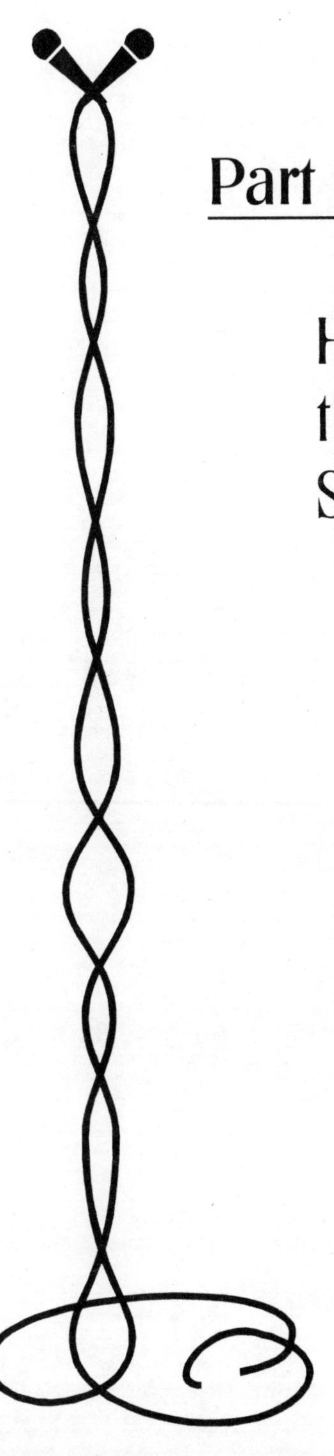

Part II

How to Overcome the 6 Major Speaking Faults

14. Have I orchestrated the question and answer period? (You may need to read Chapter 13, Professional Secrets of Question and Answer Sessions, before you can answer that question.)

Preparation Knows No Shortcuts

These 14 steps constitute the ultimate outline for a person giving a speech. Sure, you can skip one or cut a few corners, but the audience will notice. Every element of your presentation should be supported by [illegible] preparation time. It's also important to prepare for your general communications: talking to your boss about a raise or presenting something to a client. Even a telephone call requires programming. You need to know what you plan to cover and what your objectives are.

Without preparing sufficiently, the odds are you will commit one of the six deadly speaking sins, which are explained in depth in the next six chapters. Tackle each step in order and you will have the foundation for a memorable speech.

Here's a summary in the form of questions you can ask yourself:

- ☑ In one concise sentence, what is the purpose behind this speech?
- ☑ Who is the audience and what is its main interest in this topic?
- ☑ What do I already know and believe about this topic as it relates to this audience? What additional research can I do?
- ☑ What are the main points of my outline?
- ☑ What supporting information and stories can I use to support each of these main points?
- ☑ What visual aids—if any—do I need?
- ☑ Do I have an arresting opening?
- ☑ In my final summary, have I explained what I expect the audience to do with this information?
- ☑ Have I polished and practiced the language of the speech to the best of my ability?

Chapter 4

Fault #1: An Unclear Purpose

During the course of most speeches, the audience, as a rule, can figure out what the speech's subject is, but not the object.

—Anonymous

A well-thought-out purpose is so elemental it's often overlooked. Have you ever sat in an audience and asked yourself when the speaker was going to get to the point? Or heard a speech just drift—along with the audience? The subject may be compelling, the speaker even charismatic, but without determining a clear purpose, the speaker fails to lead the audience.

In front of an audience, speakers are leaders, in charge of moving that audience from one point to another. And you can only be a leader—and attain the power that goes with leadership—if you have a clear purpose in mind. No one should be in doubt for long as to your purpose unless you're saving some shock for the end, and even then, you had better make sure your audience can follow along.

The purpose of your speech is what you want to leave in the minds of those in your audience and what you want them to do as a result of hearing you. I pondered this issue. Why is this fault so prevalent? I realized that most speakers confuse the purpose with the subject. For example, when I ask my clients about the purpose of their presentations, I hear things like, "I'm going to talk about the new marketing program" or "the new guidelines for hiring." In other words, they tell me about the content of their presentations—not the purpose.

What does the speaker want his audience to do after hearing his presentation on hiring guidelines? He doesn't just want to give the audience information; he wants his listeners to hire the best people for the job.

In fact, every talk needs three elements: a title, a subject, and a purpose. For example:

Title: "Buckle Up and Live Longer."

Subject: Automotive safety.

Purpose: To make more people wear seat belts.

How to Determine Your Purpose

You can zero in on your purpose by asking: What do I want to accomplish in the minds of those in my audience? What do I want them to do, feel, or know?

Knowing clearly how you want the members of your audience to feel will affect the mood of your speech, your choice of examples and stories, and how you build the argument: Every element is influenced by the effect of your overall purpose.

Start by Stating Your Purpose

It can be surprisingly tough to set down a clear-cut statement of your purpose. In my public-speaking classes I always ask people to state their purpose; usually the speaker is not too clear on this, even after giving a speech. That doubt can stem from an attempt to convey too much, to make sure an audience gets all the facts. Don't be an overloaded speaker who drifts and, at the end, can't get back to your original message. Your purpose should be so clear that no one is left in doubt. When your purpose is defined at the outset, you can make sure all that follows supports your aims and that no one ends up wondering what point you were trying to get across.

The 6 main Purposes of Presentations

Most speeches fit into one of the six categories in the list that follows. Each requires a different tone, different types of stories, different examples, even a different choice of words. Of course, a speech can have more than one purpose, but there should be one overriding purpose that is absolutely clear to you and to your audience. The six main purposes are:

1. **To Inform.** When NASA scientists show us photos of a comet hitting Jupiter and explain its effect, they don't want us to do anything as a result (such as evacuate planet Earth). Their purpose is to *inform.* You may not be called upon to discuss such planet-shattering topics, but you may be asked to announce a colleague's promotion or retirement, to let employees know that the company has adopted a new insurance policy, or that a specific sales goal has been reached. Millions of talks are made specifically to inform people—to tell them something they will find beneficial to know. This kind of speech is usually fairly short and to the point and concentrates on the facts of the situation. The information presented should not be too complicated; your audience should be able to fully comprehend the subject matter just by listening to you speak about it. Some topics for informative speeches might be: The History of Our Company, Our Products and Services, or Introducing the New Package Design.

   Most speeches in business fall into this category. If I were giving a one-hour talk on how to become a more effective speaker, I would be informing, but if I were to deliver a two-day workshop with six to eight people who would be videotaped, my purpose would fall under the next category, to instruct.

2. **To Instruct.** Suppose, once again, you are asked to give a presentation about the company's new insurance policy. This time, instead of just being asked to announce that a new policy exists, you're asked to let employees know exactly how the plan works: how to fill out the forms, where to send them, how long to wait for reimbursement. Now your purpose is to *instruct*, to teach, to give specific directions or orders. This type of presentation is usually longer than an informational speech, but not necessarily. It must cover your topic thoroughly, so that your listeners absorb your instructions and come away with a new skill. Some sample topics include: Ten Steps to Being a Better Manager, What To Do in a Fire Emergency, and How to Use Your New Computerized Appointment Calendar.

   Whenever you are providing opportunities to hear, understand, practice, or apply, that is instructing. Instructing and informing are often joined together.

3. **To Entertain.** Unless you're a professional stand-up comic, you probably won't be making speeches solely to entertain. For most business

speakers this is a rarity, and a very difficult type of speech to deliver. However, you do want to deliver your subject and message in an entertaining, interesting way. So if you're delivering a talk on reducing stress in the workplace, you can add an entertaining slant to it, and a funny title, like "Tickle Your Funny Bone and Live Longer." A topic like that would lend itself to funny props and stories. Even a more serious topic, such as safety, can benefit from amusing cartoons. The basic features of this type of speech are vivid language, sincerity, and enthusiasm.

4. **To Inspire/Motivate.** There are many ways to inspire and/or motivate people. Some people inspire others by talking about how they have personally triumphed over hardships, such as Gerald Coffee, who spent seven years in solitary confinement in a prison camp; or Lance Armstrong, who overcame cancer to reclaim his championship at the Tour de France. They share their stories to let others know that no matter what tragedies may happen in life, it is possible to get beyond them successfully.

   Motivational speeches do not necessarily focus in on personal hardships. Susan B. Anthony motivated many in her generation to stand up for a woman's right to vote. Martin Luther King spoke to us all about his dreams of a glorious future and motivated many to become involved in the civil rights movement. These kinds of speakers desire to pull the best out of their listeners.

5. **To Activate/Stimulate.** Maybe you don't just want to inspire people, but you want to stimulate them to take action. A speech designed to *activate* presents ideas, suggestions, and arguments in such a way that the audience will believe so strongly what you tell them that they will actually carry out your suggestions. A fundraising speech is a perfect example: Your purpose is to get people to open their wallets and make a contribution. Other sample topics might be: Vote for Proposition 21! Save the Whales! and Follow the New Safety Regulations!

   To get people to act on your ideas, you must tell them what to do and stress that this action should be taken. You might point out what will happen if they do take this action, and what will happen if they don't. In order for this speech to be effective, you yourself must be firmly convinced that the course of action you are urging is the right one.

6. **To Persuade.** Capitol Punishment Should Be Abolished! Multiculturalism Is Good for Our Business! Sex Education Should Be Taught Early! These are all topics for presentations whose purpose is to *persuade*. This type of speech causes your audience to willingly accept your proposal through logic, evidence, and emotion. A persuasive speech offers a solution to a controversial problem, presenting sufficient logic, evidence, and emotion to sway the audience to your belief.

Once you know your general purpose, you need to develop a more specific, related purpose. For instance, when I present my PowerSpeak seminars, my general purpose is to inform or instruct based on the length of the presentation. My specific purpose is to give people tools and techniques so that they can be more interesting and powerful communicators. The more specific your purpose, the more powerful your presentation will be.

So how do you state your purpose? The first step is to figure out which type of purpose yours is. Will you be speaking to entertain or to impart information? Or do you need to go beyond informing and actually persuade, or even rouse your audience to action? It's quite possible your purpose will involve a combination of these goals. If it does, which one is paramount?

A good purpose is a specific one. Your general purpose may be to inform, but you must focus on exactly what you are going to get across. Do you get loads of mail on executive seminars? Look at the descriptions of courses offered: Each objective is spelled out clearly. Speaking of this book, I could say my purpose is to teach you about public speaking, but that's vague. It would be more specific to say that I want to teach you how to be a powerful speaker by avoiding the six major speaking faults.

Don't Just Inform—Persuade!

Even though we just discussed the fact that there are six major purposes, one stands out among the rest: to persuade.

Take the salesman at a large Canadian telephone company who recently told me about a presentation he was going to give. He'd been asked to observe a new telemarketers' training program for three months, then present an evaluation to company executives. When I asked him what the purpose of his presentation was, he said it was to inform the company executives on the status of the program. But as we spoke, he came to realize that he really wanted the executives to sign up for a long-term commitment to the program. His real purpose was to activate, not just inform. When his purpose changed, so did his entire presentation.

The speaker's task is seldom as simple as imparting information. Granted, informing is central to the job; speaking is an efficient way of conveying timely information to large groups. But chances are your objectives as a speaker are to *persuade,* to give your audience new information in such a way that it sees things your way. This is the purpose behind the purpose, the end result that speakers seek.

You can see these two goals—informing and persuading—at work in business and technical presentations, where the topics, the facts, and the statistics are presented with a clear objective in sight: to win that account, reorganize that department, or revamp that computer system. As tools of persuasion, speeches and presentations are everyday events. But it's not enough to be clear; you need to be compelling too.

I once heard a principal speak to the parents of his students about drunk driving, a subject of such inherent seriousness that he should have been able to lead the parents with ease. But he never made his purpose clear: His facts and presentation were jumbled; his stories weren't focused; and up until the very end, the parents were left wondering what the point was.

In fact, he had a very specific point. He wanted the audience to write letters to the legislature supporting tougher laws. But because he waited until the last few sentences to spring this request on them—instead of weaving the effect concerned citizens can have throughout his talk—his audience felt more put upon than activated.

He made the mistake of thinking that informing is the same as persuading. It's not. Informing is a preliminary step to getting people to act, but facts need support, organization, and clear communication of benefits to get results from an audience.

Don't Let Your Subject Be Too Broad

When the purpose gets too broad, it gets confused with the *subject.* Keep these two separate and you're well on your way to focusing your talk. You may have to speak on "Corporate Leadership in the 21st Century"; if you think of that as the purpose of your talk, any panic is justified. A topic like that is just a broad subject; your purpose is to make a specific point about leadership—maybe even in a specific company—through examples, anecdotes, and various facts. So tackle some key trees, not the whole forest. Your purpose in such a speech could be to inform the audience of the skills necessary to achieve leadership in a corporation. Or it could be to convince people to start preparing now for changing leadership roles in the 21st century. The possibilities in the subject are vast, so you must be very clear and specific about your purpose.

The more focused and specific your talk, the better your chances that some words will resonate. Speak vividly about the leadership of one person, and your audience can glean much about leadership in general. Let people make the leap from the specific to the general, while you continue to be vivid. Broad subjects can be wonderful assignments if you give them a narrow—and therefore memorable—purpose and focus.

Analyze the Audience

Always ask yourself how the purpose of your talk relates to your audience's interests. Knowing your audience is the only way to understand its attitudes and anticipate its objections. A dentist addressing a group of parents would talk about preventing tooth decay in their children, not about the latest equipment installed in his office. Study those in your audience; think of their needs. You must link the beliefs you are trying to impart with their existing concerns. Chapter 9 ("Not Meeting the Real Needs of Your Audience") goes into this crucial analysis in detail.

Let Purpose Lead the Argument

If you titled your leadership speech "A Group Without a Leader Is Like a Boat Without a Rudder," that title would lead naturally into your general purpose: to get those in your audience to act, to change their behavior, and adopt and use the five leadership strategies you are about to introduce. You could go on to support your purpose by explaining what could happen if they don't use them and what will happen if they do.

Get Mileage out of Your Title

Titles lend a professional air and are an opportunity to be more creative. Titles help the audience to focus, make it easier for your introducer, and look better in the program. Many speakers either omit the title altogether or tack on something at the last minute. But the title is the first thing about your speech an audience sees or hears, and it deserves a lot of care. Good speakers use titles as part of their strategy; nothing communicates creativity quicker than a well-worded title. A lively title will also help the meeting planner, who frequently will print them on whatever he or she is using to summarize or sell the meeting. One of my clients actually hired me to help them develop more interesting titles for the annual managers meeting.

A weak title is better than no title at all—barely. Compare "Safety" to "Be Safe and Live Longer: 10 Steps to a Healthy Workplace" and "Managing Well" to "How to Be a Super Boss."

Always use titles—even for a meeting you're running in your own corporation. It's your first chance to catch your audience's attention.

Fine-Tune Your Tone

Establishing your purpose is the beginning of the fine-tuning all good speakers do. And the same purpose can lend itself to talks with very different thrusts, depending on your audience. For example, a talk on leadership to senior executives will differ from one to new managers. The thrust may change from reinforcing to introducing; the examples relevant to the audience's business life will be different. Other shifts would occur if you prepared a talk on the same topic to laypeople and technical experts.

Should speeches be entertaining, strictly technical, or a little of both? Speeches have their own *tenors* that can either be inappropriate to the subject at hand or just fight. The twist you put on the facts will guide much of your audience's reaction to the information you're imparting.

A plea for humor: Even if your purpose and your tone are extremely serious, you shouldn't neglect the saving grace of humor. An amusing example or story is still one of the best ways to be memorable; even Shakespeare had comedy in the midst of his most tragic plays. I am not suggesting you work at being a stand-up comic, but that you take advantage of the bond created when speakers get audiences to laugh with them.

Compel Through Commitment

The key to being compelling lies in your own commitment to and connection to your topic. And it comes from knowing exactly what you want to say. Sound familiar? We're back to the original task of defining your purpose—knowing what you want to say. But that second step—persuading—needs a commitment from you to your topic. Funny stories, slides, and startling statistics all may help you make your case, but your own commitment as a speaker—the passion and the tangible belief that you can summon—is hard to beat when you combine it with a logical, informative presentation.

In 1976, Norman Vincent Peale (famous for his book *The Power of Positive Thinking*) wrote another book called *Enthusiasm Makes the Difference,* in which he stated that enthusiasm can not only help you cope with any problem you may face, it can help you harness the power to motive yourself and others. To be the excited—and exciting—kind of speaker people remember, you must believe in your material. This is especially true when your purpose is to convince or motivate. Your enthusiasm must be genuine and palpable; anything contrived will seem just that.

Was Your Purpose Clear? Get Feedback

Get in the habit of asking people who have heard you whether your purpose was clear. Before you give your next talk or chair a meeting, write a sentence that you feel describes your purpose. After you deliver your presentation, ask the participants what your purpose was. They should be able to tell you—easily. See how closely what they say matches what you wrote. If it doesn't, you need to work harder on making the content support and evoke the purpose you have in mind. Without feedback, you can only assume your purpose was clear—you'll never know for sure.

Focused, committed, invigorated—isn't that the kind of speaker you enjoy hearing? It is the kind you can become, and the first step is that firm grasp of purpose. Determining your purpose really is an easy step, and it makes everything that follows, including organization and selecting good supporting material, much easier. When you communicate a strong purpose, people see you as a leader with vision, which can't help but add power to your presentations.

Another Perk of a Clear Purpose: Cut Your Prep Time in Half

One of the greatest benefits of having a clear purpose is that it helps you cut down on your preparation time. Recently, I was working with an endocrinologist who was working on a speech he was going to present to other doctors. He spent a lot of preparation time gathering technical information he thought he would use. But when he realized that his real purpose was to persuade these doctors to treat diabetes more aggressively, he also realized he didn't need as much technical information as he originally thought. Had he stated his purpose in the beginning, he would have saved himself hours of prep time.

Professional Projects: Concentrate on Purpose

1. Listen to some politicians and see if you can write down a clear, one-sentence summation of the purpose of the speech you are listening to.
2. Think about your next meeting with your boss and clearly write out a purpose that will help keep you focused and assure you of better results.
3. Practice with your next voice mails by clearly stating your purpose and then listing your key points. This is a good way to build the purpose habit.

Chapter 5

Fault #2: Lack of Clear Organization and Leadership

Properly organized, even crime pays.

—Jim Fisk and Robert Barron

Eliminating the six major speaking faults from your speech is like climbing a ladder: It's a methodical, successive practice; you use each rung to get to the next. Clarifying your purpose is essential. The next thing to avoid in the climb to a powerful speech is a lack of organization.

A poorly organized speech wreaks havoc with even the most compelling ideas. You could have the most interesting topic and the most willing audience, but if you don't structure the speech, it's like slipping when you discover there's a rung missing on your ladder. You're left dangling and so is your audience. Good organization also helps prevent audience boredom. The people in your audience don't have to wonder where you are going if they see you are proceeding logically. So they remain focused on your ideas and don't get sidetracked. They put themselves in your hands much more willingly if they sense you know where you're going and how you're going to get there.

Unfortunately, organization is not a sexy or popular topic. However, there is another way to think about it that makes it more appealing. Organization puts you in a leadership position. If you want to be a leader, people have to be able to follow you—and the easiest person to follow is the one who is best organized.

3 Parts of a Speech That Make up an Organized Whole

Your speech will have an introduction, a body, and a conclusion. All three parts are equally important, but the bulk of your talk is taken up by the body of the speech. Many speakers prepare the body first, and then go back to the introduction and conclusion. Prepare your speech in the order that works for you. But don't forget what you learned in the last chapter—always start with a clear purpose as your first step. This doesn't mean you can't change the purpose, but it should be your starting point.

3 Essential Aspects of Organization: Outline, Transitions, and Patterns

There are three aspects to organization. It's important to use all three in order to keep your audience with you at all times. The first two are outlining and transitions, the third has to do with the order in which you present your information, or a pattern of organization.

Outlining: The Key to Organization

Fine speakers have various methods of approaching their material, but they all have one thing in common: a good outline. It highlights the important elements of your talk, gets rid of the excess, and helps you choose the best supporting information. An outline compels you to analyze your logic and reveals any gaps or flaws in your reasoning.

A strong outline also helps you perform your speech better because you visualize the main points in your mind. Your talk flows easily toward the conclusion without hesitation.

The biggest advantage of a good outline is that it can be modified to meet different situations and demands. With the right outline, you can change a 20-minute speech into a five-minute one, and vice versa.

Indeed, you should be prepared to deliver long, medium-length, or short versions of your speech, especially if you are the last speaker and the speakers before you ran over their time limits. A British foreign secretary was once at the mercy of a long-winded toastmaster who took up all the remaining time and most of the audience's patience. When the toastmaster finally introduced the secretary with the words "…and now our foreign secretary will give his address," the gentleman stood up and said: "I have been asked to give my entire address in the remaining five minutes. That I can do. Here it is: 10 Carlton Gardens, London, England." He then sat down, to appreciative applause.

A Good Outline Is Lean and Mean

The most frequent outline mistake is not making it simple and orderly. You may be tempted to cover many items, which all seem to be equally important. That's an understandable impulse; you don't want to leave out key facts or topics. But this approach will get you in the end. For starters, it's doubtful all those tempting items are equal in importance, and your audience just can't absorb that many points.

You must establish priorities. First, identify the three or four major points that need to be covered. Then establish subheads that will provide the framework people will use to absorb the information.

A popular management phrase these days is "lean and mean," think of a good outline as being "lean and clean." The following is a good general outline that should suit most presentations. It's designed to grab your audience, hold its attention, and provide the right amount of information.

Sample PowerSpeak Outline for a 20-Minute Presentation

I. Introduction: (5 percent of your time)
- A. Opening statement to gain attention and interest—capitalizes on audience's goodwill.
  - i. Development of opening statement.
  - ii. Other supporting material if needed.
- B. Second introductory point (if necessary).

II. Body: (90 percent of your time)
- A. First main point of your speech.
  - i. Major subpoint supporting point A.
  - ii. Subpoint supporting point A.
- B. Second main point of speech.
  - i. Major subpoint supporting point B.
  - ii. Subpoint supporting point B.
- C. Third main point of speech.
  - i. Major subpoint supporting point C.
  - ii. Subpoint supporting point C.

III. Conclusion: (5 percent of your time)
- A. Summary.
  - i. Famous last words.
  - ii. Thank the audience.

Don't Forget Transitions

Transitions are so basic that many speakers overlook them and concentrate on structuring the outline. But transitions get you from one part of the outline to another; they are the secret to a professional's speech. Look at the sample outline and realize there should be transitions between each main point and subpoint. These devices are so important to organization—and to giving good presentations—that I've devoted all of Chapter 11 to them.

After you have written down three or four key topics, keep track of everything you can think of that supports these main points (more on this under Fault #4, page 69). Anecdotes, research, clippings, and facts will all be necessary to provide the support and the color a memorable speech needs.

Choose a Pattern: Make the Sequence Your Own

Once you've grouped your subheads and examples under the main points, the next crucial job is to work out the *sequence* in which you will present them and the *style or pattern* that fits your purpose best. Your choice of sequence must build from point to point both to maintain interest and move the speech along. It might be entertaining to string 10 jokes together, but if the string doesn't add up to a ball of yarn, the audience is dissatisfied. On the other hand, it may be logical to present a series of facts in chronological order, but that can also be boring.

Select a style of organization, but don't be too predictable. The last thing you want is a complacent audience. In the middle of a presentation I made the mistake of saying, "Let me be more organized." I felt the entire audience deflate—enthusiasm just wilted. So I quickly added, "I said organized, not boring." And the audience perked right up again.

An outline may seem strict and uncompromising by definition, but it's governed by the sequence of your points, and here you are free to create. You can start with small points and build to a climax. Or you can open with an attention-getter, and follow with less startling points.

Being organized does not imply that there is only one way of doing things. Some companies train their people to use the same style and often the same visual aids for all their presentations. That's great when just one person is speaking. There are times, however, when an audience is asked to listen to a series of speakers. If all the presentations are in the same style, using the same organization, the speakers' messages will get lost (and be uninteresting to boot).

A skilled writer can achieve the same objective a hundred different ways, and as a speaker, you can do the same thing. You may organize your points by using contrast and comparison; by moving historically from the most primitive examples to the most modern; or simply by going from the simple to the complex, the smallest to the largest, or the cheapest to the most expensive.

Whatever you do, choose a pattern that sells *your* message, fits your own thinking and style, and helps the audience move along with you clearly and logically. And remember to always hold something back for your windup. All speeches should end on a high point.

The 4 Classic Organization Patterns

You will see that nowhere do I have a style of organization based on a series of slides. Stringing together a group of points is boring! It would be just like going to a play or movie where the scenes had no connection. It would be very difficult to follow.

You can present your speech in a limitless number of ways, and this fact is daunting for people looking not only for *any* way but also for a pattern of presentation that is known to be effective. Here are four basic, tried-and-true patterns. Their acceptance doesn't make them dull or predictable; those adjectives can only apply to your attitude, material, and delivery. Like outlines, patterns are blank slates, and are as powerful, or as bland, as you make them.

1. *Sequential.* Present events in the sequence they occur (that is, the steps necessary to start a new business or to install a new computer). A *chronological* sequence goes further and gives a specific time context to the event. It's inherently logical and easy for an audience to follow.

2. *Categorical.* This pattern is useful when you lack a clear pattern of organization, or your topic isn't confined to a procedure, process, or time frame.

   You assign meaningful labels to subtopics related to a general topic. For example, I deliver a speech on the topic "Sales Success" and within the speech I have four categories: "Personal Power," "Organizational Power," "Verbal Power," and "Sales Power." The categorical pattern works well when you are presenting new ideas that have not yet been put into a framework by your audience.

3. *Problem and Solution.* This pattern is commonly used in technical presentations, but it is effective for any talk where you need to show what *is,* what *ought to be,* and what *needs to be done.* When you think about it, most good presentations state a problem. Either the problem itself or the consequences of not correcting it is the attention-getter. Often this pattern includes:

   - Symptoms of the Problem. Get the audience to recognize that the problem exists and should be solved.
   - Identification of the "Real" Problem. Analyze and present your *what, when, where, how much, how many, how often,* and *why*. Show how the answers to these questions are related, and state (or restate) objectives related to the problem.
   - Possible Solutions. A talk addressing a problem of any complexity will not only list solutions but also include constraints on the solutions, an overall evaluation of them, and a recommendation of the best solution or combination of solutions.

   You can use the problem-and-solution pattern most persuasively and dramatically when you want the audience to make a decision and take action. It's also very effective for presenting your findings in a dramatic context.

4. *Contrast and Comparison.* Get your audience to evaluate alternative ideas or plans by calling its attention to differences and similarities. The success of managers with a closed mind versus those who are more flexible, "intrapreneuring" versus hiring outside consultants, and the different ways two companies face a crisis—all use comparisons not only to illustrate but also to structure the argument.

Combinations: A Final Alternative

The four basic patterns can easily combine with each other. However you present your information, your task is to develop the optimal combination in terms of your topic, your audience, and your objectives of informing and persuading.

Each pattern can also benefit from a *question approach,* where you stimulate the audience by rephrasing the point you're making as a question.

Before You Speak: Test Your Organization

You've focused, researched, outlined, written, polished, and you're ready to speak. Check your preparation against the following list of key characteristics of a well-organized speech:

☑ A clear purpose.

☑ A topic inherently interesting to the audience.

☑ Strong, logical, and clear sequence of ideas.

☑ Points presented in a consistent way that is easy to follow.

☑ Speech is adapted to the attitude of the audience and to any special circumstances.

☑ Transitions are clear, definite, and well thought out.

☑ There isn't too much information, and what is there relates directly to your main points.

☑ Plenty of support backs up your assertions.

☑ Frequent summaries aid the audience and emphasize your main points.

☑ The conclusion restates what it is you want your audience to know, do, or feel.

Once you have an outline you're comfortable with, it will be tempting to fill it in with as much information as possible to support your points. Avoiding that temptation is central to avoiding the next speaking fault, "too much information."

Professional Projects: Organizing Helps

1. You are a project manager in a large management consulting firm. You have been asked to give a presentation to a potential client on the benefits of using your company. Your purpose is to get a commitment from the client to use your company.

   You must make a presentation to your staff on the importance of teamwork.

   Develop your organization through these two methods:

   A. Comparison and contrast.

   B. Problem and solution.

2. Check out the chapter outlines in the nonfiction books you have in your library and see what other ways they could have been organized. Also look for points that could be added or omitted.

Chapter 6

Fault #3: Too Much Information

No speech can be entirely bad, if it is short enough.

—Irving S. Cobb

You will neither engage nor inspire your audience with too much information.

—Dorothy Leeds

In my workshops, when I ask,"too much information is...?" and open it up to the audience, everyone answers "BORING."

Faced with an expectant audience, speakers feel they have to provide as much detailed information as they can. This overabundance of information makes some speakers feel secure, and soon becomes their security blanket.

This love of information is understandable; as a country, we have been programmed toward overabundance—more is best. Not so with speeches. Although your speech should be rich in examples and illustrations, it should be thin in facts, figures, and lists. This is especially true for technical presentations, which tend to be overloaded with information.

Watch out for Multiplying Facts

Facts are seemingly reassuring. They back our assertions and give us ground to stand on. Worried speakers gather them for many reasons, not realizing abundance is harmful to a speech, because it's a lot easier to compile data than to make them interesting. Some speakers use facts to back up their claims, thinking that the more information the audience gets, the more believable and compelling the speech will be. They use facts to give speeches an objective—and therefore a powerful—tone. Other speakers feel the audience needs to know a lot and pile facts and lists into a speech in an attempt to give people their "money's worth."

However well intentioned, both approaches are misguided and work against both the speaker and the audience. Audience overload occurs surprisingly quickly. People retain three or four main points—nicely illustrated and explained—better than they do myriad bits of supporting information. Instead of bolstering your audience, excess facts just bog the audience down.

But the fact problem goes even deeper. An abundance of data is not the best support for your argument. Anyone can read a list of facts; your job is to make that information interesting, to give your viewpoint, using your own style and voice. Audiences don't want sheer objectivity: They want your interpretation.

Don't Dodge the Spotlight

Remember that you have been invited to speak for reasons that have nothing to do with your research abilities. You have something unique to say on the subject, some special angle.

My first job was teaching very bright high-school kids. I was a nervous wreck, because I figured that they were so much smarter than I was, which was undoubtedly true. I studied and studied before each class and ran a losing battle trying to stay ahead of them.

At the time, I didn't realize that I knew enough about the subject; I already had enough information. What I needed to do was make that information interesting and meaningful to students. They may have had more intelligence, but I had the experience to translate the facts vividly. Once I realized they were there to hear my interpretation of the subject, I was fine.

Don't Let Data Equal Boredom

Even speeches that don't overload on information can be accused of having too much—if that information isn't interpreted in an interesting way. Granted, it's a lot easier to give information than to look for ways to make it interesting and useful. (But no one said giving a speech was easy.)

The major fault in technical presentations is relying on the hard-core technical data to carry the day, and having too much of it. Everyone—scientists included—wants a presentation that doesn't throw findings at him but interprets facts and weaves a story. Almost all of the technical presentations I have seen needed their information reduced by half and their visual aids simplified.

Humanize and personalize your data. After my son took a college course on military history, I asked him what struck him as the most interesting thing he had learned. He said he was amazed by how long it took soldiers to load the early guns and how difficult they were to fire. He saw the data presented to him in terms of human consequences. Let your audiences do the same by presenting your facts in a human context.

It's also very easy to make false assumptions about the level of data appropriate for your audience. For example, in talks to upper management, speakers feel they can fill speeches with technical information, because the audience is at such a high level. In fact, by the time people get to upper management, the skills they wield are generalists' skills; they are no longer as knowledgeable of the technical details as the technicians below them.

Power Through Condensation

If you embroider your facts with the stories and support that will make them memorable, chances are you will have too much to say. Condensing a speech you've worked hard on into the allotted time may seem cruel, unusual, and impossible. But it's necessary. When you take time to condense your speech, your audience is much more likely to listen to what you say, because long-windedness leads to repetition and lack of focus.

It takes time and thought to condense everything you know about a subject into a few highly refined major points. Woodrow Wilson, the last president to write his own speeches, was once asked how long it took him to prepare a 10-minute speech. "Two weeks," he said. And how long for an hour's talk? "One week." And for a two-hour presentation? "Oh," he said, "I'm ready now."

Rules to Speak By

In my speech classes, I give what seems like a simple assignment: Prepare a three-minute speech on any topic that interests you. That's only enough time for about 450 words. When these speeches are delivered, almost no one finishes in the allotted time.

The problem is that most people have a very unrealistic idea of what they can say in a short period of time. And if people overload three minutes to such an extent, imagine what they will do with a 20-minute speech! Everyone tries to fit in too much or tries to talk faster as they realize they are running out of time. This time trap points out a key to a powerful speech or presentation: Practice—and time—your delivery. Even though the only way to really see if your speech fits a time limit is to practice it, here are some guidelines for length you can use *before* you write: If your speech should be 20 minutes, figure on covering four major points; 30 minutes leaves you room for five points; and a one-hour speech allows you to work in eight major points.

After your speech is written, you can check for time by counting words. We speak at approximately 150 words per minute. Therefore, if you count the number of words in your speech, and add a minute or two for audience reaction, you should come up with a rough estimate of how long your speech will be. Of course, the best way to estimate is to time yourself while you practice, but counting words can let you know if you're way over (or way under) before you even begin.

These limits make it sound like you don't have a lot of time and room—and you don't. It's staying power that you're after, and that means limiting yourself and choosing your main points with care.

Respect Your Audience's Limits

An audience reaches its limit a lot faster and sooner than most speakers think. The average attention span is only eight seconds. People forget 25 percent of what they hear within 24 hours, 50 percent within 48 hours, and 80 percent in four days. Not long ago, audiences had an attention span of 3.5 minutes. Today that span has shrunk to about 2.5 minutes. That's one reason we now have less time (and less show) between commercials on television.

Your words of wisdom will be competing with people's thoughts of what they did that day, what assignment is due tomorrow, and whether anyone's home to walk the dog. Being brief and concise isn't just polite, it's effective. And it helps you avoid the speaker's ultimate curse: being boring.

Professional Projects: Practice Editing

1. Select an article or editorial from your local paper. Condense it into one short paragraph. Be sure to get the main point across.
2. Take out your last 20-minute presentation. Imagine you are the last speaker of the day and have only five minutes to deliver it. Jot down the key points you will make and what you can eliminate.

Chapter 7

Fault #4: Not Enough Support for Your Ideas, Concepts, and Information

"I'm glad I attended your lecture on insomnia, doctor."
"Good. Did you find it interesting?"
"Not especially, but it did cure me of my insomnia!"

—Old joke from a humor anthology

The job of a speaker is to romance information. Emily Dickinson once said, describing another writer of her day, "She has the facts, but not the phosphorescence." That phosphorescence, that inner light that shines through a powerful presenter onto his or her listeners, only comes when you appeal to an audience's emotions—not just its intellect. Any speaker would like his or her speech to be described as interesting, memorable, powerful, and never boring. And the surest route to that kind of speaking success is using support—examples, anecdotes, and other devices—throughout your talk. Without support for your facts, audiences lose involvement in what you are saying. Many speakers work to make their introduction and conclusions memorable but neglect doing the same for the body of the speech. That's understandable: It's hard to sustain an audience's involvement as you make every point. Although it may be hard, it's also essential for powerful talks. Using examples to make your talk lively is the best way to maintain that involvement. Examples with vivid language, colorful stories, and famous sources wake up the audience and earn its attention.

PEP: The Formula for Success

Here is an important piece of information that will really aid you in speaking powerfully. And it's so simple to use. For all your major points, do this: Make your point, give a descriptive example, and then *remake* the point as creatively as possible. That's PEP—Point, Example, Point. The PEP formula is designed to let you weave in examples and illustrations. Every major point you make needs to be supported to be memorable. You're taking advantage of how people learn (through repetition and illustration). Retention is the key to a powerful speech.

My training programs recognize the importance of retention, and I turn lessons into games and role-playing—vivid, real-life examples of principles that participants will remember far more readily than a dry synopsis. The same principle is at work in a speech; because people remember vivid stories and examples, use them to increase the level of what people remember when they listen to you.

After you have applied the PEP formula and have sorted out the various support materials, you may have material left over. If your leftovers won't group around your main points, they are probably irrelevant. Throw them out. Even if they do apply, set them aside, for they will probably make the speech too long. Make it a cardinal rule to stick to your main ideas, and get rid of the clutter. Sometimes these leftovers are handy if you ever need a longer version of your talk. I give 15-minute and 45-minute talks on the same subject and find the leftovers invaluable. But only if there's a proper place for them.

It's also possible you'll wind up with some important information that doesn't seem to fit under your main points. In this case your main points may not be broad enough. Go back to square one and restate them in a larger framework.

Give Their Brains a Right Brain Break

Why does the PEP formula work? Because it appeals to both sides of the brain, the left and the right. Different sides of the brain control different styles of thinking. The chart on page 71 lists what each side of the brain governs.

Although no one is all left-brained or right-brained, most people have a distinct preference for one style of thinking over the other; some people are more "whole-brained" and use both sides equally. Left-brain subjects focus on logical thinking, analysis, and accuracy. Right-brain subjects focus on aesthetics, feeling, and creativity. If you want to inspire, you must connect to the right brain, the emotions.

You never know how many people in your audience are left-brained, and how many are right-brained. Therefore, your presentations must always appeal to both sides of the brain. If you appeal solely to the left-brain (just the facts, ma'am), even the most left-brained members of your audience will get bored and restless, and their attention will begin to drift. Every few minutes, regain their attention and wake them up with a right-brain break by including examples, stories, and creative imagery.

Left Brain Thinking	Right Brain Thinking
Logical	Intuitive
Rational	Instinctive
Analytical	Synthesizing
Objective	Subjective
Sequential	Random

The 3 Magical Phrases

One effective way to introduce a right-brain break is to use one of what I call "the three magical phrases." When I'm giving a presentation and tell people there are three magical phrases, they immediately get out their pads to make notes—no matter how many credentials they have or how experienced they are as speakers. That's because everyone wants an easy fix to be a better speaker. This is, in fact, one easy fix. And these magical phrases are: "It's like…," "For example…," "Just imagine…."

Those three phrases are perfect to get your audience's attention and lead them along the path you want them to follow. Suppose you're making a presentation trying to get your colleague to participate in a blood drive. You could make the presentation by stating all the facts about how many people need blood donations every day and how depleted the blood supply is. But think about how much more effective you could make your appeal by adding: "Just imagine that your loved one is in trouble and in need of blood, and there is not enough to go around." That right-brain example is more likely to lead to action than just the facts alone. (By the way, I used the right-brain trick by starting the sentence before last with "But think about....")

Here's a good use of the phrase "it's like." I once read an article in the *New York Times* about a probe flying to Jupiter at 106,000 miles per hour. That speed was beyond my comprehension; it did not spur my imagination at all—until the next sentence, when the author wrote that it was like going from New York to San Francisco in a minute and a half. Then I was able to picture myself sitting down in a plane, taking a deep breath, and winding up in San Francisco. The simple phrase "it's like" is a powerful example of the effect your choice of words can have on a presentation.

Examples also add power to presentations. Use them whenever you can. Suppose you wanted to tell your audience that we all have a huge amount of potential inside us; we just have to let it out. You could then add: "For example, Michelangelo claimed that he didn't create his statutes, but rather released them. Find a slab of marble, he told his younger artists, then take away everything that isn't the statue." Every time you say "for example" in a presentation, the audience's interest perks up. They know you're going to explain your idea in a different way, or a better way, or make clear something they didn't understand the first time around.

If you use the phrase "just imagine," use it only once or twice, because it stands out and people will notice if you repeat it too often. You can use "it's like" or "for example" more frequently without it becoming obvious.

Choose Your Stories With Care to Engage and Inspire

A compelling story beats a mountain of facts every time. Stories don't have to be amazing, incredible tales—often family mishaps and personal insights are very moving. Author Sue Miller stated in a 1999 *New York Times* article that "...you can make a story out of anything, anything at all. What's hard—and what's interesting—about a story is not so much the *thing* that's in it, but what's made of that thing."

Like any powerful tool, however, support can be overused and misused. The PEP formula ensures that your speech doesn't become a string of stories; support devices should bolster your main points, not vice versa.

Make sure your supporting examples and quotes are well rehearsed, accurate, and tie into your purpose. It's tempting to plunge ahead with a lively story or fact without checking it thoroughly; after all, no one is going to write down every word you say, and you are just trying to keep people interested. But in any field or endeavor, mistakes can come back to haunt you. The best speakers use accurate data, accepted definitions, and good sources. Finding authorities on your subject may take a little extra research, but it's worth it.

Selling Through Stories

Speakers are in the selling business, and they sell facts by using examples the audience is far more likely to retain than straight facts. Use your support to *focus*: All of your stories, jokes, analogies, and quotations must be related to your subject.

It's very important to get into the habit of looking for good stories that will make your speeches interesting. Audiences love people stories. During one PowerSpeak program, I asked people to tell a story about their first driving test, first day at college, or first date—in 25 words or less. I got a wonderful variety of interesting stories, and afterward people said that was the best part of the program, because it made them realize—vividly—the importance of stories.

Technical speakers must make sure they present a vivid illustration or demonstration of their process, procedure, or discovery. By doing so, they "translate" the esoteric into the relevant. Developing this kind of support isn't just more fun for your audience; it's more fun for you too. It also shows the audience that you are comfortable with your topic and your expertise and that you care about giving the audience an enjoyable speech.

Support Is Everywhere

The best way to use support is to mix humor, quotations, analogies, and other elements—offer your audience a rich brew of stories. Mix human-interest stories with factual details and vice versa. Your sources? Try newspapers, quotation collections, industry research, memories of childhood, friends' experiences, world history, and so on. Your sources are endless. And never underestimate the power of the past. I often use a quotation from Confucius to open sessions where I'm speaking on effective management. The quotation never fails to bring nods of recognition, and looks of surprise, when people hear that Confucius came up with this wisdom around 500 B.C.! Reminding people that there's nothing new under the sun and giving your presentation a historical context are good ways to make your speech something people can relate to and remember.

Tried-and-True Sources of Support

Whether you're facing a skeptical audience, have a difficult idea to communicate, or just need support to make your topic clear and engaging, here are some of the most reliable ways to give your speech staying power. You'll keep your audience involved and its interest level high if every three or four minutes during your presentation, you tell a story, ask a question, or use a combination of the support devices that follow:

- *Facts.* A fact is simply a statement that can be verified, either by referring to a third source or by direct observation. Facts give your opinions weight and add objectivity to your pronouncements. Without facts, you have no credibility. The key is not to bore your audience with too many of them.

- *Figures and Statistics.* Succinct and unblinking, numbers can provide startling punctuation to any presentation and are mandatory in many technical ones. But numbers cannot communicate on their own. Some numbers are so vast they require further illustration, such as the national deficit. A good speaker will "translate" this huge sum into a stack of $100 bills and tell the audience how tall that stack is.

- *Definitions.* They allow you to inquire into the nature of something, usually by identifying it with a general class and then specifying its particular qualities. For example, a man (the word to be defined) is a type of mammal (general class) that walks upright (particular quality).

  Using the dictionary is always a good source, though definitions can vary. Select the definition that suits you. For instance, if you want to call attention to marketing's sheer scope, you can define it as "the coordination of all activities—including planning, research, and selling—necessary to get a product or service from a seller to a buyer."

  Definitions don't have to be serious; many speakers use pithy, witty quotations to zero in on a point they want to cover. Here's how Ambrose Bierce defined *egotist*: "A person more interested in himself than in me." Sometimes it's fun (and memorable) to make up your own definitions.

- *Examples.* Usually brief, examples are incidents or objects that prove or clarify a generalization you're making. As support, examples are everywhere and often serve to introduce compelling facts and statistics. A manager trying to prove it's possible to cut costs in his division without cutting personnel will persuade his audience with examples (that is, the actual dollar savings attached to various changes in procedure).

While you will usually want to use examples to prove or elaborate on your point, you can also use them to form a positive point of view. For example, as XYZ Manufacturing Company has shown, if you don't cut personnel, here's what will result: Morale will rise, employees will work harder, and profits will increase.

- *Illustrations.* These are more detailed than examples, often offering point-by-point clarification.

  To illustrate the above stance on not cutting personnel, you could go step by step and show how the company was still able to cut costs through a better hiring process, and then take your listeners through that process.

- *Anecdotes and Personal Stories.* These are stories or experiences used to illuminate but not necessarily to prove a point. Many speakers use anecdotes and personal stories—often about themselves—to establish rapport, break the ice, or subtly reinforce the point they are making. Anecdotes tend to be human-interest stories and can have real staying power with an audience.
- *Authority.* Cite an authority when you use a reliable, recognized source to support your point.
- *Quotations.* A favorite of many speakers, quotations allow you to bring in an authority, an example, and often some humor—all at once. And because many quotations that have survived through the ages tend to be pithy and profound, speakers instantly inject both qualities into their speech. A favorite of mine is John Kenneth Galbraith's quote that modesty is a much overrated virtue. The quote (or the person quoted) doesn't have to be well known to be effective, it just has to be relevant and help you make your point.
- *Testimony.* Usually more directly relevant to the speaker's points than a quotation, testimony is corroborating evidence—proof in someone else's words that supports your view. In my talk "The Power of Questions: How to Use Questions to Lead, Succeed, and Activate Change," I quote Michael Bloomberg as sharing that there is an indivisible bond between the people who have the right information and the people who succeed. I got this quote from him several years ago, but now that he is the mayor of New York City, it makes my information even more credible.

- *Analogies.* A set of parallel conditions that throw light on what is being discussed by their similarity and familiarity, analogies are very useful in technical presentations. Use a "domestic" analogy, one that defines the esoteric in terms that are close to home. Best-selling author Dr. Richard Seizer makes medicine seem immediate when he writes phrases such as, "a surgeon, who palms the human heart as though it were some captured bird." The best analogies have a little bit of surprise—the surprise that leads to retention.
- *Restatements.* Because it is the business of a good speaker to condense and edit, restatements help you find and present the essence in a long-winded point you need to include. By putting things into your own words, which is why you were asked to speak in the first place, restatements let you speak with the authority of the facts behind the statement without losing your own talent.
- *Historical Background.* Most presentations need some sort of context to be persuasive. Be sure your audience has the background necessary to understand the implications of your presentation. Don't make the mistake of assuming the topic you're talking about is common knowledge. Astute speakers will present their background material in such a way that it also supports their contentions.

Keep Your Flourishes Coming

Speakers also get support from devices such as humor, rhetorical questions, and compliments or challenges directed toward the audience. Whether used separately or as part of an example, an analogy, or another element, these attention-getters serve to startle. They make the audience sit up and take notice, and they allow you to observe the cardinal rule of speaking: Never be boring.

A good speaker will insert some lively support every three to four minutes to keep audience involvement high and to recapture attention. A speech should be made up of a series of peaks and valleys: The peaks are the places where the speaker inserts supporting material; the valleys are the natural lows between new bits of material that make the peaks possible.

Most speakers start strong, and then plummet as they move toward the conclusion, where the excitement builds and the final point is made. But chances are that what came in the middle will be lost.

The most effective speech travels an interesting path, guiding the audience along through each section with introductions, transitions, and conclusions. Supporting material will be frequent but not so overpacked that it slows down the journey. Momentum is steady and sure, climbing up to a memorable conclusion.

The world is filled with support for your presentations. Look around, keep lists of things that strike you as appropriate, and remember to use examples to make your points effectively. Carry around a little black book to jot down support as it occurs to you. Make it an ongoing quest; you should always be looking for examples.

When we tell stories, our voices naturally become animated. Once you have amassed your support, the next step is to really use your voice, raising and lowering it for variety. Your voice is an instrument that can be used to keep your audience interested, an advantage the next chapter covers in detail.

Professional Projects: Build Interest and Involvement

1. You have been asked to deliver an orientation address to 20 new employees. In your opening, include at least one analogy and one personal story.
2. Start a file for quotations, stories, and all kinds of supporting materials.
3. Recreate a story about your first date or your most embarrassing moment.
4. For a week, read through the newspaper (*USA Today* is a source of good material) and come up with an anecdote that could be useful in your presentations or conversation.
5. Commit to telling an interesting story at the next party you go to.
6. Read the Obituaries. I found a wonderful story about Tom Landry, the former coach of the Dallas Cowboys while reading his obituary.

Chapter 8

Fault #5: Monotonous Voice and Sloppy Speech

Speech is a mirror of the soul. As a man speaks so he is.

—Publius Syrus

Your voice is your calling card. Over the phone, it's responsible for the entire impression you make on your listener. Whether you bore or enthrall—a lot depends on how you sound.

People's initial perceptions of each other break down three ways: visually (how we appear), vocally (how we sound), and verbally (what we say). The verbal aspect accounts for only 7 percent of how we are perceived; how we look forms 55 percent of the impression, and how we sound a surprising 38 percent. Yet the sound of our voice is something we give little thought to.

But you have to be conscious of your voice—and of how to change it—throughout your speech. As anyone who has heard a droning speaker knows, the wrong voice, besides making a bad impression, wrecks an otherwise compelling speech. A monotonous tone, mumbling, lack of clarity, and poor enunciation leave the audience noticing your voice and not your words.

A voice is not a neutral thing: It's either a wonderful asset or a serious liability. It either conveys control and confidence or proves a lack of both. But it should be your *greatest aid* in being interesting and exciting, because it can insert variety into a speech with such ease. To battle an audience's short attention span, speakers need to insert something interesting every three to four minutes. But that doesn't mean coming up with stories and jokes exclusively; you can use your voice to get attention immediately. You can polish your voice just as you polish your speech. All it takes is awareness and practice.

Listen to Yourself—Often

The first step to a powerful voice is getting to know yours. That's not as silly as it sounds. You may think you know your voice; after all, you're always speaking to people at work, at home, and on the phone. But in those instances you're listening to *them,* not to yourself.

Getting your voice ready for a speech means listening to the way you start sentences, form vowels, and pause after periods. You should practice speaking aloud often. Use your own words, the newspaper, anything. Read to the kids, to the dog; recite in the shower. Develop a love for good speech; listen to audiocassettes of powerful speakers reading book excerpts. Listen to how classically trained actors such as James Earl Jones or Meryl Streep use their voices, as instruments of feeling.

Look in the mirror to see how you are making the sounds. Make a habit of speaking aloud to yourself every day. Use a tape recorder and the exercises in this chapter and *listen* to your progress. Evaluate yourself often; use the form at the end of this chapter. Once you have started to listen to your voice objectively, you're ready to tackle the fine points of controlling it.

How to Build a More Interesting Voice

Speakers have many tools at their disposal for building vocal variety:

- *Volume.* Volume adds variety to whatever you say.

  Practice: Say the word *no* over and over, starting very softly (almost whispering) and working your way to very loud (almost shouting).

- *Pitch and Inflection.* Different from volume, pitch and inflection reflect your overall tone.

  Practice: Say the following, letting your voice follow the words: "Let your voice come down evenly, smoothly as a sigh. Then evenly up and ever so high. Hold our tones level and high today; then level and low tomorrow, I say. Let tones glide high, then slide down low. Learn to say, "no, no, NO." Recite the "do, re, mi" scale, going from a high tone to a low one. Or try the numbers one through eight, going up the scale and coming down again.

- *Pace and Rhythm.* How fast or slow you articulate the words and sounds.

  Practice: Read a rhyme such as "The Ballad of Green Broom." Slow down each time you say, "Broom, Green Broom" and the words that rhyme with it. Read the rest very quickly.

- *Emphasis.* This affects your word and syllable stress. The key point is to be sure people get your main ideas. Help them by subverting the less important ones. A common fault of speakers is to emphasize too many things; you should isolate the key points you want to emphasize.

  Practice: Use a simple declarative statement such as, "I am going to the store." Use the same sentence to answer a series of questions, emphasizing the appropriate word to answer the question. Subvert the unimportant words.

  Many Americans have the bad habit of fading away at the end of a sentence. This can be dangerous in certain situations. Imagine you were given the task of diffusing a bomb, and the person giving you instructions says, "Whatever you do, don't touch the…." That last word could be a lifesaver! Although the last word is not always that dramatically important, it doesn't mean you should just let it drop out of hearing altogether.

- *Attitude.* The same word or phrase can take on radically different meanings, depending on the attitude implicit in your voice.

  Practice: Say *well* as if you were: annoyed, disgusted, surprised, thrilled, in doubt, suspicious, thoughtful, and pugnacious

- *The Pause.* Powerful speakers use the pause several ways—for emphasis, effect, and mood. Pauses can be long, medium, short, or very short (when you're just drawing a breath). They can also signal a transition.

  There are four types of pauses:

  1. The Think About it Pause: Gives people a chance to digest what you have said (one to two beats long). It can be effective to pause before you deliver an important point, although it's not good if it's so overused that it becomes boring.

  2. Transitional Pause: Take a short pause between two minor points (one beat) and a longer pause (two to two and a half beats) for transitions between two more important points.

3. Emphasis Pause: Take a long pause before you make a statement or ask a question where you want people to think about the implications and meaning of what you have just said (two to three beats).
4. Pregnant Pause: Similar to the thinking pause, but used most often to create effect (two to three beats).

Practice: The next time you have to deliver good news, practice your pause. "Wait until I tell you the good news!" Stop. Count to three slowly. You'll sense the anticipation in your listeners. Enjoy it and feel its power. Then tell them the news.

Practice Your Vocal Variety

Here are seven sentences you can use to practice vocal variety. Say each sentence several times, each time using different pitch, rhythm, and word emphasis.

- Why aren't you all lying on the beach in Hawaii right now?
  (Try this as if you were angry, then as if you were motivating your team.)
- How many of you paid all of your income tax last year?
  (How does the sentence change if you emphasize the word "all"?)
- What would you do if you knew you only had one month to live?
  (Say this in a slow, measured tone. Then repeat it at a faster pace, emphasizing the words "one month." See the difference?)
- This occasion will go down in history.
  (There are two interpretations to this statement: the "occasion" might be a happy one, or it could be a day of infamy. Convey the two different meanings using pitch, volume, and attitude.)
- I'm going to tell you how you can make $25,000 in 25 minutes.
  (Pauses can make this sentence quite effective. Where would you put them?)
- I was told two years ago I had three months to live.
  (Emphasis can bring out the contrast between the words "two years" and "three months.")
- Let me tell you how I won the lottery!
  (Use all the tools to vary this sentence in as many ways as possible.)

Learn to Loosen up

Facially tense people have more monotonous voices, because they are not using their jaws and not changing their tone enough. An effective voice is relaxed and flexible; the variety so important to a lively speech will only result if you have loosened up your voice ahead of time and speak with an open throat and a loose, active lower jaw. With an open throat, sounds are no longer tight and squeezed.

To open your throat, relax the whole area around it. Rotate your head slowly to one side for a count of eight, and repeat for the other side. Think of clothes dangling on a line—limp and at ease. Then indulge in a nice big yawn. Right before you finish the yawn, lazily recite the vowels "A, E, I, O, U." All your throat exercises should be put together with very open sounds and done very lazily, effortlessly, and slowly.

Now work on getting an active jaw. Americans are known to have tight jaws, which makes for poor diction. Most American men, in fact, have "cultural lockjaw"; they speak like Clint Eastwood, who keeps his mouth almost closed when he speaks. Women tend to have more interesting and varied voices because they are more facially animated. You have to open up your jaw on certain vowel sounds and diphthongs (vowel sounds that come together, like *now).* Say *cow,* with your hand on your jaw, and notice the jaw movement.

Practice: Try "How now, brown cow." Make these sounds slowly and easily. Use a mirror to make sure you are really shaping the sounds. The tight jaw style of Gary Cooper and Clint Eastwood may be great for movies, but it's not good for public speakers.

Other Keys to Clear Diction

Our breathing, throats, and jaws all play an important role in how we sound. But clear diction is also governed by our lips, teeth, and tongue. Lips should hit against each other on the "P," "B," "M," "W," and "WH" sounds.

Practice: Create these sounds and the vowels in between by saying "PAPA," "MAMA," and "WAWA." Make sure your lips hit each other and build your speed. Try longer phrases, increasing your speed as you go along: "We have rubber baby buggy bumpers." "Peter Prangle picked pickly prangly pears."

Keep practicing until you have an open throat, an active lower jaw, strong lip muscles, and a flexible tongue that can trip lightly over tongue twisters.

Variety Through Emphasis

One of the biggest faults of American speakers is that we give everything equal emphasis. Read the following paragraph from a story by W. Cabell Greet, associate professor of English, Barnard College (and if possible, record yourself doing it).

> Once there was a young rat named Arthur, who could never make up his mind. Whenever his friends asked him if he would like to go out with them, he would only answer, "I don't know." He wouldn't say "yes" or "no" either. He would always shirk making a choice.

What is the most important point in this paragraph? It's that Arthur could never make up his mind; the places in the paragraph that make that point should be emphasized. The others can be read at a fairly quick pace.

Vocal variety is one of the most powerful weapons in a speaker's arsenal; good speakers use it to great effect. If your words were written, you would rely on punctuation to move your thoughts along and to link your ideas. In speech, all you have to make your points and to get people to understand is your voice; it is the only sort of punctuation the speaker has.

An effective speaker stresses points by limiting the main ones and by shading all the rest through vocal technique. The key words you emphasize, the pauses you insert, your shifting pitch, rhythm, loudness, tone, and rate of speech all affect how your audience interprets your words. Learn to *build*; even lists can gain drama if you let your voice add it. For example, "I came, I saw, I conquered" could be said with equal emphasis on the three verbs, and it would seem rather bland. But "I came, I saw, (pause) I *conquered*" builds to a finale and catches the audience's attention.

You should always "lean" on the new idea in your sentence. For example, if you've been mentioning sales success and are introducing the concept of life success, emphasize the word *life* vocally, because it represents a new idea, and de-emphasize success, because you've said it already. Nine times out of 10 an action word (often a verb) represents the new idea; don't leave it entirely up to the audience to grasp the new idea just because it's new; use your voice to nudge the audience along.

Another way to highlight an important point is to stop talking just before you introduce the point. The pause is one of the most effective attention-getters around. People get so used to hearing a speaker *talk* that when there is silence they sit up and take notice.

Keep Your Speech Interesting Through Articulation, Diction, and Pronunciation

When you speak, you avail yourself of words the way a musician uses notes. And like the musician, you can sound words and letters smoothly or disconcertingly. All it takes to be smooth is some awareness of language. The way we speak breaks down into three elements:

1. *Articulation* means using your articulators—lips, tongue, teeth, lower jaw, upper gums, hard and soft palate, and throat—to form the sounds of speech. The key to good articulation is keeping all these parts flexible as you speak.
2. *Diction* is the total production of your sounds. You can be sloppy or crisp, depending on how you put everything together.
3. *Pronunciation* is the manner in which you deliver words; it's where you place your accent. People in different regions pronounce differently—*car* in New York becomes *cah* in Boston. I once heard a Russian woman deliver an address on the subject of nuclear power at a public utility. When she said *mass* (frequently), it sounded to those in the audience like *mess* and they were noticeably alarmed and confused.

The clearer your articulation, diction, and pronunciation are, the more in control—and the more powerful—you will appear to be.

Don't Ignore the Basics—Vowels and Consonants

Vowels are the music of our speech; they carry the tone and must be pronounced like the open and pure letters they are. *Consonants* are the bones of speech; they must be sharp and precise. *Diphthongs* are a union of two vowels that form one syllable, but that one syllable must be formed properly.

When forming all vowels, the tip of your tongue should be behind your lower teeth. The two major problems people have with vowels are elongating the short ones and not drawing out the long ones. Keep your jaw active and your tongue flexible and you will avoid these mistakes.

Practice: Explore the differences between "he bit the dust," where the vowels are short and clipped, and "the long sleeve," where the sounds should be drawn out.

Reading out loud is still the best way to become aware of the various sounds speakers face. Inside our small, 26-letter alphabet lurk a surprising variety of combinations. We have only five vowels, but 14 vowel sounds are possible. Our 19 consonants can produce 25 consonant sounds—like the "dg" in *udge.* The more aware you are of these components, the more practiced you are at uttering them, the more polished you will sound.

Vowel, Diphthong, and Consonant Exercises

Practice the following sentences, concentrating on the underlined sounds. If you have any questions about pronunciation, consult a pronouncing dictionary to help you understand what the sounds should be.

Breathe: Your Speech Depends on It!

For your audience to hear you, you must breathe correctly. People tend to start sentences on a high note and fade out; their voices start to sound monotonous because they don't have enough breath to support variety throughout the entire sentence. A good voice has sufficient breath so that the audience hears all the important sounds.

We get into bad habits and don't use our breathing fully. To really see how to breathe, watch babies or animals. To breathe fully, like they do, take a deep breath and observe yourself. Did you use only your shoulders and chest or did your diaphragm (the area just above your waist) expand too? As you inhale, your diaphragm should expand, and it should deflate like a balloon as you exhale.

Find Your Diaphragm

To get your diaphragm going, pant like a dog out of breath. Put your hand above your waist. Now, laugh—when you laugh you are actually breathing through your diaphragm. It's like a large band all around this area of your body. To exercise your diaphragm, lie down with an object like a heavy book pressing against your chest.

Practice: Raise the book up and down and get used to breathing through your diaphragm. When you're standing, practice not lifting your shoulders as you breathe: Proper breathing isn't seen or heard by your audience.

It's not just how you take in air, but how much. If you take in too much, you are going to flood your diaphragm; if you take in too little, your voice will sound very thin. You have to learn to distribute air evenly over an entire sentence, and it's a good idea to take in a little extra so you don't run out of steam. Because the most important point usually comes at the end of a sentence, you'll want to have enough energy to really make your point there.

Get into the habit of taking air in through your nose and letting it out through your mouth; this way your mouth doesn't get dry, which is a common speaking fear. Breathing through your mouth will only accentuate whatever dryness is already there.

Build Your Endurance

Short phrases only require short breaths. But complex sentences pose challenges for speakers who don't want to weaken points by stopping in the middle and gasping—however slightly—for air. You can control your need for air just as people train themselves to stay underwater for long periods.

Start by saying a short sentence first. Then add phrases one at a time while extending your endurance.

Practice: "This is the cow, with the crumpled horn, that tossed the dog, that worried the cat, that killed the rat, that ate the food, that lay in the house that Jack built." You can also use "The Twelve Days of Christmas." Each day you practice—and lengthen the sentence—your endurance grows.

Your Path to a Powerful Voice

Although there are many voice pitfalls into which we can fall without knowing it, there are also many steps that assure us of clear and effective communication:

- Use a warm, resonant voice. Avoid sounding flat, gruff, harsh, too weak, or too loud. Strive for a clear, ringing tone and speak with vigor.
- Build your point vocally. Add emphasis and drama through the way you actually say your words by stressing the most important words and phrases and shading the less important ones.
- Vary your pitch, force, volume, rate, and rhythm. Catch people's attention by getting noticeably louder at an important point.

- Have enough breath to finish each sentence on a strong note.
- Make sure your thoughts forge ahead and build your argument.
- Display a lively amount of vocal and physical energy. Be animated; otherwise, why should your audience be enthusiastic?
- Use rhetorical questions to involve your audience, but don't overdo it.
- Clearly articulate each sentence, phrase, word, and syllable. Give full value to all the sounds in your speech.
- Do not drop consonants (for example, *gonna*, *runnin'*).
- Use correct pronunciation.
- Strive for a smooth tone; it will sustain your argument better than a choppy one.
- Avoid "oh," "uh," "okay," and "you know."
- Make sufficient use of the pause.
- Make sure your voice rises when you ask questions and falls when you make statements.
- Use emphasis, pauses, inflections, changing pitch, and loudness to shade what you have to say.

A Quick Fix for Imminent Engagements

To guard against being boring, add variety to your next speech. Here is a quick list of things you can add without much trouble—things you *should* add to ensure that your next speech will be livelier than your last.

- Put at least two rhetorical questions in your speech. Your voice will naturally rise when you come to them.
- Insert at least one dramatic pause. This device builds your power, for nothing captures the audience's attention like silence.
- Vary your speed. If you tend to speak quickly, slow down at least three times during your presentation; if you speak slowly, speed up at least three times.

- Change your voice and your attitude just before your conclusion.
- Combine an interesting variety of voice inflections within your speech to involve your audience. The next chapter goes into meeting those needs in detail. Adding variety to your voice is important in general communication as well. Colleagues will listen more closely when you color your words to give emphasis to your important points.

Relax, You Probably Sound Fine

Speaking well is an art, not a science, and there is no one formula for a compelling voice. Whether you tend to speak fast or slow, you don't have to completely change the way you present words. Just become aware of the little things you can do to change the way you sound and practice the voice exercises in this chapter. Then at your next presentation, be natural and be yourself.

Professional Projects: Develop a More Interesting Voice

1. Develop a 3- to 5-minute vocal warm-up for yourself.
2. Record your next presentation or record a practice reading. Then evaluate it using the voice and speech evaluation form on page 89.
3. Read children's stories to your kids, to your neighbors' kids, to your nieces and nephews. Volunteer to read for the blind. Use your voice to its fullest. When you are a character, really give that person a unique vocal character. You'll have fun and so will your audience.
4. Rent or buy some books on tape read by excellent British actors. Good actors such as Anthony Hopkins and Maggie Smith utilize all kinds of vocal variety. These tapes will help to train your ear, give you confidence to expand your vocal range, and will also be enjoyable listening.

Voice and Speech Evaluation Form

1. *Voice production*
   a. Support of tone
   ____Good ____Needs improvement ____Weak
   b. Proper breathing
   ____Good ____Needs improvement ____Weak
   c. Vocal quality (for example, harsh, nasal, breathy)
   ____Good ____Needs improvement ____Weak
   d. Resonance
   ____Good ____Needs improvement ____Weak
   e. Overall vocal energy
   ____Good ____Needs improvement ____Weak
2. *Producing the sounds*
   a. Sharp articulation
   ____Good ____Needs improvement ____Weak
   b. Flexible lips, jaw, and tongue
   ____Good ____Needs improvement ____Weak
   c. Clear and correct punctuation
   ____Good ____Needs improvement ____Weak
   d. Diction using long and short vowel sounds
   ____Good ____Needs improvement ____Weak
3. *Vocal variety*
   a. Volume
   ____Good ____Needs improvement ____Weak
   b. Pace or rhythm
   ____Good ____Needs improvement ____Weak
   c. Pitch
   ____Good ____Needs improvement ____Weak
   d. Inflection
   ____Good ____Needs improvement ____Weak
   e. Attitude
   ____Good ____Needs improvement ____Weak
   f. Shading and word emphasis
   ____Good ____Needs improvement ____Weak
   g. Use of the pause
   ____Good ____Needs improvement ____Weak

3\. *Main areas for improvement* ____

____

Chapter 9

Fault #6: Not Meeting the Real Needs of Your Audience

Men are not against you. They are merely for themselves.

—Gene Fowler

Picture this: You're on an expedition to climb Mt. Everest. You're leaving base camp when you hear a thunderous noise. Avalanche! The head Sherpa turns to you and your fellow climbers and says, "You may not know this, but I've been a Sherpa for many years. My group was the only one to survive the last avalanche that hit this mountain. This is what we did to make it out alive...."

How would you listen to what this Sherpa had to say? *Very carefully.* Why? Because he is meeting the needs of his audience.

I once heard a woman at a conference give a speech on what new associations could do to grow, prosper, and be valuable to members. She had an audience that really cared about the topic; people had signed up for it specifically. She meandered, went off on tangents, and seldom finished a thought. She said "you know" about 75 times in a 45-minute presentation. But *because she met the needs of members of her audience*, she got a standing ovation. They felt she cared about them and understood what interested them. That's how important it is to be tuned in to your audience. If you are, even a poorly delivered speech can be well received; if you're not, even a polished one can fall flat.

A surprising number of speeches simply don't meet the real needs of the audience. The chief reason: The speaker feels it's enough to tell people something *the speaker* thinks they need to know.

In one of my many previous careers, I was a school teacher in New York City. It didn't take long for me to realize that if I didn't make information meaningful to my students, they tuned me out almost immediately. I couldn't give them a list of boring principles; everything I taught had to be relevant to their lives. So, for instance, when I taught the subject of group discussions, I asked them to play out a scenario. I told them that they were with a group of five friends trying to decide what to do on a particular Saturday night. How would they make a decision? Would one person turn out to have more influence than the others? How could they be sure everyone in the group had a say? The kids had fun with the exercise and—whether they knew it or not—learned the principles I was trying to get across.

But you can't expect your audience to have the same excitement that you do; you must develop the audience's interest. No matter how worthy, life-enhancing, or even lifesaving your topic may be, your enthusiasm is not enough. You must make those in your audience enthusiastic. They are potential skeptics, and your task is to win them over. Because you can't say everything there is to say on your topic, you need to say the things your audience needs to hear.

The Most Compelling Subjects

Winning listeners over is easier if you know the four things people find most interesting: sex, health, money, and themselves. This is somewhat of a cynic's list, but most good speeches will tap into one of the things, usually the last item.

Inspire Your Audience: Make It Impossible *Not* to Listen

Because people do things for their own reasons, you must motivate and inspire people from *their* perspectives, not yours. If you speak to their real needs, they will be compelled to listen, and listen well. In my own seminars and speeches, I always find out one or two specific problems that the audience currently faces. Then I construct a speech that solves—or shows people how to solve—those problems. This is the speaker as hero or heroine, the problem-solver approach, and I recommend it highly. If you're speaking to middle managers on running their departments more efficiently, and you determine that one of their problems is motivating clerical employees, then give them a strategy to do just that, with results that tie in to what the corporation expects of them.

Whether your audience is one person or one thousand, you should focus on its needs. Being successful in one-on-one situations requires you to focus on the other person. Start any general communication by putting yourself in that other person's shoes and proceed from there.

Addressing problems your audience faces illustrates the importance of *context*. So does this story: Suppose you came to a seminar and, instead of the promised speaker, you were met by a desert survival expert. You probably would not listen too closely. But if the pilot of a plane being forced to land in the desert gave that lecture, you would view that formerly irrelevant information quite differently. Context is caring—what does your audience care about? Figure that out, and you're well on your way.

Tune Into WIIFM and Sell Benefits

Speakers should always be motivated by their desire to please the audience; audiences are motivated by their own self-interest. Both forms of self-interest come together well if you realize that every person you're talking to is thinking, "Why should I care about this speech?" Everyone has a secret radio station called WIIFM, otherwise known as "What's In It For Me?" An effective speaker anticipates this built-in bias and shapes a speech by always thinking, "What benefit or benefits can I offer this particular audience?"

You sell an audience with benefits, not facts. To use the old expression, you buy a drill not for the drill but for the hole it will make. A ballpoint pen has a retractable point (fact), so you don't get ink on you (benefit). But be careful of just throwing benefits at your audience; the connection between the product and the benefit—in this case the retractable point—must always be clear, because that's often the item or outlook you are trying to promote. Never assume that the members of the audience will make the connection themselves.

At first glance, this advice may sound cynical: People are so narrow-minded that everything must be fed to them in terms of self-interest. Not everything; just your speech. Think about it from this perspective: As a speaker, you are taking up people's time; you are asking them to listen closely to you for a period of time and to think hard about what you are saying. It may be cynical (and practical) to appeal to their needs, but it's also polite. They are giving you their time; you must respond with something worthy of that honor. In the end, everyone benefits, especially you, because you will have succeeded in making your points in a vivid, convincing, and memorable fashion.

Engage Your Audience With Facts and Feelings

You connect best with your audience by using a combination of facts and feelings. We need facts to get the information across. But we also need an emotional component, because every communication is trying to get someone to buy something—whether it's something tangible (such as a product or service), or intangible (such as an idea or principle).

How do you combine facts and feelings? By appealing to both left- and right-brain functions. When you state the facts, you're appealing to your listeners' left brains. When you state feelings, you're appealing to the right sides of their brains. In sales terms, facts and feelings are known as features and benefits. Features appeal to the intellectual, detail-oriented part of the brain. No one would buy an air conditioner, for instance, on its features alone. It's a big gray box that fits into a window. But it's benefit—that it cools you off on a hot summer's day—makes it worth an investment.

Features stay the same for everyone: A big gray box is a big gray box. But benefits change for different people. One person might need an air conditioner to cool off the room, while another might need it to provide clean air for an asthmatic child. It's important to know your listeners' needs so that you can emphasize the benefits that are most important to them.

When I conduct my PowerSpeak workshops, one of the first things I do is ask the participants what they can gain by becoming a better speaker. They give me a variety of answers, but the three that come up the most are the "three *C*s": Confidence, Credibility, and Cash. With these benefits in mind, it's easy to motivate them on to success.

7 Steps to Audience Involvement

By addressing the needs of the people in your audience, you are *involving* them in your speech. The more you can make them participants and not passive listeners, the more effective you will be. By participants I don't mean people who bombard you during a question-and-answer session, but people who are thinking, reacting, and taking mental notes as you speak. Here are seven steps that help instill the participation that leads to the persuasion that occurs when the audience follows your argument and actually accepts your ideas:

1. Prepare your speech with care, so your listeners will know you care about them and their needs.
2. Make the audience want to hear you; devise an intriguing, startling opening and a title you know will fit that audience.

3. Present your ideas dramatically with stories, examples, and facts. You want people to remember what you say, and the support stories provide goes a long way toward making your speech vivid.
4. Show how those ideas affect the people in your audience and what the benefits are. They now have the facts—you've supplied them. Now bridge the gap between your words and their lives. If you want your department to make formal use of job descriptions when hiring, tell them why: how these documents will help them find qualified people, save time, work more efficiently with the personnel department, and so on.
5. Use language's most appealing words: *discovery, easy, guaranteed, health, love, money, new, proven, results, safety, save*, and *you*.
6. Draw them in; ask the listeners to study or contemplate these ideas further. Involve them. Show them your ideas have a relevant context; they aren't just your private, unsubstantiated thoughts.
7. Ask the audience to act on your ideas. The best speeches carry over—into petitions, changed minds, reorganizations, elections, new ways of doing things.

Your end can be the point where you reveal that formerly hidden purpose that guided your speech from the beginning. But it was never meant to be kept a secret. By the end of your speech, you should have built the logic, the facts, and the stories to such a point that no one doubts your commitment. Now you are trying to enlist the troops.

Technical Presentation Pitfalls

I do a lot of consulting work with large corporations such as Verizon, Paine Webber, UBS, Duke Energy, and Pfizer. More often than not, executives there, who have to make presentations, assume they can just give the facts, however technical, because their audience is technically inclined.

Don't make the same mistake; don't assume benefits are irrelevant to a technical presentation or that they are readily apparent. They often aren't, as they lie buried in technical jargon. Making the benefits link is seldom stating the obvious; instead, it results in clarity and persuasion.

Technical speakers also often assume a level of expertise—or vocabulary—in the audience that is just too high. Play it safe and never let your audience's level of education trick you into thinking you don't have to define your terms, make good analogies, and clarify benefits. I once gave a talk to a high-level management group—or so I was told. I had prepared a speech that I thought would also be suitably high-level, but it quickly became apparent that my audience—mostly professional staff and new to management—wasn't following me. I quickly adjusted the speech before I had lost the audience's interest entirely.

25 Tricks of the Selling Trade

As a speaker you are a salesperson, and the item you're pushing is information. Your audience might be temporarily captive, but it isn't converted. You can sell your information more effectively if you remember that people buy for emotional reasons, not factual ones. When you do give facts, try to tie them to the emotional needs of your audience.

Psychologist Abraham Maslow discovered that all people have a hierarchy of needs, which rank from the most basic to the loftiest: physiological (sheer survival), security, social, self-esteem, and self-actualization (those rare moments when what we are doing and who we are seems exactly right). To sell through your speech or presentation you should keep these needs in the back of your mind, for they underlie the more obvious reasons people make decisions.

Here is by no means an exhaustive list of 25 reasons why people are persuaded to buy or say yes to something. You'll see that most relate directly to one of Maslow's steps in the hierarchy. Ask yourself if your speech ties in to at least one of these emotional needs:

1. To make money.
2. To save money.
3. To save time.
4. To avoid effort.
5. To gain comfort.
6. To improve health.
7. To escape pain.
8. To be popular.

9. To attract the opposite sex.
10. To gain praise.
11. To conserve our possessions.
12. To increase our enjoyment.
13. To satisfy curiosity.
14. To protect our family.
15. To be in style.
16. To satisfy an appetite.
17. To emulate others.
18. To have beautiful things.
19. To avoid criticism.
20. To avoid trouble.
21. To take advantage of opportunities.
22. To be individual and unique.
23. To protect our reputation.
24. To gain control over aspects of our lives.
25. To be safe.

Get to Know Your Audience

You're trying to appeal to the members of your audience. Who are they? Generally speaking, they have needs, goals, troubles, and short attention spans. But what are those needs, goals, and troubles? Start your audience research by asking the questions in the Audience Analysis on page 98.

Be One of Them

More than anything, a well-prepared speaker is aware, not only of the audience's quirks and concerns, but also of the larger picture: how current events may affect the presentation, or what preconceived notions the members of the audience might have of the speaker's topic or reputation. But don't make the mistake of assuming your audience has knowledge about recent events such as the Korean War or the Vietnam War; a growing number of young people don't remember the assassination of President Kennedy because they were born after it. It's a fine line to walk: Although you shouldn't overestimate what your audience knows, you can't underestimate its knowledge, either.

Once you have constructed a speech that truly addresses your audience's needs, you're ready to add the basics—an opening, transitions, and a conclusion—that reinforce the importance of the material you are giving them.

Professional Projects: Persuade Through Benefits

1. You are making a pitch for a raise. List three facts as to why you deserve it; along with the facts, list the benefits that your boss will enjoy by granting it.
2. Imagine you are a Jeep salesperson. Divide a sheet of paper into two columns. Head one column Features, the other one Benefits. List four features of your vehicle. For each feature, list at least one benefit. For example, if you list a convertible top as a feature, list the benefits along side it.

Audience Analysis—Preliminary: What You Need to Know

1. Audience's major needs, problems, concerns at this moment:

____

2. Subject knowledge and vocabulary level: ______________

3. Their relationship to me as speaker: ______________

4. Level of education: ______________

5. Age: ______________

6. Sex; Ratio of men to women: ______________

7. Ethnic background: ______________

8. Occupation: ______________

9. Audience size: ______________

10. Any special interests or purpose of meeting? ______________

11. Religion: ______________

12. Political persuasion: ______________

13. Special organization projects and current events: ______________

14. Are there any other speakers before or after me on the program? ____

15. Will there be drinking or eating before my speech? ______________

16. Have other speakers addressed this audience on a similar topic? ____

    Audience's reaction? ______________

17. What has audience responded to most positively? ______________

18. What has audience responded to least positively? ______________

19. What data and support will persuade my audience (for example, statistics, anecdotes, demonstrations, or colorful visuals)?

____

____

____

Below is a questionnaire I have found works very well with clients who hire me to speak. Whether you have someone fill it out, or you research the information yourself, all of these questions should be answered before you face your audience.

Audience Analysis—Customized

This questionnaire is designed to help us prepare a program specifically suited to the needs of your group. Please take a moment to answer fully all the questions and return the form to our office. Thank you for your help!

Special Request: Please send all available printed material on your company, division, employees, and product/service line.

(If additional space is needed, use a blank sheet of paper and attach it to this questionnaire.)

1. What is the theme of your meeting?

   ____

2. What are the top three challenges or problems faced by the members of your group?

   (a)______________________________

   (b)______________________________

   (c)______________________________

3. What, approximately, are the characteristics of your average member?

   Age:______________ Occupation:______________

   Sex:______________ Annual personal income:__________

   Educational background:______________

4. Will there be any special guests? Please explain:

   ____

5. How many people will be in the audience?______________
6. Why is your group attending this meeting?______________
7. How will they be notified?______________

8. What is their overall opinion regarding the subject, for example, favorable, hostile, etc.?

____

____

9. What three facts should I know about your group before addressing them?

   a. ____________________________________

   b. ____________________________________

   c. ____________________________________

10. What speakers have you used in the recent past and what did they discuss?

   a. ____________________________________

   b. ____________________________________

   c. ____________________________________

11. What programs/speakers have been most enthusiastically received?

____

____

12. Please list the names and positions of three people in the organization who are well known and well liked within the group, who will be present at the speech, and who I can joke with or call on if the need arises.

Name ________________ Position ______________

Name ________________ Position ______________

Name ________________ Position ______________

13. What are the three most significant events to have occurred in your industry, or within your group, during the past year?

   a. ____________________________________

   b. ____________________________________

   c. ____________________________________

14. Please share with me any "local color" you can think of relating to the location where my speech will be held.

____

____

____

____

15. Please share with me any "industry color" you can think of relating to your organization or industry.

____

____

____

____

16. Specifically, what are you trying to accomplish at this meeting?

a. ____

b. ____

c. ____

17. What are your specific objectives for my part of the meeting?

a. ____

b. ____

c. ____

18. Are there any issues/topics in particular that you think I should discuss during the program?

a. ____

b. ____

c. ____

19. Are there any issues/topics that you think I should avoid during the program?

    a. ______________________________

    b. ______________________________

    c. ______________________________

20. Do you have any suggestions to help me make this presentation the best your audience has ever heard?

    a. ______________________________

    b. ______________________________

    c. ______________________________

Part III

Conquer the Trouble Spots: The Basics—Openings, Transitions, Conclusions, Questions and Answers, and Visual Aids

Chapter 10

Starting on the Right Foot: Openings That Capture Your Audience

Things are always at their best in the beginning.

—Blaise Pascal

Powerful speakers start powerfully. They engage their audiences immediately. You must gain the audience's attention and interest the moment you walk on the stage. Without that attention, you won't get your message across, you'll have trouble sustaining whatever interest there is, and you won't have established your leadership and control—the keys to being a powerful speaker.

As a speaker, you are an unknown quantity, but only for the first 30 seconds of your speech. After that, everything you say will be heard in the context of that first impression, those first sentences. So it's very important to memorize your opening and practice it many times. Because this is your first contact with your audience, you need to keep from looking down at your notes, which does not help you seem warm, powerful, or persuasive. Your eyes are the most important way to keep people's attention, so make sure you know your opening well.

Grab This Time of Heightened Expectations

At the start of your talk, you have a big attention advantage. You've been formally and perhaps enthusiastically introduced; the men and women at your presentation are hoping it will be interesting, hoping they will get something out of it, and hoping it will not be a waste of their time. Your audience is in a state of expectation, and all you have to do is be reasonably confident, knowledgeable, and prepared *at the beginning,* and you'll have the audience on your side.

The opening is your appetizer; it is not meant to satisfy but to tempt, titillate, and arouse, and whet appetites for the next course. If you fail to get your audience's attention at the very beginning, it will take you at least three minutes to get it back, and people will already be less than excited about what is to come.

Compare these two openings:

1. "Um...hello, I'm your speaker, Dorothy Leeds, and I'm here to give some, or a few, clues on what foods to avoid so you can have less disease and less stress."
2. "Ladies and gentlemen: Would you like to add 20 quality years to your life? Then THINK before reaching for your salt shaker. I'm Dorothy Leeds, and I'm going to share with you 10 easy, proven steps to add those 20 years to your life."

Years ago, the great architect Frank Lloyd Wright gave a speech in Pittsburgh. His attention-getting opening was, "This is the ugliest city I have ever seen." Pittsburgh paid attention—to the opening and to the rest of the speech. In a recent survey, the city was ranked as one of the most desirable places to live in the United States. Wright knew not to start out with, "Good afternoon, it's a pleasure to be here," or with an irrelevant joke just for the sake of opening with humor. He came out swinging, and even if the people in the audience didn't agree with him, he had them listening.

Let Them Know You're NOT A BORE!

When you give a presentation, you're not always the first person the audience will see. There's usually someone else who introduces you. If that person is a good speaker, and knows the facts about you, you're off to a good start. But that's not always the case. So get off on the right foot: Write your own introduction.

Your introduction is the first thing your audience hears about you and your first chance to make an impression. Professional speakers known for a personal style don't leave these crucial first words in the hands of others. An introduction you write yourself (for someone else to deliver) warms up the audience, lists appropriate qualifications, and acts as a bridge that lets you cross over directly into your speech. And if you write it yourself, you know it will be accurate. Many a speaker has had to begin a speech by correcting a biographical flaw in an introduction written by someone who did not carefully check the facts.

There are still risks when you write your own introduction—someone may mess up the humor you're trying to insert, or even mispronounce something—but you reduce the chance of mistakes if you provide the text yourself.

Always send your introduction in advance with a note saying that it ties into your speech and should be read as is. You can leave some space for your presenter to add something if he or she wishes; just indicate the best place for this. Type the introduction in caps and double-space it so it's easy to read. Make it short and to the point. A standard introduction includes these four points and not much more: your name and title, your qualifications, why the speech can benefit the audience, and why you've been asked to speak. When you list your qualifications, name only the best three or four examples, or the ones that pertain to that particular audience.

Here's a sample self-introduction written by Joel Weldon, a well-known speaker.

> Our speaker this morning is Joel Weldon. His subject is titled, "Elephants Don't Bite: It's the Little Things That Get You." Joel comes to us from Scottsdale, Arizona, where he heads up his own personal development company. In the past six years, he has conducted over 1,000 seminars and workshops for some of America's top organizations.
>
> The reason we have him here today is because of his unique ability to help successful speakers become even more successful. He's creative and fun to listen to. And his unusual business card tells you, "Success comes in cans, not in cannots." Speaking on "Elephants Don't Bite: It's the Little Things That Get You," help me welcome Joel Weldon.
>
> (Printed materials given out during presentation at the 1981 National Speakers Association Convention [July 28, 1981]. © 1981 by Joel H. Weldon & Associates, Inc.)

That's an introduction that does a lot: It's short, simple, and vivid.

I often close my introductions with a pleasant touch I learned from some Southern hosts: "Please join me in welcoming Dorothy Leeds and PowerSpeak." Ending with a comment like that always brings a nice round of applause, which gives you support as you approach the platform.

Blow Your Own Horn

There are times, however, when no one is available to introduce you. In that case, you'll have to do it yourself. When this happens, most people come out on stage and say, "Good evening, ladies and gentlemen. I'm Dorothy Leeds, and I'm here today to talk to you about...." BORING! And it's what the audience expects you to do. You want to surprise them into paying attention, and let them know that you're not a typical speaker. Start off with your appetizer; give them a little tease before you tell them who you are.

Look at the two openings on page 106. The tease in version number two is only two sentences long, but it's enough to get the listeners hooked. Then you can go on to tell the audience who you are. Usually your name is enough; this is not the time or place to go through your entire resume. You can include one interesting fact about you if it is relevant. For example, I sometimes follow my attention-getter with, "I'm Dorothy Leeds, and I'm known as the Questioning Crusader."

10 "Can't Miss" Opening Strategies

Openings have more crucial responsibilities than any other part of your speech. Although the following list may seem daunting, remember that one well-crafted opening can combine many tasks into just a few minutes or sentences. Getting attention is the key task of any opening, but it's not the extent of your opening's responsibilities. Here's a list of criteria for a powerful opening:

1. Get the audience's attention. How you get it is not nearly as important as making sure you get it.

2. Build a bridge between what went on before and what is to come—your presentation. That's why people thank the introducer or refer back to previous speakers.

3. Let the audience know your purpose and objectives.

4. Get the members of your audience involved in your topic, your mission. You want their support, and you want them on your side.

5. Build expectations for what is to follow. Be careful about starting with a great joke you've practiced and then going into a list of facts and figures; your audience will feel let down.

6. Build a connection with the audience. Warm up the audience; relax them and show them they will have a good time listening to you, that you won't bore them. You're not putting them to sleep; you're saying, "It's okay, you're in good hands."
7. Make the listeners confident in you by showing how they will profit from and enjoy what they're about to hear.
8. Let the audience know you are in control. Give any necessary directions, such as how and when you will deal with questions or handouts. Explain everything up front.
9. Disclose something about yourself to further gain the audience's support by showing that you are human, fallible, or whatever is appropriate to the occasion.
10. Let the people in the audience know you're glad to be with them. This can be evident from your own enthusiasm; you can also address a compliment directly to the members of your audience, or disclose something about yourself in a way that shows you are relaxed around them.

Openings have to do a lot, but speakers have great freedom in crafting them—an advantage that other writers, such as playwrights and novelists, lack. You don't have to confine your story to a character's personality or to history. You can use all kinds of visual and audio aids. You don't have to keep the action tied to a specific place and time. You can roam from past to present to future, all in one sentence. You can draw your sources from almost any context. Above all, you can adjust and tailor your message to the specific audience you're addressing.

Quick and Easy Ways to Get Attention

All this leeway means the criteria for a good opening consist of one question: Does it grab the audience's attention? It's like the tree falling in the forest: Does it make a sound if no one is there to hear it? You may be up on a platform, ready to speak, but without your audience's attention, the speech will reach deaf ears.

Although a lot of your opening success comes down to your delivery style, and the passion you bring to your subject, the following 14 devices can be especially effective when incorporated into your opening:

- *Audience Compliment.* Don't use sheer flattery with no relevant purpose, but insert a sincere comment on some positive quality of the people before you. You want them to like you; show you already like them. I often use the following comment when I'm speaking: "I'm especially pleased to be here today, because I totally agree with the 5-foot, 6-inch Kansas City shortstop who said, 'I'd rather be the shortest player in the majors than the tallest one in the minors.'" (This works well because I am 5 ft. 1 in. tall.)

- *Audience Response.* As the author of *Smart Questions: The Essential Strategy for Successful Managers* and *The 7 Powers of Questions,* I am a strong believer in the power of questions. Direct questions get your audience involved—the key to a good opening. Staff and motivational speakers often use them because people will pay more attention to things they think of rather than to what you put forth. Asking the audience is a good technique if you have the style to get a response—it is distressing, and you lose credibility, if you ask a question and no one answers. You must let them know with your tone that you expect a response—and pause just long enough to get it. Always have an alternate plan, or answer the question yourself, quickly enough to give the message that you aren't upset about not getting answer. Any questions you ask should be interesting but not too difficult.

  Starting your speech with a question is good way to get the audience involved right from the beginning. I used to start my presentations with, "How many of you would like to be more successful?" When I start my talk on PowerSpeak, I often start by asking, "How many of you have heard the expression 'step outside the box'?" Almost everyone raises a hand, and with just one sentence, I've got the whole audience participating.

- *Audience Surveys.* Another related way to get the audience involved is to take a survey. It's often a good technique to use after lunch or dinner because it gets people moving a bit; they all look around to see who's raising a hand. For instance, I often ask my PowerSpeak audiences: "How many of you give formal presentations?" "How many speak up at meetings?" "How many leave voice mail?" "How many of you wouldn't answer no matter what I asked?" A survey is one of my favorite openings, because it gives me good information and gets the audience involved. (I borrowed the last question from another speaker, and I now lend it to you. It always gets a chuckle.)

If you think carefully about your questions, this technique can give you valuable information. For instance, if you were speaking to an audience of doctors, you might ask: "How many of you treat diabetic patients?" "How many of you feel the majority of your patients' diabetes is controlled?" "How many of you believe we should treat diabetes more aggressively?" The answers you get can help you focus your speech so that it meets the needs of each specific audience.

- *Rhetorical Questions.* By asking a rhetorical question (one that doesn't require an answer), you can restate your point in a dramatic way. Rhetorical questions make people think. After a presentation where I discuss the power and effectiveness of asking questions, I ask, "If questions are so powerful, why don't we use them more?" These questions can involve your audience and get people to think about the answer in their own minds. You focus their attention without engaging in the give-and-take of a true question-and-answer session.

  Before you incorporate a question, analyze it for rhetorical effect: Will it make your audience think? Will it get them mentally—and even physically—involved.

- *Startling Statement.* "My mother is the oldest living person on the face of the Earth." Use that at the beginning of a speech about health care for the aging and you're bound to get the audience's attention. You could follow it up by saying, "At least that's the way she feels most of the time." Anything that takes the audience by surprise will have them hanging on your every word until they get an explanation or further details from you.

- *Startling Statistic.* Combine brevity with a degree of shock—two powerful qualities for any opening—by leading off with a startling statistic. For example, if your topic was about the high cost of healthcare, you might open with, "Did you know that back pain alone costs society $20 billion a year?" Be careful not to use too many statistics at once, because people only remember one or two at a time.

- *Joke.* Many people feel they have to start with a joke, perhaps because they have heard so many other speakers do so. But as I mentioned earlier, you must be careful about setting up expectations of more jokes to come. The best time to use a joke is if it fits in with your topic just beautifully and you can tell it well, or if you intend to intersperse jokes throughout the speech.

Even with the risks, jokes can be a very good way to begin. I once attended a presentation on tunnel vision—a topic that can easily slip into predictable admonishments. The speaker began by telling a joke about two ostriches running away from two other ostriches. They couldn't run fast enough, so they decided to hide. She then looked at the audience and said, "Do you know how ostriches hide? Do you know how vulnerable you are in that position?" The audience chuckled, and she had made her point—that tunnel vision can be disastrous—effectively.

- *Visual Aid.* Visual aids can get attention quickly. I once saw a presentation on the advantages of nuclear power where the speaker held up a picture of a smiling Arab holding oil and U.S. dollars in his hands. Instantly, the speaker had made his point about nuclear power freeing us from some of the expense of importing. (More about visual aids in Chapter 14.)
- *Personal Experience.* Starting with a relevant story about yourself establishes empathy and rapport, and also confirms your qualifications to address the topic.
- *Reference to an Occasion.* If you are addressing the 100th anniversary of an association, work it into your opening. Your speech will instantly seem tailor-made for the members of the group, and they will sense what's coming up will also focus on them.
- *Reference to a Current Event.* Few speeches are given in a void; show off the links between your topic and the world at large. Doing so gives the audience a larger context in which to listen and to remember your words. Try to avoid being overly controversial, because you never know the current mind-set of your audience.
- *Quotation.* Quotations are popular, and with reason: The hard-earned wisdom of renowned people tends to be succinct, witty, and memorable. And a quotation can focus the attention of your audience much faster than traditional exposition. A quote from your grandmother, "When all is said and done, more is usually said than done," can be just as effective as a quote from someone famous, as long as it is relevant and helps make your point.
- *Citing an Authority.* You can often gain attention if you align yourself with a higher authority, whether it's a prize-winning scientist or the

head of your department. For instance, an educator might do well to quote legendary anthropologist Margaret Mead, who said, "Children must be taught how to think, not what to think."

- *Audience Challenge.* Don't be afraid to startle people; conflict is at the center of every successful play, and it can work equally well in a talk. You involve people even if they don't agree with you. Just make sure your challenge to the audience relates to the subject of the speech; otherwise, it will seem inappropriate. I use this challenge in my training sessions with managers improving their communication skills: "I dare you to put me out of business!"
- *Story.* Make your opening come alive by telling a story; stories tend to be things audiences remember with ease. John F. Kennedy told a story about a taxi ride before his election. He got out and was about to tip lavishly and tell the cabbie to vote Democratic. Then he remembered some advice from his father. He got out of the cab, didn't tip at all, and told the cabbie to vote Republican.
- *Comparison.* Comparisons are especially vivid if they relate to some daily aspect of your audience's life. I have heard cost-of-living expenses used to point out disparities between different parts of the country. They also help people have a visual image, which helps make your point. For instance, in the September 19, 2000, issue of the *New York Times*, Jane Brody wrote an article called "With a Little Help from Friends, Pandas Hang On." In it, she stated that a newborn panda is a "half-developed creature" of 4 or 5 ounces, cared for "by a 200-pound momma, who, if she is not extraordinarily gentle and devoted, can easily crush her newborn. If human mothers and babies had the same weight ratio, a 120-pound woman would give birth to a 2.5-ounce baby. Or, put another way, the mother of a 7.5-pound baby would weigh about 6,000 pounds." These comparisons make it easy for us to understand the enormous difference in size between momma panda and her baby.
- *An Unusual Definition.* These definitions are everywhere, and you can find the best ones in anthologies and quotation books. An example: "Men are like cellophane: hard to get rid of once you get wrapped in them." The more vivid the definition is, the more your audience will remember it.

Openings to Avoid

Just as there are ways to grab an audience's attention, there are traps even experienced speakers fall into that work swiftly to halt whatever momentum you're building:

- *Don't use the opening to restate the title of the speech or to reiterate information.* You need every moment to create interest and suspense; don't go over what is already known. Don't start by saying, "I am going to talk to you today about…safety."
- *Don't open your speech with an apology.* You may think it makes you sound friendly and not pompous, but apologies set up your audience to listen for your weaknesses.
- *Don't greet the "important" people in the audience.* Forget saying "Thank you, Mr. Chairman, Mayor Jones, Senator Smith…." The only time you would use such a formal opening is as a political candidate speaking before a very distinguished audience. If you want to bring attention to certain people in the audience, use their names in the context of your speech.
- *Don't explain your presence.* Don't offer explanations about why you *think* the chairman asked you to address the group. Remember that you are there for a good reason; you know it, and the audience knows it. Also remember the maxim covering explanations: "Your friends don't need it, and your enemies won't believe you anyway."
- *Don't say how difficult it was to choose the subject.* As far as the audience is concerned, your topic should be so vital that you never doubted its importance, and you should communicate that vital nature.

Practical Steps to Open With Ease and Impact

Beginnings are always difficult. But you can make starting your speech a little easier by following these steps, including the six steps to positive body language and the seven steps of the opening block.

Establish Your Credibility With Positive Body Language

1. Breathe (remember the prana, or deep breathing technique discussed in Chapter 2).
2. Walk to the "platform." (Take calm, easy strides. Don't run out unless you're making a super-high-energy presentation.)

3. Thank the introducer (if there is one).
4. Get yourself set up, arranged, and remove any distractions or previous visuals (this is especially important if you're following someone else).
5. Take a few beats to look around the audience (give them a chance to look at you, too).
6. Smile if appropriate; and you can do it naturally.

Begin With a Strong Opening Block

1. Greet the audience.
2. Begin with your attention-getter.
3. Introduce yourself, if someone is not doing it for you.
4. Let the audience know your purpose.
5. Give the audience a road map of your presentation; give them a brief preview of what you'll be talking about.
6. Let the audience know you're in control—give them all necessary directions, handouts, procedures, etc.
7. Transition into the body of the speech.

Hook your listeners at the outset, and you're well on your way to winning the battle for their attention. At the very least, like a good suspense novelist, you will have aroused enough curiosity that they will want to see what comes next.

Professional Projects: Sharpen Your Openings

1. Your topic is "We Can Beat Inflation." Devise three different attention-getters: a rhetorical question, a startling statistic, and a quote.
2. Your topic is "Change We Must." Start with a personal story about how change has had an impact on you or tell an appropriate and applicable joke about the subject.

Chapter 11

Bridging the Gap: Building Smooth Transitions

Good transitions can make a speech more important to the audience because they feel they are being taken to a positive conclusion without having to travel a bumpy road.

—Joe Griffith

It's true. The smoother the road you lead your listeners along, the more willing they are to follow. Transitions make the road smoother because they are one of the three aspects to organization. The first two are outlining and sequencing (putting the ideas in the order in which you will present your information). But transitions are also important for several reasons. They are logical extensions of the thoughts that came before; they help you get from one idea to the next. They also act as signposts to tell your audience that a new idea is coming.

Imagine that you are driving through the state of Florida, and you want to visit Key West, America's southernmost city. There's one problem. Key West is located at the end of a series of islands. Once you reach the tip of the Florida mainland, you're sunk—or you would be, if it wasn't for the bridges. Each Key is linked to the next by a succession of overseas bridges that make it possible to travel easily from one island to the next (and the next and the next) until you reach your destination.

Presentations are like the Florida Keys in that they're made up of a series of separate ideas that have to be linked together. The only way to get from one to another is by building linguistic bridges; those bridges are what we call *transitions*.

Speakers tell me that transitions present some of the biggest problems they have in their presentations. Many speakers concentrate all their ammunition on the opening, thinking that with a strong start, the rest can just follow. Not true. While an attention-getting opening is crucial to the beginning of a detail, the challenge is to keep the ideas that follow just as vivid.

Map out Your Speech With Transitions

Transitions are usually put in as an afterthought. But keeping transitions in mind can help you organize your presentation before you begin. Suppose you were putting together a presentation. One of your first tasks would be to make a list of the ideas you want to include. Take this list, for example:

Oranges

Apples

Fruit salad

Haircut

Pears

The subject of this speech is how to make a fruit salad. If you take the first two items on the list, oranges and apples, it's easy to see how you could transition from one idea to the next. It would also be a logical step to the next idea, fruit salad. But what happens when you come to "haircut"? You'd have to travel some awfully winding paths to get to that topic from fruit salad. If you can't easily make a transition from one point to the next, it means there's something wrong with your organization—it might even mean the point doesn't belong in there at all.

If we take haircut off the list, we've got: oranges, apples, fruit salad, pears. Although you could do it, you might have a bit of trouble moving from the combined fruit salad back into the solitary pear. It would be easier to transition from apples to oranges to pears, and finally to fruit salad. So the most logical order of ideas for this presentation would end up being: apples, oranges, pears, fruit salad. Considering the relative ease or difficulty of transitions before you put your presentation together saves you a lot of time that would otherwise be spent in editing and rewriting.

This fruit salad list is a simple example, but one that shows how you can use the concept of transitions to help you construct a clear, logical, easy-to-follow presentation.

Keep Your Ideas Connected

Transitions are what make an average speech seem polished and professional. When I tell participants in my speaking classes that overlooked transitions are one of public speakers most common problems, I can see the look of collective recognition as people remember the moments when they paused and stammered because they didn't know how to get from point A to point B. I am often asked, "What is the difference between a memorable talk and an average presentation?" Other than having a clear, well stated, well thought out purpose—I would have to say transitions.

You can't just present ideas; you must *lead* your audience. And that's where transitions come in; they are the maps you use when you are leading a group and you need to tell them which direction to go in next. The better organized you are, the easier it will be for you to develop smooth transitions. And the leadership evidenced when you're clearly in control adds to your power as a presenter.

Transitions: So Crucial, So Overlooked

Transitions are important in any type of communication, but they're even more essential to speaking than they are in writing. If you miss something in written material, you can always go back and reread. Haven't you ever found yourself reading along when you suddenly discover you're on a new topic, with no idea how you got there? So you turn back the page and try to re-establish the path the author took. Your audience can't rewind you when you're speaking live in front of them, so you have to make it as easy as possible for them to follow along.

As we've learned, speeches are made up of many parts that must fit well together. And transitions are responsible for much of that fitting: They take you from your opening into the body of your speech and provide a smooth passage between your main points, while also serving as smaller links between minor ideas. Yet transitions are so useful and frequent that they are often overlooked. If you hear a speaker stumble, chances are it's over a transition.

Um, Uh, What Did You Say? Watch out, People Are Counting!

Audiences are so savvy today that they often sit and count the number of times a speaker says "um" or "uh" or any other space-filling sound. In a *New York Times* article, (September 26, 1996) by Sandra Blakeslee, called "Traffic Jams in Brain Network May Result in Verbal Stumbles," linguist Dr. Willem Levelt says that the process of generating thought into speech goes through several layers of networks in the brain. If the process is interrupted at any one of the levels, "...many things can go wrong." And it is especially when our thoughts are not connecting properly that we run into trouble. Dr. Levelt states that "...speech errors can occur in the transition of a thought between the lemma network [which handles syntax] and the lexeme network [which manages spoken sound]." It is at that point that, according to Dr. Levelt, we use "'um' and 'er' to signal that trouble is afoot." In other words, when we have trouble connecting one thought to another, we stumble over our words and shift gears using "um," "ah," and phrases such as "let's see, and "our next point is." Effective transitions help you avoid those stumbling blocks. Look at your outline for a speech and see how many topics and subtopics you have. Each one requires a transition before you plunge your audience into it.

And be sure you don't start your speech with an "uh"—it's a cardinal sin that everyone notices. If you know that you have the "uh" habit, no matter what other speaking faults you have, eliminate the "uhs" first.

Successful Transition Techniques

It's always a good idea to memorize your major transitions or to write them clearly on the note cards you will have with you during your speech. Label these cards "transition cards" so you know when they are coming and can get ready to shift gears.

Frequent transitions carry your story forward, and they also help you to keep the audience's attention from drooping by strengthening logic, aiding retention, and helping you build to a climax. Frequent transitions add peaks to the curve of your speech and keep it interesting. The best ones will lead your audience in a subtle and natural way. You don't want your audience to feel it is being led, but you do want it to be alerted to new points you are about to introduce.

I once heard a speaker trying to persuade his audience to exercise. He used this transition into his conclusion: "And so, ladies and gentlemen, why exercise?" He then listed all the terrible consequences of inactivity and then said quietly, "The quality and quantity of the rest of your life is up to you." It was very effective.

The important thing is to spot where you need transitions. A rule of thumb is to use one any time you finish a thought and are ready to move on to a new idea. Major shifts—where your topic is really changing or you are introducing a new area—require unmistakable transitions. Give yourself at least a sentence to bring this shift to your audience's attention.

Crossing Bridges With Three Transitions: Verbal, Vocal, Visual

When most of us think of transitions, we usually think of a word or a phrase that will lead from one idea to the next. In fact, there are three distinct types of transitions; using all three will give your presentation added interest, vitality, and energy. The three types are:

1. *Verbal:* These are the actual words you use and are the most common forms of transitions. Some transitional words and phrases include:

However	There is an even better way	For example
But		Another reason is
And	Here's where ____ fits in	In addition
Although	On the other hand	In the same way
So you see	These are just a few of the	Think of it
In short	To show you what I mean	Besides
That's why	All things considered	A case in point is

2. *Vocal:* Your voice can be a transition all by itself. You can use your voice as a transitional tool by changing pitch, rhythm, and tone. It can very effective to suddenly get louder at an emotional point in your presentation—but you can also make a strong impact by getting softer and slower (as long as you're sure that the audience can still hear you). Below you'll find an excerpt from Hamlet's "To be or not to be" soliloquy. Try using a variety of vocal techniques (review Chapter 5 if necessary) to transition from one idea to the next in this text.

   To be, or not to be: that is the question:
   Whether 'tis nobler in the mind to suffer
   The slings and arrows of outrageous fortune,
   Or to take arms against a sea of troubles,
   And by opposing end them? To die: to sleep;
   No more; and by a sleep to say we end
   The heart-ache and the thousand natural shocks
   That flesh is heir to, 'tis a consummation
   Devoutly to be wish'd. To die, to sleep;
   To sleep: perchance to dream: ay, there's the rub...

Vocal transitions can be particularly effective when repetition is involved; try speaking the "To die: to sleep" loudly the first, and softly the second (or vice versa) and see what effect it has in moving on the next idea. Use your voice to command attention. Speaking too quickly or breathlessly translates into reduced credibility. Give vocal weight to your key points and transitions.

3. *Visual:* This is a physical transition that your audience can actually see. Don't be afraid to use physical movements that reinforce your transitions. It could be moving from one side of the room to another (or simply taking one or two steps forward or back), standing from a sitting position (or vice versa), or using a prop or visual aid. When the speaker on exercise reached the concluding transition I described previously, he also moved from one side of the stage to the other, which emphasized the shift he was making as he spoke. This can be very effective when combined with the pause. For instance: "Asking questions can change your life. I know (pause, two steps forward) because it changed mine."

Keep Your Signposts Visible: Transitions Are Meant to Be Noticed

In writing, transitions are subtle. The knitting together of character, thoughts, and action into a narrative should be almost invisible. But in a speech, transitions that bridge the gaps from one topic to another are much more obvious because you have to be sure your listeners cross the bridge with you. If the transition is too subtle, they may miss it and remain on topic A, while you are well launched into topic B. An effective transition always lets the audience know you are moving from one point to another. The process can be straightforward or creative, depending on the device you use.

A Central Theme Will Keep You—and Your Audience—on the Right Track

One way to gain control and to keep your audience's attention going throughout your presentation is to develop a central theme that links your ideas together. Many presentations start off with a reasonable attention level, which drops off sharply as the presentation continues. The reason being that presentations tend to be like reading a list: "Good morning, everyone. Here I am today to talk about the three best ways to save on auto insurance. Here's suggestion number one. Now here's suggestion number two. And now here's suggestion number three." The audience knows from the outset that there's nothing to look forward to but a boring list of ideas.

On the other hand, look carefully at this chapter, for instance. The "central theme" is based on "traveling." There are several references to moving and driving, and to maps, signs, paths, and especially bridges. Every time we use one of these references to transition from one thought to another, we are helping you—the reader—follow along. This is a "left brain, right brain" trick you can use too. The left side of the brain controls logic and reasoning. The right brain is more creative. Giving an audience a simple list of drugs is a left-brain activity. You can spice up that list, and make it easier to remember, by adding in bits of right-brain imagery (for example, maps, cars, and bridges) to help the audience focus on and remember your points.

Your theme doesn't have to be complicated. And if you can tie it into an audience's particular interest, all the better. I work with many pharmaceutical representatives who have to make presentations to doctors. It's well known that many doctors play golf. So they might open their presentation by asking, "How is prescribing the right drug like using the right club to hit a hole in one?" Then they would say, "You wouldn't use a putter to try for a hole in one. Choosing the right club can make all the difference in your game. That's why we want to help you make the best prescribing decision, to make sure you're choosing the best drug for your patients." They would then sprinkle the presentation with golf-related images to keep the doctor's attention throughout. (Just don't overdo it; you don't want to come off too cutesy.)

10 Transitions for an Effortless and Enjoyable Journey

Good speakers vary their transition style and avoid being predictable. Here are 10 types of transitions that are easy to use:

1. The simplest transitions are *bridge words*—words that alert the listener that you are changing direction or moving on to a new thought. Examples of bridge words include: *furthermore, meanwhile, however, in addition, nevertheless, moreover, therefore, consequently*, and *finally*.

2. A *trigger transition* relies on repetition, using the same word twice to connect one topic with the next. "That wraps up our assessment of product A. A similar assessment can be made of product B" is an example of this type of transition.

3. A *question* can serve as a good transition. It can be broad or quite specific. At a seminar on productivity, I shifted people's attention by saying, "Now that we have seen what an effective team is, what can we do to *build* that better team within this organization?" It was a large question that I was about to address one part at a time, using smaller transitions between those parts.

4. A *flashback* can be a transition and can also create movement within your talk with its sudden shift to the past in the midst of what the audience may think is a predictable sequence. The flashback doesn't have to be far in the past; use a transition such as, "You remember that I mentioned the major changes in our workforce a few minutes ago. Another example of the dramatic changes we will face this year is...." This is not one of my favorites because most audiences do not like to be reminded that they should know something. Often people use "as I said before," but I have not found that to be effective either. Better just to repeat a statement rather than tell the audience you are doing so. A more effective way to handle it would be to direct your audience to "flashback to all the changes we've been working through and how well we've handled them. This experience will prepare us for the dramatic changes we will face next year."

   Flashbacks can serve as mini-summaries sprinkled throughout a speech. They are especially helpful transitions because they aid your listeners in remembering your ideas and seeing how everything fits together. They also let you build your argument by summarizing the points you have made before. A simple example is: "So far we've talked about hiring new people and training our existing staff. Another possibility is a reorganization that would...."

5. A *point-by-point* transition can also work, if you don't have too many points. Saying, "There are three important reasons this product will sell in the Midwest," and then listing them is a quick way to shift from generalities into specificity. These transitions can also serve as mini conclusions that sum up what you have said in a previous section of your speech.

Be careful not to overuse point-by-point transitions, because they are the least dynamic and can easily bore audiences unless you have lots of lively examples with emotional appeal. Good visual aids also liven up a presentation that depends on point-by-point transitions.

6. *Visual aids* are transitional by their very nature. Shifting from unaided speech to the mechanics of visual aids carries a built-in transition, as you turn down lights or start to use whatever equipment you have chosen. And when you use visual aids to illuminate complex points quickly and vividly (instead of just using slides to restate what you could easily convey verbally), you are making visual aids a transition that also enlightens.
7. *Pausing* is a nonverbal transition that helps your audience shift with you. Good use of a pause—if done sparingly—helps your listeners focus on what you are about to say. But be careful, too many pauses will make your delivery seem frustratingly slow and stilted.
8. *Physical movement*—such as moving to another part of a platform—also acts as a transition between parts of your speech. As I mentioned, just shifting from one prop or visual aid to another is its own transition, because it refocuses the audience.

   Effective nonverbal transitions entail doing the opposite of what your audience has gotten used to. If you have been pacing, suddenly stand still. If you have been standing in one place behind a lectern, move about suddenly. Either way, you call attention to what is about to come—which is the essence of a good transition.
9. A *joke* or a *story* can act as an interesting transition. In a talk to managers on why and how to become better listeners, I used the Epictetus quotation: "God has given us two ears and one mouth—so we may hear twice as much as we speak." I added: "Now, because people talk twice as much as they listen, we must reverse the process and listen twice as much as we talk." The quotation helped me make my point and provided a way for me to shift to my next idea.
10. The *PEP formula*—Point, Example, Point—is a valuable transition in itself, because it makes connections between points for your audience.

Transitions are the seams that keep the parts of your speech fitting smoothly together. They let you take the audience by the hand and guide it in the direction you want to go, and they also reinforce your main points.

Transitions also reenergize and reactivate an audience. It is a place to gain renewed attention. Mastering transitions means realizing the best ones are frequent, varied, clear, and compelling. Transitions are the maps you use to persuade your audience to follow your thoughts and buy into your ideas. Transitions turn an outline, with its abrupt switches, into a smooth, memorable presentation—and turn you into a persuasive, powerful presenter.

Professional Projects: Tackling Transitions

1. You are giving a talk titled "Little Acorns Grow Into Mighty Oaks." And your very serious purpose is to get your department to economize on the little things that add up to big expenses. Your opening will explain the title and state your purpose. Write the transition that leads from the opening into the body of your talk.
2. You are talking about the problems related to the new computer system. The second part of your talk deals with the solutions. Write a transition to get from the problems to the solutions. Try one serious one and one humorous one.
3. You are introducing your boss to new employees at an orientation meeting. You have shared his credentials. Now devise an interesting, unique transition to her and her talk. Avoid the commonly used, "Please join me in welcoming."
4. People often get into bad habits with transitions and repeat words like "so" and "and." Start listening with more concentration to your transitioning habits and work to add more variety.

Chapter 12

Finish With Style: The Importance of Powerful Conclusions

Great is the art of beginning, but greater the art is of ending.

—Henry Wadsworth Longfellow

You've grabbed attention in the opening, sustained it through the transitions, and now all you have to do is close. It may seem like a time to wind down, to simply sum up and breathe a sigh of relief. And, of course, it's not. For no matter how vivid the words that came before, your conclusion is your prime time; it's what your whole speech should build toward. Don't throw it away. Instead, build up to it, and make sure it is stimulating and memorable.

What do people remember most? What they hear last. Yet so few speakers devote any thought or preparation to their ending. They just fade away and they and their messages are soon forgotten. To be truly memorable you must end as strongly as you began.

I've seen people so relieved their stint on the podium is over that they start to pack up before they finish speaking. Powerful speakers save a lot of energy and concern for the audience until the end, and make the conclusion their dessert: something delicious, with a memorable aftertaste.

Fitting Conclusions Don't Just Happen

The best time to prepare your conclusion is when you begin thinking about your speech. Memorize and practice your conclusion just as you do for your opening. Your conclusion must tie in with your opening and your overall purpose; it's an ending that must connect naturally with your beginning, and that's where organization continues to be important. Conclusions are your destination: You begin a speech where your audience is, but you end where *you* want them to be. The body of the speech is a bridge, and the speaker must always know what that bridge links. Always conclude with your own ideas, especially after a question-and-answer session. Alert the audience in the beginning of your speech that you will reserve the last few minutes to tie things up.

Ask for the Order

A good sales pitch will not only ask people to order, but also tell them how. When you buy a car, the dealer explains the auto's features, points out why it is better than the one you already own, and *then* tells you how you can pay for it.

Speakers, as you now know, are also in the selling business, and the conclusion is the time to ask for the order. Nothing will happen if you don't ask. And you ask by telling your audience what you want it to do with the information you've presented and *how* it can take that action. An effective speaker presenting a central idea ends by pointing out to those in his audience exactly what is needed from them to put that idea to work. For example, if you have been talking about on-the-job safety, end with an emotional and specific appeal showing why safety is important to the people in front of you, and how they can ensure safe operations by applying the information you've presented. If you've been persuading them to give blood, tell them where. And make it sound easy to get there.

Getting a visible demonstration of support is an effective technique. If you shared 10 reasons why your staff must operate their vehicles in a specific manner, end by telling them how lives could be saved, including theirs. End by asking, then and there, for a show of hands from those committed to the new procedures. This is not the time to be shy, but to be rousing.

Action doesn't always have to be literal. If you simply want the people in your audience to mull over your ideas, tell them this is what you want them to do. Summarize your important thoughts in sequence; in doing so, you give them a verbal pocket digest they can carry away with them. If you fail to ask for a specific action, you may end up giving a wonderful speech that builds up to nothing.

One way to zero in on a dynamic closing is to ask yourself, "What do I want the members of my audience to think about as they leave?" Remember that the conclusion is not a second chance: If you've failed to get your ideas across in the body of your talk, it's too late now. You've presented your message; now is the time to fix that message in your listeners' minds.

A Quartet of Quintessential Elements for a Strong Conclusion

There are four essential elements that go into constructing an effective conclusion:

1. *Never say "in conclusion...."* It's not necessary to announce your intention to conclude. If people get a lot of advance warning that you are going to conclude, they wind up your speech in their mind and start to tune you out. Be more subtle: Lead into your conclusion with a creative transition instead of the not very dynamic "and so, in conclusion, I would like to point out...." It's better to use a word such as summary— then all the people who haven't been paying attention perk up and listen to hear what they've missed.

   The best way to regain the audience's attention and lend greater credibility to your message is to use this phrase (or paraphrase this phrase): "The most essential points, the ones that will benefit you most, are...." The more important people think the message is, and the more meaningful to them, the more they will hang on your every last word.

   A good conclusion needs a lot of energy: It may be a stirring statement, a joke, a call to action. Some conclusions try to motivate through a challenge issued directly to the audience.

   I once heard an executive outlining new organizational changes after a takeover. Predictably, the members of his audience were nervous, and rumors of layoffs were rampant. He described the changes and ended his presentation by saying, "I dare you to come in tomorrow, to put aside your fears and apprehensions and to give your all." That direct challenge to the unspoken reservations the members held roused them and let him end on a strong, memorable, and positive note.

2. *Construct your speech in the form of a circle.* Referring back to your opening comments ties your whole speech together. Your audience sees your talk as a satisfying whole rather than a series of points without any particular direction.

Opening-Conclusion Circle

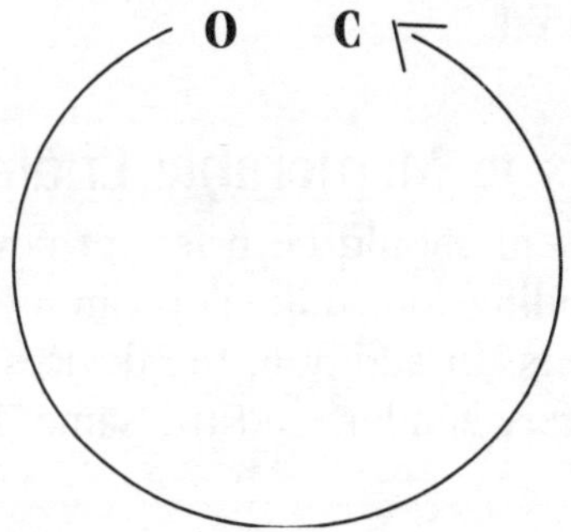

I once heard an executive conclude simply—and very effectively—with her opening words: "Now really is the time for all good people to come to the aid of their company." Opening statements often refer to the purpose of the talk, and conclusions that return to and reinforce that purpose can make effective endings. A speech on customer service started with the advice to treat the customer the way you would want to be treated and ended with the speaker asking the members of the audience to think back and remember how they felt when they were customers and were treated rudely.

Most people who give technical talks—the ones who base their presentations on a series of slides—end badly. They simply present their last bit of information on a slide and never have a conclusion at all.

3. *Reenergize yourself, and your audience, with a strong, memorable conclusion.* Don't rush to the end. To make the greatest impact, your ending should be vocally strong and verbally colorful. Use persuasive language and vivid imagery so that your audience has a clear memory of your presentation and your message.

4. *Use the two-conclusion strategy.* One mistake that many speakers make is to end their presentation with a strong conclusion, and then take questions from the audience. After the last question, the speaker might say, "No more questions? Goodnight then." What does the audience go out remembering? What they heard last, which means they remember the last question and answer. That's not always a good thing, especially if the question was one that stumped you or that someone else in the audience answered for you.

So if you're taking questions at the end of your presentation, be sure you have a second powerful conclusion to use after the last question has been answered.

6 Aids to Memorable Endings

Your closing statement should be brief yet powerful. There are six major devices for concluding your talk. You can use each alone, or combine them with the others. In addition, the devices for openings, transitions, and closings are very similar, and the same device can be used in numerous places.

1. *Summarize your major ideas.* Conclusions should contain a summary. Don't make it a total rehash; instead, add some new thoughts or elements and a final statement. A summary is especially effective if the primary purpose of your talk is to give information. By restating your ideas, you may fill in some blanks for listeners who didn't fully grasp or respond to your entire presentation.

2. *Make a direct appeal.* You have told the people in your audience what you want them to do, why, and how. Now stir them to action with a ringing declaration or challenge. This can be as simple as saying, in a rousing tone, "Now let's get up and make this work!"

3. *Look ahead.* You may want to close with a prediction that holds forth hope and promise of better things to come. So turn your audience's thoughts to the future. If your talk has focused on disastrous corporate events, find some positive alternatives to end with. A talk on reshaping a marketing division could end, "With this new advertising approach, we can avoid the losses facing our industry, and next year we will be able to see black instead of red."

4. *Ask a rhetorical question.* This device lets people fill in the answer for themselves, and you can combine it with other methods of closing. During a talk on safety, a rhetorical question might be, "Do you want to be the next statistic?" These questions make your speech a two-way street by actively inviting the audience's mental participation. They allow you to steer the audience's response in your direction. And while many rhetorical questions have evident answers, that very obviousness can give them a vividness and sense of urgency.

5. *Conclude your speech with a quotation.* An appropriate quotation can conclude many kinds of talks and provides a graceful ending. Quotations also let you borrow the prestige of a higher source and help to crystallize the audience's thinking.

   Sources for stirring summations are no further away than a good directory of quotations. Voltaire was succinct when he said, "No problem can withstand the assault of sustained thinking." A seminar on hiring could end on a good note with this bit of wisdom from R. H. Rands: "When you hire people smarter than you are, you prove that you are smarter than they are." John Charles Salak defined failure two ways, with particular pertinence to business, when he said there were two kinds of failures: those who thought and never did and those who did and never thought. Persistence, motivation, generosity, the rewards of hard work—all these universal topics have been addressed by eloquent people, and their words are yours to use to great effect.

6. *Think outside of the box.* When I close my PowerSpeak program, I often do it with a song, sung to the tune of "Yankee Doodle Dandy":

   Energy will keep 'em focused,
   Their attention will stay high.
   If I stay intr'ested, then they will too.
   E-ve-ry woman and guy.
   Be entertaining and engaging,
   Till the end of my address
   Keep my energy as sharp as Tuscan provolone
   My speech will be a big success!

You may not choose to use a song or dance to end your program, but you might try another creative venue. One speaker I know makes his final points while doing a demonstration of Tai Kwan Do! It's exciting, engaging, and helps the audience leave in an upbeat mood.

Combine Closing Techniques

Many conclusions will borrow from a combination of the above techniques. A fund-raising presentation I attended had a three-part conclusion: It started with a summary of reasons why the cause was especially worthy and led into this quotation from Ralph Waldo Emerson: "No man can truly help another man without helping himself." The speaker then launched into a direct appeal: "So please reach into your hearts and checkbooks so that tomorrow really will be a better day for the needy."

These techniques also apply in general communication. For example, after a meeting with a client you might need to sum up your discussion or ask for the order. Never let important conversations or discussions just drift away.

Whatever technique you use, strive for a conclusion that will stay with your listeners long after they leave their seats and return to their private lives.

Professional Projects: Concentrate on Conclusions

1. You are a Boy or Girl Scout troop leader on a day-long swimming trip. You've given a talk about the importance of the "buddy system." End by summarizing your key points and include a strong call to action.
2. You are a fund-raiser for your favorite charity. You are speaking to a group of investors and have shared several reasons why yours is a worthy charity. Transition into your ending with a strong, direct appeal.
3. Your talk opened with the statement, "We must exceed last year's production!" You've listed all the reasons why and how it can be done. Now write a strong motivational ending making a circle back to your opening statement.

Chapter 13

Professional Secrets of Question-and-Answer Sessions

More trouble is caused in the world by indiscreet answers than by indiscreet questions.

—Sydney Harris

A professor at Columbia University's Teachers College once gave me this humorous but accurate advice: "In every class you will have a student eager to argue, who will ask a lot of questions. Your first impulse will be to silence that pupil, but I strongly advise you to think carefully before doing so—that kid may be the only one listening."

Few speakers would say the question-and-answer period is the best, or most enjoyable, part of their speech. On the contrary, even some of the best speakers panic when it's time for the audience to talk back. They view question-and-answer periods as barriers looming between the presentation itself and applause and acceptance. But these sessions are proof your audience is involved and interested. In fact, Bill Lee, former chairman of Duke Power Company (now Duke Energy), has given speeches just to engage in a question-and-answer session, because it lets him get his audience involved.

Those few minutes at the end of a speech let you fill in gaps, emphasize certain ideas, and clear up misunderstandings. And the details you go back over and clarify are chosen by the people you are trying to persuade. It's participation, not confrontation. The active give-and-take of a question period yanks your audience out of that passive state known as listening. And you benefit—if you're prepared.

You Can Finish, But You Can't Hide

When people come to hear you speak, they expect two things: to hear your presentation and to raise questions about it. They may wish to know more about the subject, or they may want to contest some points. It's true that when you permit questions, you risk losing control to the audience, because for that moment the questioner is in the driver's seat. But remember that as the speaker you are automatically in a position of authority and *you* have the advantage. If you handle the questions—and the questioners—well, you extend the power of your speech and leave your audience not only informed but also impressed.

Your objective is to retain as much control for yourself as possible. You can say, "I will take any reasonable question on the information I'm sharing with you." Later on, if you get a difficult question, you can humorously add, "I said any *reasonable* question," and move on. The main drawbacks of the question period are your risk of being exposed to questions for which you are not prepared and the danger that questions may come from unfriendly, or even hostile, members of the audience. But you can virtually eliminate these risks through careful preparation.

Be Prepared for the Worst

You should practice the question-and-answer session just as you practice the rest of your talk. When you rehearse your speech before friends and family, encourage them to ask questions—tough ones—at the end. Think up hard questions yourself. Get to know your subject so well that you anticipate possible questions, and get ready to answer them. Find your most argumentative colleagues and friends and give them a field day: Chances are they will throw trickier stuff your way than your audience will.

Anticipating questions in advance means you are unlikely to be completely stumped or taken by surprise by a question from the audience. You can't predict and control everything, but when you operate from a position of strength and full preparation, there is nothing wrong with simply answering, "I don't know, but I can find out." Remember that you're in charge of the speech *and* the answers. As Calvin Coolidge put it, "I have never been hurt by anything I didn't say."

You're Still the Leader

People's fears about question-and-answer sessions revolve around these worries:

- You will lose control when you open the floor to questions.
- You will get a question you are not prepared for.
- You will have to answer whatever question comes along.

These fears vanish if you think of the question-and-answer session as something *you* control. The better your presentation is and the more direction you give the audience concerning questions, the more control you retain. Start by limiting the kinds of questions you have time for: "I will be dealing with questions that pertain to the subject I have covered." Laying the ground rules isn't defensive, it's a sign of organization and leadership. You're still the chosen speaker; you've been leading your audience throughout your speech, and that guidance should continue through the question-and-answer session.

In today's information age, it is impossible to have all the information on a given subject, especially if it's a broad one. As I stated earlier, there is nothing wrong with saying you don't know. But if you set boundaries and guidelines at the outset, you will limit the number of questions that fall outside your area of expertise.

Do you have to answer every question? No. If you feel you do have to catch everything, no matter how off-the-wall, you've already lost your leadership role. Set limits with grace, but set them. There is nothing wrong with telling someone his question isn't covered by your presentation, but that you would be glad to provide him with further information afterward. Your audience will respect you for it.

Banish these preconceptions about questions and you'll find yourself relaxing in spite of yourself. I've seen videotapes of people giving speeches and handling questions afterward; they look more comfortable during the question-and-answer sessions than during the speeches. That's not hard to understand; there is a naturalness to engaging in a dialogue that a speech can't match. Think of your audience as interested, not hostile, and you won't have to worry about what turn out to be good-natured dialogues.

The Right Time for Questions

Because the question period comes at the end of your speech, it's important to do it right and leave the audience with a good impression. Follow these tips to ensure your organization doesn't lapse during this period:

- Announce both at the very beginning of your talk and at the start of the question-and-answer (Q&A) session when you are going to take questions. You can also tell your audience that you will cover topics only related to your talk and subject.
- Don't give a set amount of time for questions—that way you can stay flexible and if you really run into trouble you can get off the hook by saying, "I'm sorry, we seem to be running out of time."

  Remember to keep the final minutes of a speech for yourself. They are the prime time; why turn them over to someone else? Whether you're concluding with a summary or some provocative, additional food for thought, prevent a messy ending by asking for questions before you present the real conclusion of your speech. A simple statement like, "I'll be happy to answer any questions you may have, but I would like to hold the final two or three minutes for a summary," will keep you in control.

  Those few extra moments at the end will also give you a chance to recover from any irrelevant or awkward questions, and send the members of your audience home with your ideas on their mind, not someone else's.
- Stay flexible. If you happen to get a great question that ties in perfectly with your speech, by all means use it.

Exceptions to the Rules

Business presentations and training sessions can be far more interactive then speeches, and presenters often don't face a traditional question-and-answer session. In many business presentations (especially informal ones during meetings), the best time for questions can be during the talk, as they come up. This is tricky for speakers, who risk losing their place and momentum. Try this approach only as you become a more experienced speaker. Allow yourself to be interrupted if you have to; if the boss asks a question that fits in, answer it, but as a rule, explain why you would like to hold questions until the end.

There are two general strategies for taking questions in training sessions: You can stop and answer as you go along, or you can take questions after each section of your presentation. The first strategy can get you sidetracked unless you control it carefully; however, the second one doesn't let people ask questions as freely as they can if you take queries as they arise. How to organize the Q&A period is always a dilemma for a speaker. The way you take questions must be decided by analyzing your purpose, the extent of your content, the size of the audience, and the amount of time you have been allotted.

Training meetings have a tangible goal: to transfer a skill or technique to the audience. If people don't have questions answered as you go along, you will lose them as their understanding and grasp of the new material slips. As a general rule, ask people to jot questions down as you go along, and stop every 20 minutes or so to take them. If you have someone who just isn't keeping up, don't allow the whole session to drag; you'll alienate the rest of your audience. I tell the person I realize the concept is difficult and that it took me a long time to master it. I then ask him or her to talk with me during the next break.

What if No One Asks?

What if you ask for questions and nobody responds? This is unusual, unless the speech is on a topic that people are just not emotionally involved in. But if it does happen, it's usually for two reasons: You have answered all potential questions in your speech (pretty unlikely), or your audience feels uncomfortable about asking. Your job is to make them more comfortable. Even if the initial silence simply means no one wants to be first, it can be embarrassing for you. There are many good ways to get out of this spot:

- Handing out question cards at the beginning of your speech gives people a way of jotting down thoughts as they occur. If you are going to read from these cards, ask for short questions and for people to print clearly. These cards also let people know you really do want questions. They encourage participation in large and formal presentations.
- Take an information survey (which you have thought about in advance) by saying, "Let's see, by a show of hands, how you all would answer the following questions." The results of a question such as, "How many of you feel corporations should do more about day care?" can give you new information to discuss and also gets the audience involved.

These impromptu surveys are good icebreakers; they start the ball rolling.

- Pose your own question by saying, "A question I'm frequently asked that might interest you is...." This method gives you more points to cover and buys time for your listeners to think up their own questions. If you ask your own question, make it provocative and of interest to many people, such as, "How can I handle customer resistance?"
- Make the first question one you heard from an audience member: "On my way here this evening, your chairman asked me a question I thought would be interesting to everyone," or "In preparing for this talk, I interviewed some of your colleagues. Here are a few of the questions they asked me."
- Deliberately leave out an obvious part of your speech—an omission that will stimulate responses. If you are talking about north, east, and west, but leave out south, someone will be sure to bring it up. You will also find out who is listening. Use this technique carefully, and be sure it works well with your presentation, because if you don't get to the omitted material quickly enough, people will think you are just poorly organized.
- Arrange with the program chairman to select a member of the audience ahead of time to ask the first question. So if you ask for questions and no one responds, the prearranged "plant" will get things going. You don't have to plant the actual question; you just need a willing audience member to help out. But be careful: If the question is very neutral, or if the plant sounds like he or she is reciting a memorized question, you will lose your credibility. As a rule, it's better to choose one of the other methods and opt for spontaneity.
- If you have saved the conclusion of your speech, you can simply get on with it by saying, "If there are no questions, let me share this essential thought with you."

Watch Your Manners

The manner in which you accept and answer questions is even more important than what you actually say. You set the tone and atmosphere with your very first answer, and the best way to send the right signal is to have a positive attitude toward all questions. If one person asks a question, it is probably on other people's minds, so when you answer that one person, you're answering everyone.

Because you probably can't decipher the motive underlying a question, you can't take each question at face value. Not all questions are sincere requests for information. Often people want to express their opinion, to show you up, and to demonstrate their wisdom and great intelligence. Your analysis of a question should focus on three things:

1. The content of the question.
2. The intent of the question.
3. The person asking the question.

Never launch into an explanation without fully clarifying the question or being absolutely certain that you understand the question thoroughly. It's all too easy to *think* you understand what someone else is thinking. For example, if someone asks, "How much time should an employee spend on professional development?" a smart speaker would clarify first by asking, "Do you mean during regular working hours?"

Vague questions are traps for both the speaker and the audience. We are so used to them that we tend to answer too quickly. A classic is the inevitable job interview request: "Tell me about yourself." How can we know what the questioner wants? Yet most people plunge in and talk themselves into all sorts of trouble. Just as people try to count to 10 before losing their temper, the smart speaker will count to three while asking him- or herself whether the question needs to be clarified.

When you analyze the intent and the person behind the question, remember that argumentative people may be looking for recognition. Give it to them, but don't let them take over. You may lose a few points, but telling them that their question really requires more time and asking, "Can we get together after the meeting?" may be the best way to deal with these people. Long-winded people must be cut off, but you have to do it politely and tactfully. And if you get a real troublemaker who causes a disturbance, chances are your audience will express disapproval and ask him or her to sit down.

Make sure that you treat every question seriously and courteously. The occasional bad apple aside, most people are sincere in their desire for more information. The people in your audience have heard your ideas, and you can be sure they have reacted to them, especially if they are new, difficult, or controversial. Always remember that questions mean the audience is involved with you. Even if the question sounds negative, the questioner may just be expressing some anxiety or doubt. The question may just be the person's way of asking for reassurance. Answer politely and you reassure the whole audience, too.

3 Objectives to Assure Control During Q&A

It's just as important to get your points across in a question-and-answer session as it is during your speech; if you don't, you lose an important opportunity to persuade and lead your audience. You've got three *interdependent* objectives to keep in mind at all times when taking questions. The objectives are hard to separate from each other, and you will stay in control of the question-and-answer session only if you keep all three in mind.

1. Maintain your credibility and control, no matter what happens. Any time you are not believable, you cast doubt on your entire presentation. And if you get angry or defensive, you lose control. Repeat the question—your audience needs to hear it clearly—and hearing it in your own voice will calm you down.

   My definition of assertive is knowing what you want and getting it effectively while you consider the rights of others. The key to success through assertiveness is staying calm, not being defensive, and being courteous. A powerful speaker is one who keeps control of a situation. If you lose that control by losing your temper, you'll never be able to reassert yourself with your audience.

2. Satisfy the questioner. But remember, you don't have to answer the question *fully.* Don't spend too much time with one person. Unfortunately, most of us want to see that look of total approval and acceptance in the eyes of our questioners. But if you spend the time necessary to achieve that look, you will lose the rest of the audience. Answer in a way that makes your best point in relation to your overall objective, break eye contact, and move on. Saying "Jennifer, you've asked an excellent, complex question. Because we have many other people asking questions, this is the way I can answer it in a limited time" is a polite, honest response that keeps things moving along.

3. Keep the rest of the audience on your side at all costs. Consider the entire audience. You have to let people know you're always considering their time and patience. If you're asked a multiple question such as, "How can I cope with not enough staff, not enough space, and a boss who gives me no real authority?" you might say, "You've asked me three very good questions. Because there are other people in the audience with questions, let me answer one and come back to the others if we have time." That way, you partially answer and still keep the audience with you. The audience will respect you for not letting the questioner monopolize the little time you have to spend with them.

If you get a question out of left field, pause and ask, "Does anyone else here have a similar concern?" If people don't, answer the question briefly and tell the questioner you'll be happy to stay and speak with him or her after the presentation. This technique also works well with hostile questioners.

One More "Never"

In addition to never be boring, and never say "in conclusion," here's another never: Never ask, "Did that answer your question?" This is often a trap and one that is very difficult to escape. Do you think an argumentative person is going to say yes? A dynamic or argumentative questioner will try to hold on to the spotlight and ask for more clarification. Remember that there is no law that says you must answer every question fully. In a training session you should certainly try, but there are times when it is not possible. The most important of the preceding three objectives is to keep the rest of the audience on your side—too much time with one person will reduce your credibility and effectiveness with the rest of the group

Keep these objectives in mind and you will do fine. All revolve around consideration for members of your audience; and the more considerate you are of them, the more they will be on your side.

Coping With Commonly Asked Problem-Causing Questions

Upon occasion, you may find that you've been asked a question that puts you in a sticky situation. Here are some of these types of questions, and ways you can answer them quickly and professionally.

Loaded Question

Q: How much damage has this allegation done to your agency?

A: With respect, I don't agree with your premise. In fact...

Don't accept the premise by trying to ignore it.

Instead, challenge the premise politely, but firmly.

Then move on to your message.

Personal Opinion

Q: What about your personal opinion?

A: I don't believe the issue is my personal opinion. The issue is...

Keep your personal opinion out of it.

Question—Don't Know Answer

Q: How much was the investment?

A: I wouldn't want to give you off-hand information. I will get the right information for you.

Say you don't know/offer to get it.

Never lie; never guess.

Questions—You Know the Answer but You Are Not Allowed to Say

Q: What was the amount of the offer?

A: I'm not in a position to say because: (that information is confidential; the issue is before the courts; it would be inappropriate for me to comment; the issue is very sensitive; the issue is currently under discussion/review/negotiation).

Give reason why you can't answer.

Getting Boxed In (2 Options From Which to Choose)

Q: Are you going to increase funding or maintain the status quo?

A: Our goal is to provide quality service.

Ignore two options.

Begin with straightforward statement or theme.

Persistent Questioning

Q: ...then why won't you reveal the strategy?

A: As I mentioned, the strategy is in place, ready to go, and we'll announce it at the appropriate time. So with all due respect, it's pointless to go over the same ground again.

Politely but firmly signal you're not going to give in.

Repeat your message.

Open-Ended/Vague Question

Q: Tell me about your organization.

A: What specific aspect are you interested in?

Ask for clarification/focus.

Rumor

Q: There's rumor that other companies may be interested in developing a similar product ...

A: It would be inappropriate to respond to rumors; we'll just have to deal with that issue if and when it arises *or* I've seen no evidence to support that rumor.

Multi-Part Question

Q: What impact will the changes make…and will you be able to continue to…at the same time or will you have to…?

A: Let me begin with your first question. The changes will make us more efficient and more responsive to the public. With regard to the question of….

Choose the question that is easiest for you and will help make your point.

You don't have to answer them all at once.

Never Underestimate the Power of Warmth

Some speakers set a positive tone by complimenting the questioner: "That's a perceptive question" or "That question goes right to the heart of the matter" establishes a warm, receptive atmosphere. Even if the question sounds truly hostile, you can still compliment the questioner: "We can always look to Jack to go straight for the jugular." This tactic is best used occasionally; if you begin every answer with a compliment, you will start to sound insincere. Try varying your adjectives and your phrases: "That's a really touchy question," "That's a truly appropriate question," or "I was hoping some one would ask that." There is no law that you have to preface each question with a compliment—just answer the question. If you do a good job that should be enough.

Save Your Jokes (or Use Them in Your Speech)

Resist the temptation to be witty or clever when answering questions. Audiences will think you are not taking them seriously, and they will identify, and sympathize, not with you, but with the brave soul who struggled to his or her feet and asked the question that you seem to think is silly.

Handling the Hostile Questioner

In general, speakers shouldn't worry that every questioner is out to get them; this is speaker paranoia. But occasionally a genuinely hostile question will get thrown your way. There is only one way to behave if this happens: Be courteous. And here's another "Never." Never—under any circumstances—become defensive, angry, or snide. If someone deliberately tries to embarrass you, being polite is especially effective. Audiences appreciate fair play and good manners. They will automatically reject the person who is making trouble and be on your side—if you continue to be polite and unruffled.

If you are dealing with a tough subject and expect a hostile audience, asking people to state their names, companies, and so on, can reduce the amount of questions, because many people do not like to volunteer this kind of personal information. This tactic can work at large rallies or in groups where people are not already acquainted.

Being polite doesn't mean you have to be a patsy. If the questioner is out of hand, you can cut him off. If he is especially provocative, you might consider the kind of reply General Hugh Johnson used occasionally: "I'll answer any fair question, but I won't answer a loaded question like this one."

You Don't Have to Go it Alone: Create a Mini-Panel

Many of my clients tell me this is very helpful because it takes the pressure off them and makes the Q&A portion more interesting for the rest of the audience. Here's how it works: Before your presentation ask a few intelligent, informed people if they would serve on your panel. Before starting the Q&A session, tell your audience that to make the session more valuable for them, you have asked some experts to provide answers and input. Then just call on the panel members as the need arises.

The Fine Points of Mastering Questions

Speakers who handle question-and-answer sessions well have mastered the fine points too:

- Give clear directions at the start of the question-and-answer session. Unless you have ground rules already laid, you can't resort to them without sounding like you are dodging questions.
- Truly listen. Listening well is not a strong suit among many executives, but it's a crucial skill for an effective speaker.
- Hear from everyone who has a question before returning to someone with a second question. If someone tries to monopolize, say you'll come back to that person after you've heard from other contributors, and make sure you've established this rule at the outset. You can hold off aggressive hand wavers by saying, "Will you hold it a moment, please? I believe this person on my far left is next."
- Always recognize questions in order. When two or more people hold up their hands at the same time, recognize the first one you see, then mentally note the others and come back to them in order.

- Don't develop any blind spots as you look for questions. Let your eyes roam over the entire room, including the head table or rostrum.
- When you're asked a question, always repeat it before answering, because many people in the audience might not have heard it. I've been advising people to paraphrase the question. This assures you of a full understanding of the question. If necessary, ask for clarification. Repeating or restating the question is one way to clarify it: "As I understand it, you are asking..." Don't feel you have to repeat verbatim; you can always restate in a way that gives an impression you want to give. End by thanking the questioner.
- Always look every questioner straight in the eye. Then answer the question briefly and accurately. Don't wander away from the point. Some questions may tempt you to make a speech in reply. Don't! You have already made your speech.
- If you don't know the answer, don't bluff your way through it. Your listeners will have more respect for you if you're candid and say you don't know, but you can find out and get back to that person.
- You may be able to score some important points by asking someone else in the audience to answer. For example, if you are asked a technical question and you know that Jack Jones in the back row is an expert, deflect the question to him: "That's a good question, but it is out of my range. Perhaps Jack can comment." You satisfy your questioner, and win the support of Jack Jones at the same time.
- Save your second conclusion for the end of the question-and-answer session. Only end with someone else's question if it fully supports your position in a very memorable way. And even if that's the (rare) case, I still like to end the session myself. After all the time and effort you put into preparing your speech, why end on someone else's note?

Rules for Testing Your Answers

There are three tests every answer you give should pass: It should (1) inform, (2) persuade, and (3) tie in with your main purpose and objective. To be informed and persuaded is why your audience is present in the first place; the question-and-answer session is an extension and elaboration of your basic purpose. Make it work for you, and no matter how rough—or how pleasant—your reception is, always sincerely thank the audience for the time and effort they gave to the question-and-answer session and for the ideas they contributed.

End With Conviction

If you do end your talk with the question-and-answer session, do so before all the questions dwindle away. Try to end with a question from the audience that restates your position. Never keep going until some people are putting on their coats and shuffling up the aisles while one or two last questioners are lingering behind. "Has she finished yet?" one suffering listener asked another as she was departing the auditorium. "Yes," was the answer, "she finished long ago, but just won't stop." Stay in control. End the session yourself by saying, "That's all we have time for today; I want to thank you all for your contributions." Then deliver your conclusion with warmth and confidence. Come forward and mingle with the audience, especially if you have been standing behind a lectern.

If you prepare for questions, take them in stride, treat your audience courteously, and stay in control, the question-and-answer session changes from a time of dread to an enjoyable opportunity. Make it work for you. The back-and-forth nature of question sessions adds to your credibility: You're not just talking to people, you're engaging them. Enjoy it, and your audience will remember you for it.

Professional Projects: Prepare in Advance

1. You have been asked to give a speech on a highly controversial subject—how to keep drug use out of professional sports. List two tough questions you expect and your answers to them.

2. Observe people dealing with questions at the several presentations and meetings you attend. Try to find at least three techniques you can use and at least five that were ineffective.

Chapter 14

Visual Aids: When a Picture Is Worth a Thousand Words

A picture is indeed worth a thousand words. But it must be a good one.

—Dorothy Leeds

We are a visual society; if you want your words to be remembered, give your audience something it can *see.* You have a complex idea to get across: Is there some way to display it visually? People remember 50 percent more of what they see *and* hear than of what they only hear. It's no wonder that visual aids are integral to the majority of speeches and presentations. Visual aids are everywhere today, and this chapter will give you lots of ideas about how to use them—and how not to.

A visual aid is any sort of prop you use to support your speech. Charts, graphs, slides, photographs, handouts, and demonstration models are all visual aids. But always remember—you are your own best visual aid. The way you look, walk, use arm motions, and show expression (in other words, your body language) is a key part of your talk.

Visual aids are especially helpful to novice or nervous speakers, who may not have the confidence that their own movements and animation will carry the show. Aids also help diffuse any nervous energy by giving you something physical to do. But as with any aspect of your speech, practice is vital. Visual aids that weren't rehearsed will show the lack of preparation, and will accentuate a speaker's lack of experience. If practiced thoroughly, visual aids greatly enhance your professionalism. In fact, I advise my clients and students to use visual aids in all of their presentations.

However, visual aids do have their dark side: As any speaker who has had to come up with some will tell you, they take up a great deal of time and thought; they can take attention away from what you are saying; they are costly; and if anything goes wrong, they can be a catastrophe.

So why use visual aids at all? We use them because a picture really is worth a thousand words. They portray—vividly and instantly—things that would take volumes to explain verbally. They save time, create interest, add variety, and help your audience remember your main points.

My Revealing Research

Over the years that I have been conducting PowerSpeak workshops, visual aids have changed. There's more technology involved today. But some things have not changed. I've spent a lot of time researching the art and science of using visual aids, and here are some of the discoveries I've made:

- You must vary your visual aids. One of the problems with using slides from programs such as Microsoft PowerPoint (which we'll discuss more later) is that—especially for novice users—the slides all tend to look the same. Just because you're an expert in your particular subject, doesn't mean you're an expert at creating slides. If you show a series of lists, for instance, you'll lose the audience's attention after the second or third slide.
- Talk about the information that's coming up before you actually show it. You lose 90 percent of the audience's attention if you put the visual up first and then start talking. You must orient the audience first; give them a chance to switch from their left brain (following your speech in a logical order) to their right brain function (taking in a picture or an image—even an aid with text only is still visual). The more directive you are, the better chance you have of being in control.
- Don't read your slide after you present it; it's patronizing and it wastes time. They can read it themselves. Most people in the audience can read almost five times faster than you can speak. That means they'll be way ahead of you, and your reading will only be a distraction. If you think there's too much information on the slide for them to read, you're right. You should eliminate some of the points on the slide, not read it for them.
- The less information you put on the slide—the more you have to say yourself—the more believable you are.

Remember that a visual aid is an *aid* to the presentation, not the presentation itself. A good presentation with visual aids is more effective than a good presentation without them, but remember that a visual aid is not a replacement for part of your speech. Done properly, visual aids can assist you in getting your message across. Done poorly, they can blur your message and lessen your credibility.

Put Your Visual Aids to the Test

To make sure each visual aid you are contemplating will really add to your presentation, ask yourself these two questions:

- ☑ Can I do just as well without it? A visual aid you don't really need creates clutter. Each aid must have a purpose that goes beyond livening up your presentation. Make sure each one you use is related to the subject and adds value to your presentation. Always design visual aids to perform a specific function, and make sure each is self-explanatory and can stand by itself.
- ☑ Is this really a visual aid, or a *verbal* visual? Words printed on a chart are not visual aids; words are what *you* are there to provide. Sometimes you can find dramatic ways to use words in a visual aid, and they can help the audience identify pictures, but for the most part, use as few words as possible when creating visual aids.

How to Create Visual Aids

A good visual aid springs to life after its creator has followed some basic steps:

1. Go back to the outline of your speech and jot down ideas for visual aids. How could a visual aid help clarify an idea? What kind will work best—chart, model, graph, or illustration? Always design a visual aid to perform a specific function. Use visual aids only where they are needed and make sure they are related to the subject. They should not only liven up your speech but also have a purpose.
2. Write down the essence of the visual aid on a piece of paper and start to work out the way it will look. The paper represents the visual aid; limit yourself to the one or two points you want to emphasize.

3. Sketch out the visual aid itself. You will give this rough sketch to an artist if you're working with one. Whether you are creating your own visual aids or working with a professional artist, always make a rough sketch before you create your final version.

4. Avoid clutter; make your visual aids simple and easy to grasp. If you must combine words and type, strive for a good, balanced layout. Each visual aid should have a title, and should cover no more than three main points. If you have more points to make, create additional visual aids. Limit yourself to no more than six lines on each visual aid; less is definitely best!

   If you're using numbers and words on the visual aid, make them large and easy to read; take advantage of the ways graphics can reduce the number of words. Make sure each visual aid emphasizes your main ideas.

5. Use color in three ways: to please the eye, add emphasis, and differentiate one point from another. Even a little bit of color can spruce up a dull visual aid: Underline headings in color and put colored bullets in front of major points. But don't overdo it: A lot of color can lead to confusion. Using too much color is far worse than using too little.

   Color has a psychological impact on most people; we are drawn to the colored portions of advertisements and sales letters. Blue and black are both good for headlines; blue is also good for highlighting and underlining. Green implies *go ahead* and tends to be perceived favorably. Red is an excellent eye-catching accent; however, it is harder to see than the others and implies both *stop* and *losses* (red ink).

   So when you work out your rough sketches, use color and practice with it. Try out different colors and get reactions from your friends. In other words, work out the bugs before you finish the visual aids.

Rules to Remember

Ineffective visual aids—and there are a surprising number of them out there—all share mistakes that the good ones manage to avoid. Here are some tricks of the trade to help you make your visual aids and your presentation look professional:

1. Make all the visual aids consistent but NEVER boring. Titles should be the same size, and type styles should not vary wildly. All charts should use color in the same way: If you use blue bullets for emphasis in onc chart, use them in all charts. Never use more than three colors in a visual aid.

2. Keep the visual aid out of sight until you are ready to use it. You want it to support you, not beat you to the punch line.
3. Always talk to the audience, not to the visual aid. Don't let the visual aid become a security blanket; powerful speakers use powerful visual aids, but they also maintain eye contact with the audience.
4. Stand to the side of what you're showing; not in front of it.
5. Don't forget to *stage* the visual aid: Consider the room size, where the audience will be, the easel, power cord, lights, and so on. Clear away visual aids used by other presenters so that you can start fresh. Make sure your visual aids are high enough for people in the back rows to see. If you don't have a stand or an easel, hold the visual aid up yourself, but don't block your face. When you're finished, put all the visual aids aside; don't let them clutter the platform when you give your concluding remarks.
6. Practice using your visual aids as you practice your whole talk. It's a mistake to practice your speech first and add the visual aids later. Use them as you develop your talk and each time you practice. Make sure they work—and work *for* you.

The Power (or Misuse) of PowerPoint

Technology is a wonderful thing. Most of the time. In the field of visual aids, the development of PowerPoint and other computer-aided graphics programs allow you to create powerful visual aids yourself, without having to depend on IT professionals to create them for you. Like any technical advance, however, programs such as PowerPoint don't solve every problem. Many presenters now rely on a computer program for success or to give them an excuse for failure. You can NEVER rely on a visual aid to make or break your presentation. It is not the slide, the animation, or the bells and whistles that spell success—it's the individual who is speaking.

One of the problems with using presentation software is that everyone else is using it too. In an article in the February 2001 issue of *Business 2.0* called "Ban it Now! Friends Don't Let Friends Use PowerPoint," author Thomas Stewart wrote that conference organizers will often offer to transfer your overhead transparencies to PowerPoint because they "want a uniform look."

"Why in the world would you want a uniform look?" says Stewart, who, as a presenter himself, also has to listen to a lot of other presentations.

"They're all the same. One speaker finishes, his last slide saying thank you and giving his e-mail address. There is applause. The lights go up, he unplugs his laptop and leave the podium, the emcee introduces the next speaker. She walks up, mumbles inconsequentially while she plugs in her laptop. The lights dim and she shows her first slide. It reads good morning. This starts at eight, goes to 12, resumes at one, and ends at five."

So why use PowerPoint or any other presentation software? Because, done right, it can help your presentation be effective and professional. PowerPoint can be used for four different kinds of presentations:

1. Overhead transparencies: You can use this program to create transparencies that are used with an overhead projector. If you don't have a color printer, you can save your work on a disk, take it to a printing center (either in-house or outside), and have color overheads printed.

2. 35mm slides: Most commercial copy centers can convert PowerPoint presentations to 35mm slides if that's what you need for your presentation.

3. Computer-driven slide shows: This is the most common use of presentation programs, where they are presented via a laptop computer. This is the most effective use of a presentation program, because it allows you to add movement and even sound to your presentation.

4. Web slide shows: You can turn your PowerPoint presentation into a Website; this is particularly useful when you are using the presentation for distance-learning classes.

Some presenters seem to think that a slide is a slide is a slide, and that simply having computer-generated slides makes the presentation interesting. The audience knows better. Here are some tips for making your PowerPoint slides most effective:

- Take your audience into account. To whom are you speaking? What impression do you want them to get from your presentation? If you want a serious, professional presentation, be sure your slides reflect that image. Don't use bright colors or playful graphics. On the other hand, if you're doing a presentation to a group of children, or you're speaking on a fun topic, do use brighter colors and lots of pictures.

- Consider the space. Where will you be speaking? If it's in a large hall or auditorium, use simple backgrounds and the largest fonts you can provide. Don't include too much detail; if you want to augment what you have on the slides, provide it in a handout.
- Be constrained with your use of bulleted lists. Because this is the easiest type of slide to create, presenters tend to go overboard, using too many in a row with too much information on each one. NEVER put more than three bullets on a slide. And keep your bulleted items as short and succinct as possible.
- Choose your fonts wisely. Fancy fonts may seem creative, but they are often hard to read. Make sure the font you choose is large enough to be read from the back of the hall (especially if it's long and narrow). Don't use more than two fonts on any one slide. And generally speaking, use a sans-serif font for titles, and a serif font for text.
- Choose your titles wisely to gain maximum interest. Most slides should have a title. For example, if you're giving a talk describing the progression of an illness and you show various diagrams and pie charts for each stage. Each one should have a title such as "Stage 1: The Infection," "Stage 2: The Onset," "Stage 3: The Symptoms," and so on. However, if you're using pictures, as I do in my presentations, you don't always need them. You can let the pictures speak for themselves.
- Use caution when inserting clip art or other graphics. An appropriate graphic can add punch and pizzazz to your presentation, but don't let it take away from your message. Think about all those television commercials people talk about for weeks—but can't remember what they were advertising. If people walk away from your presentation saying, "Boy, those graphics were great!" you have not fulfilled your purpose.

It's your purpose that counts, of course. That's why you should NEVER start designing your presentation by designing your slides first. By the end of my workshops, most participants end up eliminating at least half the slides they have created. Begin with a sheet of paper or a blank computer screen and start outlining what you want to say. Get the content first, and add the graphics later.

Don't Keep Your Audience in the Dark: Avoiding the Pitfalls of Slides

Slides are a double-edged sword: They can effectively dramatize a difficult concept, but they also turn the audience's attention away from *you,* and your visual self is your most effective weapon as a speaker. So if you're going to use slides, they have to be very good for two reasons: to make up for the fact that you're plunging yourself and your audience into darkness, and to counter the tendency of most people to lose interest when they hear they're going to see slides. I have seen members of an audience deflate when they hear that slides are part of the presentation, and it's up to you to prove to them—very quickly—that what's coming up won't be disappointing.

Your voice has to be especially lively and dynamic if your presentation takes place in total darkness after a meal. Try to leave some light on; what you lose in slide clarity you more than gain back in audience involvement and alertness.

Despite the drawbacks, slides can work very well and are good visual aids for large audiences. Some situations really call for their use; for example, a surgeon demonstrating a new surgical technique, an engineer showing the ground around a new facility, and a real estate dealer presenting a property would all welcome the ability of slides to present in an instant what would take many words to convey. Sophisticated computer-generated graphics are common in both slide and overhead projector presentations and help speakers convey complicated concepts elegantly.

Slides also give repeat speakers flexibility; they can update their presentation by adding or subtracting slides without changing the entire display.

In fact, fewer and fewer people are using slides today—but they are still prevalent in some industries. If you have a good application for slides and are not using them to print words that you are already saying, the following rules of thumb will help you produce effective ones:

- Target what you want the audience to remember, and build your slides around these points.
- Use only as many slides as you really need. Don't waste the audience's attention by inundating it with superfluous slides.
- Practice your slide presentation. If you show a slide, make sure you refer to it; don't show a complex slide and continue talking without explaining it. Otherwise, your audience will be trying to figure it out while you're talking about something else.

- Don't leave a slide on the screen longer than you have to. When you're through talking about it or explaining it, go on to the next one.
- Prepare the technical aspects carefully. Make sure ahead of time that your slides are in the correct sequence with the right side up. Number them clearly and make sure your projector and slide carousel are in good condition. Double check everything before you begin: Are the electrical outlets in the right places? Do you have extension cords if you need them?
- Establish good communication with your listeners before you begin the slide show. Let them know you're the expert, not the slides, and that you really want to be there. Many audiences have sat through boring slide presentations, and you must counterbalance that experience. Show them you are a good presenter who uses slides because you *want* to, not because you have to.
- Look for places within the presentation to turn the lights back on. Some presenters feel that you should turn the lights off only once, that flicking them on and off is very disorienting for the audience. I disagree. I think that turning the lights back on can serve as a pick-me-up for the audience, and keep their attention moving forward.
- Don't start your "slide show" without talking to the audience—with the lights on—for at least two minutes.
- Because you don't want to put the slide up before orienting the audience to it, you may need a default slide, one that goes up while you are making a transition. For example, in my presentation, I might put up a slide that says, "NEVER BE BORING." If your presentation was about change, your "transition" slide could read: CHANGE = GROWTH AND PROSPERITY. A company like Nike, with the recognizable slogan, "Just Do It," might use this slide as their default so that people see it many times. You can add to the effectiveness and impact of your message by using the default strategy.
- Be careful when using slides to give the audience a break. Some presenters like to use cartoons when going through a transition, just to break things up a bit. However, unless the cartoon is directly related to your topic, it can be distracting and make it difficult for the audience to get back on track. Used well, however, "break" slides can be very effective. I once attended a presentation on osteoporosis, where, during transitions, the speaker showed photos of a woman from age 50 to age

80, and how she changed. Another speaker, a financial planner trying to convince her audience to keep up with inflation, used break slides showing what $100 bought in 1940, 1955, 1980, 2002, etc.

- If something goes wrong with the slides—if you drop the carousel, or they are out of order, or the switches fail, or there is some other emergency—take a five-minute break to fix it; don't try to muddle through the problem. Before you speak, plan in your mind what you will do if you suddenly can't use your slides.

The Overhead Projector: Not Yet Obsolete

That old standby, the overhead projector, is still a helpful tool for many presentations. I use it because I do not use words on my visuals—only drawings. Many of my clients who are very involved in delivering teaching presentations have joined the ranks of companies that prefer overhead projectors. Here's why:

- You can produce transparencies easily and inexpensively.
- Transparencies are easy for the audience to read and can be used with large groups. You can project images from a few feet to more than 15 feet away.
- You can "interact" with this visual by marking on the transparency during your presentation.
- The projector is easy to carry, at least the portable ones.
- Duplication is easy and inexpensive.
- You don't have to turn off the lights to use an overhead projector, which lets you maintain eye contact with your audience. This is a major advantage.
- You can use a white wall instead of a screen if necessary.
- You never have to turn away from your audience.

Keys to good transparencies include limiting yourself to six words per line and using display-size print that is large enough to ensure good visibility. You can also use clip art, preprinted borders, and attention-getting designs. Overlays can provide color for even more interesting visuals. Number your transparencies so that if they are somehow shuffled, you can sort them out easily.

Enhance Your Delivery

When you add the extra element of an overhead projector, you need to adjust your delivery accordingly. Here are some tips for a smooth presentation:

- Stay in control. If you leave an image on the screen, you're inviting competition, because audience attention is then divided between you and the screen. But you can control attention by turning the projector's switch on and off. For each transparency, you can keep your audience from getting ahead of you by covering specific points with a sheet of paper, and then exposing each point when you're ready to discuss it.
- Don't annoy the audience by turning the machine on without a transparency on the light table. Learn to transfer smoothly from one transparency to the next, or turn the machine off if you need to pause between transparencies.
- Don't look at the screen and don't keep pointing at it; when you do either, you lose eye contact with the audience. To emphasize something, point to the transparency with a pointer or pen, and leave it on the transparency. If you are nervous and worried about the pointer shaking, rest it on the projector until you are ready to use it.
- Decide how you are going to use the projector and place it accordingly. Usually the best place for it is catercorner, stage right for a right-handed person and stage left for a left-handed person. If you will be writing on the transparencies, you might want the projector directly behind you.
- Don't weaken your conclusion by starting to pack up your transparencies while you're still speaking. Turn off the machine and leave the transparencies alone. Then move forward slightly to deliver your closing remarks.
- Use borders around your transparencies (you can buy them at any office supply store). You can write notes on them (which the audience can't see) and you will appear well prepared. The borders also make it easy for changing transparencies. You can then eliminate the annoying and time consuming paper separators. I have seen more speakers loose an audience while they take off the paper separator, put it down, put down the transparency, pick up the separator, etc.

Plan for the Unexpected

You can avoid most common problems with overhead projectors through careful preparation and by assuming responsibility for the logistical details:

- Arrive early to oversee setup procedures.
- Verify for yourself that everything is ready; don't rely on someone else's word.
- Locate the on/off switch, because each projector is different, and many have switches in hard-to-find locations. For example, some machines use a bar instead of a switch.
- Bring an extra light bulb for the projector.
- Be sure you order an overhead projector on a proper stand that has room on each side of the projector for your transparencies. You need space for your visuals before you use them and a place to put the already viewed slides. Even though I request this on my audiovisual list, 75 percent of the time I have to come up with an alternate plan.
- Carry an extension cord, just in case. Also carry a kit of other supplies—an extra roll of acetates, tape, scissors, and so on.
- Set up and test equipment.
- Test the lighting with a transparency on the light table.
- Have a contingency plan.

Points About Laser Pointers

Commercial laser pointers were designed to assist speakers when giving lectures or business presentations. The laser pointer beam produces a small dot of light on any object at which it is aimed. It can be an effective tool for drawing an audience's attention to a particular point on a slide or overhead, especially when you're speaking to a large audience and the slide is projected at a great distance.

However, like all other technological advances, it has its down side. It's difficult to hold the pointer steadily focused on the point you're stressing. What happens then is that the laser beam goes jumping around the slide like Tinkerbell flying around the Lost Boys, and the audience gets lost trying to follow the light.

Also, remember that a laser pointer is not a toy. The Laser Institute of America points out that the laser light can pose a risk to the eye if used incorrectly. They recommend:

- Never shine a laser pointer at anyone. Laser pointers are designed to illustrate inanimate objects.
- Do not point a laser pointer at mirror-like surfaces. A reflected beam can act like a direct beam on the eye.
- Do not allow minors to use a pointer unsupervised.

Videos

Videos are being used increasingly by firms with sizable production budgets. This medium is characterized by high price and a lack of flexibility: Videos are not only hard to update inexpensively, but also can't be controlled by the presenter. Because the speaker has to stop the video to comment, most video presentations are designed for continuous viewing.

Videos make up for their drawbacks in sophistication and power. They most closely resemble the television and cinema experiences by which people are so swayed, and production can be very slick indeed. When both budget and occasion call for a powerful presentation, videos are particularly effective. If you ever use video, get to the site well in advance to check the setup. Nothing messes up a presentation faster than a VCR or DVD player that won't work.

Flip Charts

Believe it not, a flip chart is my favorite visual aid—actually two flip charts on either side of the stage or speaking area. They force you to move horizontally, which creates greater action and attention than moving forward and backward.

Flip charts are very good for smaller audiences. You can prepare them beforehand, or illustrate them as you go along. They can be actual cardboard displays, or simply an easel and a large pad. Follow these steps as you use flip charts:

- Set up the flip chart ahead of time, but keep it covered until you need it.
- Always start with a title so people know what the information refers to. This is a step most people eliminate. Print the title in capital letters.
- Make the drawings bold and simple.

- Don't talk and write at the same time unless you really have command of the audience and have a strong voice that will carry while your back is turned.
- For drawing, use big, heavy lines. Lightly sketch in complicated designs ahead of time so you can go over them quickly and expertly during the presentation.
- Don't use red unless you're speaking to a very small group—it's especially difficult to see on flip charts.
- If ink goes through the paper, use every other sheet. It's also easier to flip two pages at a time.
- If you're speaking in a long, narrow room, put the flip chart on a raised platform, or else people in the back of the room will have trouble seeing the bottom of your pages.
- When you're pointing to the chart, and you're standing with it to your left, use your left arm to point. If you use your right arm, you close yourself off from your audience by placing your right arm across your body. If you're right-handed, place the chart to your right.
- One of the main values of the flip is that you can leave your message up their while you're speaking about other things, which is not true of a slide or computer-graphic presentation.
- Make your presentation multi-media by using flip charts along with your other graphics.

As with any visual aid, once you've used your flip chart, you need to find a way to get rid of it. You might want to use your flip chart at different times in your talk, so the best thing to do is to have a neutral page after every picture or sequence. This can be a blank page, or one containing a symbol or picture relevant to your whole presentation.

Chalkboards

Chalkboards are also good visual aids for small audiences, if you follow these hints:

- Always check the chalkboard ahead of time to make sure the legs and pegs are stable.
- Have plenty of yellow chalk available, and keep a spare piece in your pocket. Yellow shows up better than white.

- Use damp, not dry, dusters.
- If you use a pointer, don't let it waver around the board. Point at what you want to emphasize, leave the pointer there for a moment, and then take away the pointer.
- Never try to draw or write for more than a few seconds at a time; avoid talking while you're drawing. When you want to explain what you're doing, turn and face the audience before speaking.
- Clear the board as soon as you're finished with what's on it and have moved on to a new topic. Old drawings will distract your audience.

Special Hint for Chalkboards and Flip Charts

To draw straight lines and perfect circles, trace them very faintly in pencil or with chalk before your presentation. Then draw over the lines during your speech; your audience will think you're a latter-day Leonardo da Vinci.

Models and Objects

Models and objects are limited to small groups. Good ones tend to be expensive, costly to duplicate, and often unwieldy. Models require ongoing narration from the speaker to come to life, but this need means that the presenter has flexibility and can change the speech to fit the audience. As with videos, models work best when the situation really calls for them.

When you pass out objects, samples, handouts, or other materials as visual aids, you lose attention as you do so. Don't introduce vital new points at that time; rather, use the time to summarize or to describe the object being distributed.

Handouts

Handouts are visual aids the audience can manipulate, so it's important to manage their presentation in a way that keeps you in control. Make it clear what you expect your audience to do with your handouts. Don't give them out without first talking about the ideas they contain, or people will start to read ahead of where you are and you'll lose control.

Audience members are a lot more likely to remember things when they write them down, even if they never go back and look at their notes again.

That's why handouts with questions and fill-in-the-blanks can be a good way to help an audience retain your information and message.

Save time and confusion and create a polished impression by counting handouts ahead of time. You'll need to know the number of rows and the number of people in each row. Try to be creative with your handouts. Avoid using typed lists, use drawings or other artwork where appropriate. The cardinal rule for visual aids also applies to handouts: They must have a clear purpose and contribute something you could not convey verbally.

Pictures That Tell Your Story

The best visual aids are a kind of shorthand. Charts and illustrations are the visual aids used most commonly and effectively by the creators of slides, transparencies, and flip charts.

Charts are inherently flexible and can show graphs (bar, pie, or line), organizational relationships, cause and effect, and how one event relates to another (flow chart). It's up to your imagination. Whether a diagram, cartoon, map, or original artwork, illustrations make visual aids *visual* and keep them from looking like typed restatements of your speech.

Not Just for Public Speakers

Visual aids—especially flip charts—are helpful for staff meetings and client discussions. They help reinforce your points and make you appear more polished and better prepared. You will make an impact because not many people use visual aids in these situations. Just watch everyone perk up the first time you use visual aids at a staff meeting.

A Final Caveat From Murphy

Bill Gates, founder of Microsoft, stood up on stage before a worldwide audience to introduce his newest program, Windows98. He and a colleague were demonstrating how easy it was to add peripheries onto the program. The colleague plugged in a scanner and waited for a message saying, "your new device has been loaded" to pop up on the giant screen behind him. Instead, the screen went blue and the dreaded "fatal error" message flashed behind them. There was some sort of glitch, and his powerful computer-aided graphics programs were not working. If the richest man in the world, the man who invented much of the way we use computers today, had problems with his presentations, chances are that, at some point, you will encounter an embarrassing problem or two.

Nowhere does Murphy's Law apply so well as with visual aids: If anything can go wrong, it will. To help you counter this law, I have included the checklist that follows on page 164. Use it and you'll always be prepared.

Just as Boy Scouts have their motto—"Always be prepared"—a speaker using visual aids must also have a motto—"Always have an alternative plan." And often that alternative plan rests with you. Visual aids can be wonderful devices, but you should never feel you can't deliver a good speech without them; you can. And at all times, just in case, you should be able to.

Vivid, instantaneous, exciting, and *colorful* are adjectives that can apply to your speech if you use good visual aids. Of course, a master of words can get praise like this for prose alone. But powerful speakers use visual aids to get themselves that much closer to presentation excellence. The next chapter, on stage managing, will show you how to ensure excellence and a smooth show by controlling environmental factors that affect your speech in general and your visual aids in particular.

Professional Projects: Creative Visuals

1. Discuss the visual aids you would use for a humorous and informative presentation on the pitfalls of visual aids. Try to sketch them out, and show how you would make each point.
2. You've been asked to give a three-minute orientation speech to new employees. Describe the visual aids you will use and why you have chosen them.
3. Make a commitment to yourself that during the next six months you will try to use each type of visual aid. This will build your confidence and flexibility. Try to use multimedia (at least two different types of visual aids) for your next presentation.

Audiovisual Checklist

Here is a list of questions that you can use before every presentation to make sure that your visual aids are relevant, effective, and help make your message clear.

	Yes	No
1. Do my visual aids enhance my presentation?		
2. Can I concisely explain the purpose of each visual?		
3. Are my visuals clear, simple, and bold?		
4. Are they visible to each member of the audience?		
5. Are they numbered?		
6. Are they in order?		
7. Have I accounted for additional needs (for example, felt markets or flip charts)?		
8. Do I have an alternate plan?		
9. Am I comfortable enough to talk to the audience and not the visual?		
10. Do I have a way to orient the audience and to lead it clearly through each point of the visual aids?		
11. Am I prepared to explain each step in my own colorful words rather than to read verbatim from the visual aid?		
12. If I am using slides and darkening the room, have I given extra practice to my vocal variety?		
13. If I am using handouts, have I counted them and prepared the logistics of distribution?		
14. Have I noted on my confidence cards when to turn on and turn off each visual aid?		
15. Have I carefully timed the distribution of any objects or models to avoid losing the audience's attention?		
16. Have I accounted for Murphy's law?		
17. Have I accounted for O'Toole's law ("Murphy was an optimist")?		

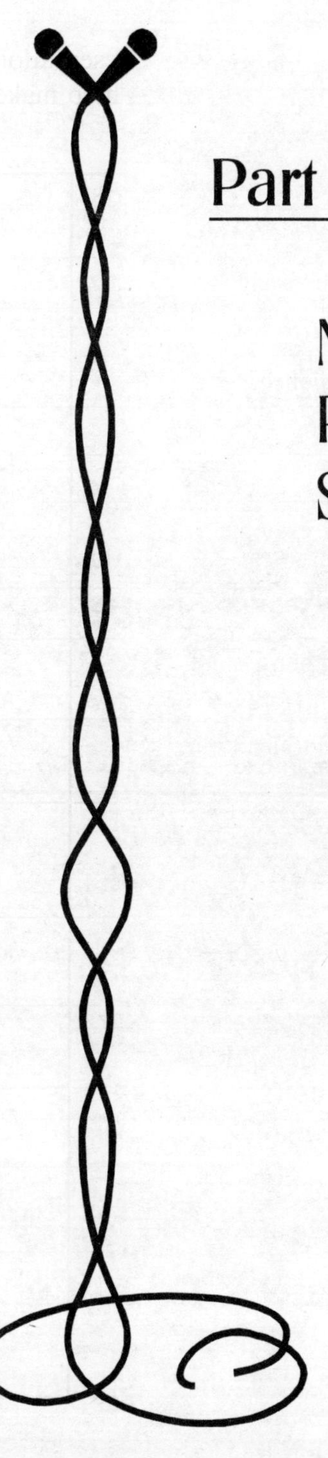

Part IV

Master the Fine Points of Powerful Speaking

Chapter 15

Power Language: Turn Everyday Words Into Persuasion

Poetry is ordinary language raised to the Nth power.

—Paul Engle

What's the difference between a pleasant, serviceable speech and a great one? Between a speech that does the job and one that makes your heart beat faster? A speech that you listen to politely, and one that persuades you to change your thinking?

By now you know enough to go out and give a good working speech. But why stop at the basics? It's only a few steps more to a speech that has the power to persuade and influence your listeners. The difference between a good speech and a great speech is *language.*

But don't panic. By language I don't mean grammar or vocabulary but the way you use simple, everyday language. This chapter will show you some of the best ways to make your everyday language both eloquent and persuasive.

Avoid the Passive Voice

Choosing the active voice—instead of the passive voice—is your most important step to a powerful speech. The active voice relies on *verbs.* "The boy ran" is more powerful than "the boy was seen running." The active voice has a clear subject, and in speeches that subject is usually *you.* In an active sentence, the subject is "doing" something (for example,

The boss vetoed John's idea). In a passive sentence, the subject is receiving the action—something is happening to the subject (for example, John's idea was vetoed by the boss).

Paint a picture in your mind of what you want to say, and choose the brighter, bolder image. Think of it as a movie. Here are two scenes: In the first, Tim comes into a room. He's angry. He wants to complain to someone. He takes out his pen and begins to write. In the second version, the camera pans slowly across the room and settles on a blank piece of white paper. We see someone's hand holding a pen, and words begin to appear on the page. Scene two can be effective, if that's what you're going for, but it you want the audience to get your point immediately, scene one is going to be much more powerful.

The active voice also gives the subject responsibility; the passive voice takes it away. If I use the passive voice and say, "The dishes must be washed before we leave," who is responsible for washing them? It's hard to tell. If I use the active voice and say, "You must wash the dishes before we leave," there is no question that "you" must take the action. You take responsibility by saying "I saw," or "I believe." The passive and impersonal "It has been seen that," rather than "I saw," may remove you from the line of fire, but it makes for boring speeches. If Caesar had spoken that way, his powerful *Veni, Vidi, Vici"* ("I came, I saw, I conquered") would have been: "The place was arrived at, was observed, and was duly overtaken."

One way to keep your language active is to eliminate verbs that end in *"-ing."* "I run" is stronger than "I am running." A title such as "How to Run a Meeting" is stronger than "Running a Meeting."

The active voice takes the more direct route to your destination. That doesn't mean you never want to use the passive voice. There may be times when you want to slow the action down, to paint a picture, or go get a different rhythm.

Modifiers Sap Your Strength

Powerful speeches eliminate the words and phrases that weaken language. And these little phrases are everywhere: People use "perhaps" and "I think that maybe" almost without realizing it. Powerless speakers use "It seems like" and "you know." Their language is filled with modifiers like "kind of" and "sort of." Compare the difference between saying "I hope I can get that done for you" and "I know I can get that done for you." One little word can make a great difference. If you feel strongly about something, use strong words. "I think" is not strong. It automatically weakens what follows, even though what usually follows is an assertion. "This is the best solution" is much stronger than "I think this is the best solution."

Social scientists at Duke University have been able to pinpoint a specific pattern that identifies powerless speech. Intensifiers such as *very, definitely,* and *surely* do the opposite of what they are supposed to do: They weaken the descriptive adjective that follows by not letting it stand on its own. "The car is fast" is a stronger statement than "The car is very fast."

Powerless speakers also hesitate often, relying on fillers such as "uh," "umm," and "well…" to get them from point to point. They are overly polite, and often use "sir" and "please." Obviously, politeness has its place, but if you are too polite, you seem timid and worried that what you are going to say will offend. And if *you* seem to have doubts about what you have to say about your subject, your audience won't be far behind.

Monitor the Misplaced Modifier

Modifiers can cause problems in other ways. Pay attention to the placement of words and phrases in your sentences. There is a wonderful old film called "The Thin Man" about a detective named Nick and his wife Nora. At one point Nora tells her husband, "I read where you were shot five times in the tabloids." Nick replies, "It's not true. He didn't come anywhere near my tabloids." Obviously, the correct way to phrase the first sentence is to say, "I read in the tabloids that you were shot five times." Obviously, the writers purposely misplaced the modifying phrase "in the tabloids" to make the line funny. But you don't want to make the mistake unless you mean to.

Beware the Ponderous Trap

Modifiers may weaken language to the point of forgettable speech, but equally bad is the style of speech politicians and social scientists adopt when they're cornered or simply trying to impress. I call it *babblespeak.* The essence of this style is using a lot of words that say as little as possible. Unfortunately, this tendency isn't limited to specialists; many people feel they must use big words to make an impression, when, in reality, vivid language is simple and direct.

The good platform speaker avoids this babbling style as if it were poison. To avoid becoming a babbler:

- Use single syllable words, which are often more powerful than words with three or more syllables.

- Make your point in the fewest words.

- Use common words instead of stilted words and jargon.
- Avoid the passive voice: Use lots of active verbs.
- Don't beat around the bush; be direct.

Much of this cloudy language has bureaucratic sources. A plumber in New York wrote to the Bureau of Standards in Washington. He said that he found hydrochloric acid was great for cleaning drains, but was it safe? A bureaucrat answered: "The efficacy of hydrochloric acid is indisputable, but the chlorine residue is incompatible with metallic permanence."

The plumber replied he was glad that Washington thought he was right. He got another reply: "We cannot assume responsibility for the production of toxic and noxious residues with hydrochloric acid." Right, the plumber answered, it's good stuff.

Finally, the Bureau sent the plumber a note saying what it had meant all along: "Don't use hydrochloric acid; it eats the hell out of the pipes!"

The worst thing about this sort of babble is that once you start, it's very easy to fall into its trap. One complicated sentence leads to another and before long, you have a whole speech—but it will be one that audiences will have a tough time listening to.

Use the Right Words—and Words That Are Right for You

Let me emphasize a point I made earlier: Anyone—regardless of his or her vocabulary—can be an outstanding speaker. You don't have to know unusual or complicated words to use power language. The important thing is to use language that is comfortable for you and to use it in a creative, colorful way.

If you do use complicated words, make sure they're completely familiar to you. The president of a football team forgot this rule when he introduced a recently acquired player: "His influence on the state's economy will be inconceivable," he crowed. Then he thought a bit. "I mean incontrovertible. No…inconsequential. Well, here he is." Misusing a word in an attempt to appear learned has led many speakers into a Malapropism: "My wife tells me I'm an invertebrate smoker."

It's not only complicated words that get us in trouble. Politicians are well known for using the wrong word in the wrong place. Mayor Daley (again) once said, "The police are not here to create disorder. They're here to preserve disorder." Many people questioned the intelligence of

President George W. Bush when he said things such as, "I know how hard it is to put food on your family," "Will the highways on the Internet become more few?" "I have made good judgments in the past. I have made good judgments in the future," and "The future will be better tomorrow." And then there is the champion of the misused word, former Vice President Dan Quayle, who once said, "Republicans understand the importance of bondage between parent and child."

Sometimes a slip of the tongue is good for a laugh. Kenneth Keating was once invited to give a speech with this charming invitation: "I hope you can come, Senator, because we would all like to hear the dope from Washington." Senator Keating turned that into a classic story and used it repeatedly in future speeches. Will Rogers was one gifted speaker who used the wrong word on purpose very effectively: "In some states they no longer hang murderers—they kill them by elocution." In both cases, the speaker used a word that surprised, and that came at the end of a sentence—a perfect combination for memorable sentences.

Watch Where You Put Your Words

Power comes from powerful phrases; it also comes from knowing where to put those phrases. Good speakers use an influential technique used by trial lawyers—people who sway audiences for high stakes. It's called *the doctrine of primacy and recency,* and it refers to people's tendency to remember beginnings and endings.

Given this tendency in listeners, effective speakers will put their crucial information at the beginning and end of each sentence, and paragraph, for the entire speech. Whatever comes in the middle tends to get lost. Listeners' concentration is high with the first word, wavers as a statement continues, and is high again with the last word or phrase. If you say the sentence "My boss is fair, observant, considerate, and generous," people will remember *fair* and *generous.* Evocative exceptions to this rule are phrases or lists with three parts: "I came, I saw, I conquered" uses the natural rhythm found in trinities. Listen to comics and humorists, whose deliveries often take advantage of the rhythmic properties of balanced sentences.

There is no universal agreement about which position—the beginning or the end—is the most powerful. The doctrine of primacy says lead off with your strongest statement. The recency argument says finish with your most powerful punch. Usually it's a matter of using your strongest point in one place, and your next strongest in the other.

Words That Reverberate

There are two components to creating powerful language: eliminating the words that detract from your message and adding language that, although ordinary, resonates. Great speakers use language the same way songwriters do: They use imagery to create mental pictures, repetition to make ideas stick in your mind, and rhythm to stir your emotions.

The key to power language is to recognize that words have something more than their basic meaning; they have emotional content too. And it's the emotion you're going for. Henry James said the most beautiful words in the English language were *summer afternoon.* Those two simple words convey a nostalgic picture to almost everyone. And the picture is universally pleasant because most people will remember one idyllic summer's day at the seashore or the ball game, rather than a sweltering journey in a crowded train or bus. The words *summer afternoon* simply make you feel good.

Even the *sound* of certain words conveys more than meaning. The word *buzz* not only means a whirring sound but also sounds like one. *Bombastic, bamboozles, blunderbuss, nincompoop, lackadaisical, rambunctious, scalawag—all* sound just like their definitions.

Aim for the Emotions

Fear, love, anger, compassion—they all have the power to stir anyone in front of you. If you want to influence your audience you must search for language that has emotional appeal. These appeals don't have to be blatant and obvious; in fact, the best ones are subtle. You can create emotional appeals by using impact phrases—memorable groups of words that shake listeners from lethargy and stay in their minds. Ideally, these phrases touch basic human emotions and help your listeners empathize with your perspective. A fund-raiser for the homeless says, "Think how you would feel if you had no home." An opponent of airline deregulation asks, "Remember how angry you felt the last time your plane got canceled, or you sat on the runway for hours?"

When Abraham Lincoln finished the Gettysburg Address, many listeners had tears in their eyes. But tears are not the only, or even the most important, measure of emotional impact. Laughter is also a basic emotion, and impact phrases can be humorous. Describing his own tendency to procrastinate, one speaker said, "I am rather like a mosquito in a nudist camp: I know what I ought to do, but I don't know where to begin."

Never underestimate rhetoric's ability to move an audience; it's been doing just that for centuries. Gorgias, a Greek who lived in the fourth century B.C., was renowned in Athens for using language so beautiful people thought it was magic. Three centuries earlier, Archilochus, another master of words, had a reputation for caustic phrases. After he spoke witheringly of his in-laws one day, they were so upset by his words that they killed themselves. Although the average businessperson no doubt has less severe reactions in mind, nonetheless it's good to realize that words can and do go straight for the emotions, even in the most routine presentation. Memorable speakers harness the inherent power of words.

The 12 Most Persuasive Words in the English Language

While you're aiming for the emotions, you'll find these words coming to your aid over and over again.

1. *Discover.* With shades of childhood treasures, this word conveys excitement and adventure. If you tell the people in your audience that you want to share a discovery with them, you start to make your enthusiasm contagious.
2. *Easy.* Many people are basically lazy and will look for a quick, uncomplicated answer. The success of books such as Richard Feynman's *Six Easy Pieces: Essential of Physics Explained by Its Most Brilliant Teacher* and Mel Klieman's *Hire Tough, Manage Easy: How to Find and Hire the Best Hourly Employees* are proof of this tendency.
3. *Guarantee.* We are all reluctant to try something new because of the risk involved. Take away that fear by guaranteeing a sure thing, and you can sell your audience on the point you're trying to make.
4. *Health.* Self-preservation is a great motivator. We gravitate toward anything that will improve our condition or make us feel better.
5. *Love.* The thing we can't do without, and the one word that evokes all kinds of romantic fantasies.
6. *Money.* People react perceptibly at the thought of making money.
7. *New.* Having something new, knowing something new—this word has an intrinsic appeal. Speakers are always striving to impart new facts and figures in their presentations.
8. *Proven.* Another no-risk word. *Proven* assures listeners that something has already been tested and given the go-ahead.

9. *Results.* This is the bottom line—where you tell people about what they will get, what will happen, what they can expect.
10. *Safety.* Unless your audience has a death wish, the idea of safety is very comforting.
11. *Save.* Even the wealthiest people shop for bargains. It's not just money that entices; people also want to hear about saving time.
12. *You.* I've saved the most important word for last. Persuasive speakers personalize their talks and use this word often. Try to avoid too many personal pronouns—I, we, our—and the anonymity of "today's session." Make it *"your* session today," and carry that emphasis on *your* throughout your presentation. You can't stir your audience up if you don't address them directly.

Power Phrases Add Emphasis

Power expressions join power words in their ability to command attention—whether overtly or subliminally. The phrases that follow pique listeners' interest and keep them listening for what's to come: "Here's how you will benefit." "Here are the results you have been waiting for." "This will answer your questions." "I have a new plan to put before you." "You will discover how you can..."

Reach for Vivid Comparisons

All impact phrases use imagery. Imagery helps your listeners understand and remember. When you want to explain an idea, draw a mental picture and then color it in. Your job as a speaker is to get people to imagine, think, and *feel.* Saying something longed for was as "welcome as a glass of cool water after eating a very hot pepper" conjures up taste, heat, relief, and refreshment in your listeners' minds. Speakers have many verbal tools to paint pictures with, and two of the best are *metaphors* and *similes.*

These two popular figures of speech are similar to each other, and most speakers don't find it necessary to distinguish between them. Certainly their purpose is the same: to create a striking, vivid picture with few words. Metaphors and similes transfer the image of one thing to another. "Man is still the most extraordinary computer of all," is the metaphor John F. Kennedy used to describe L. Gordon Cooper. These devices are fast and effective. Ralph Waldo Emerson's "Hitch your wagon to a star" conveys instant advice to the ambitious and to dreamers. A sports writer for the *New York Times* described Barry Bond as being as warm and fuzzy as a frozen pool ball.

When you do create a metaphor or simile, make sure it is appropriate to your audience and style. And do your best to make it original. A worn-out cliché—"dead as a doornail" or "white as a sheet"—is weak. We have heard it so often that it no longer has impact. Try "dead as a dissected frog" or "white as the tips of a French manicure." Original figures of speech are the ones that attract attention and make the image stick in your listeners' minds. One speaker trying to duck hostile questions at a news conference said, "I somehow feel there's a boomerang loose in the room." That's a good, original metaphor.

Try not to mix up your images. "Now that Jim is back in the saddle, everything will be smooth sailing" is a mixed metaphor that paints a confusing picture of cowboys on the high seas.

A metaphor is a more direct, less subtle version of a simile. "Power is poison" and "Room for improvement is the biggest room in the house," are short, sharp metaphors. A simile compares unlike things, usually with connecting words such as *like, as,* or *is.* "He keeps himself in the public eye like a cinder" is a perfect, ear-catching simile. Here's a vivid one: Truman Capote once said, "Venice is like eating an entire box of chocolate liqueurs in one go."

People use metaphors and similes in virtually every speaking situation. Charles de Gaulle used one to make a political statement: "Treaties are like roses and young girls. They last while they last." I once heard a woman address a group for the second time; she said, "My stories are like good wine and good women—they improve with age."

Another useful figure of speech that creates magnificent imagery is hyperbole, which is purposeful exaggeration. "He could sell refrigerators to Eskimos" is a classic example. When Dorothy Parker shared office space with Robert Benchley she said they had an office "so tiny that an inch smaller and it would have been adultery."

Apt Analogies

One of the most useful figures of speech for platform speakers, an analogy lets you quickly explain a new idea by comparing it with something familiar and simple. Benjamin Franklin said, "Fish and visitors start to smell in three days," and gave a concise picture of why people should not overstay their welcomes. Writing about Frank Sinatra, author E.B. White once wrote: "To Sinatra, a microphone is as real as a girl waiting to be kissed."

Analogies are especially useful for speakers who have to present technical or scientific information. By comparing the complex with something ordinary and familiar, your listeners understand by association. One speaker effectively explained a computer by comparing it with a secretary. The essayist, Lewis Thomas explained the universe by comparing it with the life of a single cell. There are many other figures of speech that speakers use to create powerful images—parables, fables, epithets, icons, and personifications to name a few.

Other Tricks of Language

Other colorful devices can get attention. Sound makes a strong impression, and speakers often use alliteration (using several words that begin with the same letter) to implant a phrase in the collective mind of the audience. Winston Churchill was a master of alliteration: "He was a man of light and learning." "We cannot fail or falter." Listeners can remember those phrases because of the alliteration and also because the nouns and verbs are simple and direct. These phrases also persuade.

Repetition is another powerful speaking device. George M. Cohan created one of the most stirring and memorable calls to action through the exclusive use of repetition: "Over there, over there…the Yanks are coming, the Yanks are coming, the drums drum drumming everywhere…So beware, so beware…." The cadence—or rhythm—of language also has an emotional pull. Churchill used cadence to create a stirring image: "Let us to the task, to the battle, to the toil."

Borrowed Eloquence

The trend in today's public speaking is much more conversational than the arm-waving oratory of old. Even so, powerful speech is often eloquent. A few select, powerful phrases in a speech can be the spice needed to make what you say memorable, rather than just easy to listen to.

One way to achieve eloquence is to quote from those who have been eloquent before you. When Sir Isaac Newton was asked how he saw things so clearly, he said, "I can stand on the shoulders of men like Galileo." Good speakers stand to great effect on the shoulders of William Shakespeare, Abraham Lincoln, Winston Churchill, Groucho Marx, Martin Luther King, even Mae West and Katherine Graham.

Using someone's eloquent statement about a subject accomplishes two things: It adds eloquence to your own talk and it endorses whatever you are saying. President Reagan rarely quoted from past speakers who might be expected to have agreed with him, such as Calvin Coolidge. Instead, he often quoted the words of Democrats such as Franklin Roosevelt and John F. Kennedy. The words of these "liberal" presidents not only added eloquence to Reagan's statements but also endorsed his more conservative positions by inference.

When you choose quotations to enrich your own talk, be creative. Don't use the same ones you've heard over and over. Go to more modern sources and find a witty or elegant phrase that you can use to support your position. Remember, you're using not only the words, but also the person.

All figures of speech have the same purpose—to use a few words to create vivid pictures, touch the emotions, and stay in people's minds. Power language is aptly named; use it well, and people will tend to think you are as powerful as the language you use. As Mae West so aptly put it, "It's not what I say, but how I say it." And what you do as you say it. The next chapter will help you gain power from the nonverbal communication that characterizes you as quickly as anything you say.

Professional Projects: Powerful Language

1. Create a simile or metaphor that describes how you feel when caught in traffic, when your plane is delayed, and when your computer crashes.
2. Think of a complex procedure in your office and devise a simple analogy to help clarify it.
3. Create a title for a presentation on the importance of teamwork using alliteration.
4. Create synonyms for the 12 most powerful words.

Chapter 16

Positive Body Language

As I grow older, I pay less attention to what men say; I just watch what they do.

—Andrew Carnegie

Although power language can make people notice your words, body language affects your presentation the moment you come into view. Have you ever heard a speaker cover an important topic that was of interest to you, but the style of presentation was so sloppy that you just didn't quite believe what he or she was saying? If your body language is not synchronized with your words, your message will not be clear; people will believe your body language, not your spoken message.

We are a visual society; people start to make judgments based on your body language the moment they see you. No words can convey confidence—or lack of it—as quickly as body language does, and it takes many brilliant words to change poor impressions made by your nonverbal signals. Effective speakers know they must not only master their verbal presentation, but also make their nonverbal communication work for them in a positive way.

Albert Mehrabian has said that we are perceived three ways: 55 percent visually, 38 percent vocally, and 7 percent verbally. Audiences are making their hard-to-shake first impressions as you are setting up, waiting to be introduced, and walking to the platform to begin your speech. In short, you are your own best visual aid—or your worst.

Most negative body language is a result of nervousness or lack of preparation. If you are well prepared, the audience will sense it, and your own movements will be far more reassuring than those of the person who doesn't even know how to locate the switch on the overhead projector. And as Chapter 2 noted about fear, a lot of nervousness can be eliminated if you realize audiences *want* to enjoy themselves; meet them halfway with positive instead of distracting body language and the verbal part of your speech will go that much better.

Tackling the Larger Issues

Mastery of body language involves taking control of both the broad aspects of nonverbal communication and the smaller gestures and mannerisms that we often resort to subconsciously. I'll start with the larger points that can add to or detract from your effectiveness:

Preparation

Besides making you confident and in control, nothing lets your audience know you care like thorough preparation. It's the foundation for building positive body language.

Posture

Sloppy posture conveys a lack of confidence and possibly a lack of discipline, and it's surprising how many people neglect this crucial aspect of their presentation. Standing erect, balanced between both feet, and with your shoulders back, you convey an alert and enthusiastic manner—even if that's a far cry from how you really feel.

Approaching the Platform

As you wait your turn, maintain a confident but relaxed posture. While you're being introduced, first look just at the introducer and then slowly look over the audience as the host delivers the rest of your (brief) introduction. As you approach the lectern, look as though you would rather be there, about to speak to this particular group, more than any other place in the world. Walk with confidence. There's no particular rule about who you look at as you approach the speaker's platform. It depends on how much space you have to walk across, whether you have to set up your microphone, whether the audience is applauding, and so on. One approach is to acknowledge your introduction by first looking at the audience, smiling, looking back at the person who introduced you, and then walking toward him or her.

Once you reach the lectern, slow down a little and collect yourself. Always respond to the introduction, but make it brief. You can simply say "thank you so much" and move right into your speech. If you are using a lectern, put your notes as high as possible on the stand, so your eyes won't have to travel a long distance. This allows you to maintain greater eye contact with the audience. You should have already checked the microphone (if you are using one). If you have to adjust it, take the necessary time to do so. Stay calm and in control.

Once your notes and microphone are set, set yourself as well. Balance your weight on both feet; stand up straight with your stomach in. You can place your hands lightly on the lectern but don't lean on it. Don't worry if your knees are knocking. Remember, even if you are a nervous wreck, it doesn't matter as long as your audience doesn't know.

A final note on lecterns: Avoid using them if you don't need them. Lecterns impose distance and elevation; they are barriers between you and the audience. Any book on selling talks about the need to break down barriers between you and your customers, so why create them? Some speakers insist they have to use lecterns in order to feel comfortable. But that's another very good reason *not* to use them, because your audience will sense that you are ill at ease.

How to Use Eye Contact

Your eyes are your most important physical feature as a speaker, because they are crucial in establishing rapport. Before you begin to speak, let your eyes sweep the room; look from one side to the other and from front to back. This pause will let your audience know you're relaxed and well prepared. Make eye contact with as many people as you can. Your initial message is that you're glad to be here; your eyes are your first direct contact with the people in your audience—make them support you. Establish rapport with eye contact *before* you begin to speak.

You must always be looking directly at the audience whenever you are making direct statements and key points. For example, if you say, "this project will impact our entire team, for the eyes of the entire company will be on us—and you look away or are looking down or walking away—people will not believe you. If you say, "This is vitally important," and are not giving direct contact, your words will not be credible.

It helps to focus on a friendly face, especially if you feel you have an unfriendly audience. Think of yourself as talking to that open, accepting person; look at him or her as often as you need to.

Most people have a bias toward one side of a room. To discover yours, have someone watch you speak. Then when you make your speech, place your feet toward the side of the room you usually miss: You'll naturally turn around and force yourself to face these people. To appear that you are looking at the entire room, divide the room into quadrants and make sure you look into each one. Find a friendly face in each quadrant and focus on that person but not in an obvious fashion—be unpredictable.

Dress

Comfortable and appropriate are the two key words. Adapt your dress to the people you are addressing; you don't want to dress exactly like them but choose a style similar to theirs. I used to dress quite formally at all times, and as soon as I dropped the formality and dressed stylishly but casually, my ratings improved. When in doubt, dress on the formal side, but try to add some flair; audiences don't want to look at deliberately drab speakers.

Men should stick to the basics—dark suit and white or light-colored shirt for contrast—unless they're speaking at an outdoor picnic where everyone is wearing casual clothes.

Women have more wardrobe options and are more subject to fashion trends. The real key for women is to make sure *you* wear the clothes and not vice versa. Choose clothes that feel comfortable and make you feel at ease. Unless you are known for high fashion or a particular look, it's best to avoid extremes of any sort. Women can wear bright colors: You should not only stand out but also fit in. In front of a conservative audience, you could add some dash by wearing a red scarf with your suit. I know of one woman who stands out—properly—by always wearing a white suit.

Above all, don't wear clothes that need to be adjusted when you stand up or sit down. If you wear a hat, make sure it doesn't hide your face. If you wear jewelry, keep it simple and clank-free. Big bracelets or dangling earrings are taboo, because jewelry can be enormously distracting for an audience.

Nowadays, many companies are in the business casual mode. Keep that in mind as you plan your speaking wardrobe. When I give a speech, if the dress is business casual, I wear a pants suit. If it is more formal, I dress it up or wear a suit with a skirt. For company presentations you don't want to overdress. A good rule of thumb is to be one degree more formal or better dressed than your audience. You want to be one of them yet stand out just a little.

Women should also try to wear something with a pocket to keep notes and a handkerchief in. Leave your handbag at your seat when you approach the lectern.

Controlling Your Hands

Novice speakers often ask about what to do with their hands while they're talking. Hands can take care of themselves if you know what *not* to do:

- Don't grip the lectern and hold on for dear life.
- Don't keep your hands in your pockets all the time or folded rigidly across your chest.
- Don't fiddle with your jewelry or props.

Even though your hands suddenly seem to be much bigger than they ever were before, they can be a tremendous asset. There are four ways in which you can use them to communicate ideas better—to emphasize shape, size, number, and direction. Practice your hand gestures until they feel comfortable and natural. Chances are you will feel more relaxed if you have something for your hands to do. If you've got your eyes glued to your notes, your hands will feel like dead weights at the ends of your arms. It's easier to use your hands naturally when you maintain eye contact with the audience.

Practice gestures in front of a mirror—get a feel for what you are doing and what you look like. Strong gestures come from the shoulders, not the elbows. Try it in front of the mirror, with your hands facing the sky and you'll see how a gesture from the elbow is much weaker than that from your shoulder.

Use hand gestures carefully, because too many of them are very distracting. When I train people for public speaking I tell them to keep their arms and hands at their sides if they feel uncomfortable. We discover when we play back the videos of practice sessions that this position doesn't look awkward at all, and in fact comes across quite relaxed. So if you're really uncomfortable about using your hands, just let them rest at your sides.

Your Smile

Unless you are dealing with a life-or-death issue, smile often. It projects warmth and loosens up your facial muscles. Most people look better when they smile, and it makes your audience more comfortable because you appear more natural and confident. A grim-faced speaker isn't going to develop much rapport. Even so, in my public-speaking classes of 20 students, I have to tell at least 15 of them to smile more often. Try to visualize your audience as warm and friendly, and you will find it easier to smile.

Glasses

If you wear glasses, you have to deal with how they can appear to the audience. Glasses with heavy rims will hide your face and interfere with eye contact. Half-lens glasses give the unpleasant impression that you're looking down your nose at the audience. The next time you change your glasses, try the kind with large lenses and narrow frames. Stay away from strong tinting or light-sensitive lenses that darken under lighting. Many professional speakers avoid these problems by opting for contact lenses.

You can also use your glasses for effect by taking them off once or twice during the speech, or at the end, when you're getting ready to take questions from the audience. If you've got glasses, use them to give your gestures added impact.

To Move or Not to Move

If you've ever watched an amateur theatrical performance, you know that nervous people give themselves away with their awkward movements. It's obvious that they have been told to take two steps to the left on a certain line, and then sit on a specific chair. You get so caught up in watching the clumsiness of the actor that you cannot concentrate on the lines of dialogue.

Needless to say, you don't want your audience to be concentrating on your movements and not your words. That's why some speakers choose to stand in one spot; they're afraid they'll be clumsy or fall down or somehow detract from their message. However, standing in one spot throughout a presentation can be just as much of a distraction, especially if the speaker is so still and statue-like that you're just waiting for a pigeon to come roost on his shoulder.

There are a number of reasons why you should move during your presentations:

- To get closer and build a physical connection with the audience.
- To create a stronger sense of emotion.
- To change the visual pattern.
- To make a physical transition.

- To change the rhythm of the speech. (If you have a frenetic type of delivery and move constantly, then when you stop it will be twice as effective.)
- To make a point more intense or emphatic.
- To create greater audience attention.
- To create a flow.

Use lateral movements whenever possible (moving from side to side rather than from front to back). They're not only easier for the audience to see, they create more visual interest. When you do move, move purposely—don't inch or sidle.

When we're in conversation with one another, we're always moving. We shift in our seats, or move a few feet to the left or right, or turn our heads to look in a different direction. It's natural. Your movements on stage should be natural as well—and that comes with practice. When you're rehearsing your presentation, practice your movements, gestures, and mannerisms as well.

The Fine Points: Gestures and Mannerisms

Your gestures and mannerisms can help you gain the support and confidence of your audience, or they can make people uncomfortable and even antagonistic. By far the best way to spot your gestures—both good and bad—is to videotape yourself practicing or giving your presentation. Replay your speech until you have broken it down into the series of gestures and mannerisms you rely on. Here's a list of the most common ones and how they are perceived:

Defensiveness

Arms crossed on chest	Crossing legs
Fistlike gestures	Pointing index finger
Karate chops	The fig leaf position

Reflective

Hand-to-face gestures	Head tilted
Stroking chin	Peering over glasses
Taking glasses off—cleaning	Putting earpiece of glasses in mouth
Pipe smoker gestures	Putting hand to bridge of nose

Suspicion

- Arms crossed
- Touching or rubbing nose
- Sideways glance
- Rubbing eyes

Openness and Cooperation

- Open hands
- Sitting on edge of chair
- Unbuttoned coat
- Upper body in sprinter's position
- Hand-to-face gestures
- Tilted head

Confidence

- Hands behind back
- Steepled hands
- Hands on lapels of coat

Insecurity and Nervousness

- Chewing pen or pencil
- Biting fingernails
- Elbow bent, closed gestures
- "Whew" sound
- Fidgeting in chair
- Poor eye contact
- Jingling money in pockets
- Perspiring, wringing hands
- Swaying
- Smacking lips
- Rubbing thumb over thumb
- Hands in pockets
- Clearing throat
- Picking or pinching flesh
- Hand covering mouth while speaking
- Tugging at pants while seated
- Tugging at ear
- Playing with hair
- Playing with the pointer, or marker
- Sighing

Frustration

- Short breaths
- Tightly clenched hands
- Pointing index finger
- Rubbing back of neck
- "Tsk" sound
- Fistlike gestures
- Rubbing hand through hair

To control your body language, all the points discussed in this chapter have to come together and work for you. How frustrating it must be for a speaker to deliver a speech with a grand, pressing purpose, only to have the delivery marred by nonverbal mannerisms that alienate the audience. Positive and powerful body language should support your verbal message and help you appear confident, caring, and in control in any situation—whether you are talking to a large audience, your boss, your colleagues, or your family.

Controlled body language that reinforces your strengths as a speaker carries your audience along with you to the point where it gets your message—loud, clear, and compelling. A good way to make that message even more compelling is to add a proper dose of humor, and Chapter 17 will show you how.

Professional Projects: Moving With Ease

1. Practice walking out with confidence at your next presentation. Do not rush and look around—take in the entire audience before your opening words.
2. Analyze your body language. Have a colleague videotape your next presentation. Carefully analyze your gestures, mannerisms, smile, posture, stride, and eye contact.

Chapter 17

Harness the Power of Humor

There are three things which are real—God, human folly, and laughter. The first two are beyond our comprehension, so we must do what we can with the third.

—John Fitzgerald Kennedy

I remember the first joke I ever heard. My father told it frequently, whenever my sister and I got particularly annoying:

> Three elderly women were sitting on the beach in Miami. Two were talking about their children. The first one said, "Ah, my son is a lawyer, makes $250,000 a year, drives a Jaguar, and sends me down here to enjoy the sun for one month every year, and he and my two grandchildren call me up every other week to see how I'm doing." The second woman said, "That's nice, but my son is a plastic surgeon, and makes $500,000 a year. He and his wife have twin Mercedes Benzes, and he sends me here for three months every year and my adoring grandchildren call me every week to see how I'm doing." They turned expectantly to the third woman, who said, "I'm sorry to disappoint you, but I have no children." In unison, the other women said, "What on Earth do you do for aggravation?"

This joke, which sticks so relentlessly in my mind, seems to me a model of technique. A joke is a short short story, one carefully propelled by skillful clues and deliberate miscues. Most jokes are designed to reach a sudden, surprising climax, one that triggers an explosion of laughter.

Why can humor be such an effective device for a public speaker? The most obvious reason is that a good story entertains your listeners. It makes them feel good, makes them more responsive to what you have to say, and convinces them that you're a "regular" person with a good sense of humor. Used with restraint, humor can also make your ideas more memorable, clarify your points, and persuade your listeners.

Restraint is the key word. Go for smiles and chuckles, not belly laughs. You want people to pay attention, not to roll in the aisles (unless, of course, you're a humorist and your main purpose is to entertain). The goal of a powerful speaker's humor is to keep the audience involved.

Make Your Point—Memorably

The best humor makes a point, and accomplished speakers favor illustrative humor over jokes that liven things up but serve no real purpose. The best way to use humor effectively is to change the PEP formula—Point, Example, Point—to the PHP formula—Point, Humorous example, Point.

Winston Churchill once advised the Prince of Wales: "Use a pile driver and hit the point once, and then come back and hit it again, and then hit it a third time with a mighty whack." Speakers who use humor to reinforce their points make members of the audience focus in an entertaining way, without making them feel like they are being hit over the head repeatedly with the same point. Whether they remember the joke is not important. What they do remember is the idea that the joke illustrated.

Use Laughter Early in Your Speech

Many speakers use humor at the beginning of their speech, because introductory humor can be a great attention getter. A funny opening sells both the speaker and the speech to the audience. Someone introducing Thomas Edison dwelled at length on the talking machine. When Edison was finally allowed to rise he said, "I thank the gentleman for his kind remarks, though I must insist upon a correction. God invented the talking machine; I invented the first one that can be shut off."

Humor, early in the speech, works well to establish a rapport, but only if it fits in well with your presentation. Too many speeches start out with humor for humor's sake, and the audience gets put off or sidetracked, instead of involved in your topic.

One of the best places to make a humorous point is in the title of your speech. Every title should make a point, and a little humor can make your audience anticipate the speech to come. You don't need to be matter-of-fact or dull when you can title a speech for telephone salespeople, "Why

Am I Still on Hold?" or a speech on public speaking, "If I'm the Speaker, Why Is the Audience Snoring?" One of my favorite titles was for a speech on tax deductions. The accountant who presented the information called his speech, "Everything You've Always Wanted to Know About Charitable Deductions, but Were Too Cheap to Ask." If your talk is basically serious and has no other humor, you should avoid starting with humor. You don't want to raise false expectations.

The beginning isn't the only time that humor can add punch (or a punch line) to your presentation. You can use it at the end of your presentation as well, to provide an uplifting moment after a heavy or grave subject matter, or to raise spirits when needed. You can inject humor in the middle of a presentation at a significant transition or a change of subject—this is like a fresh beginning in some ways. But do not make humor the subject; merely use it as garnish!

How to Ease Your Way Into Humor

If you're convinced that using humor is a good idea, but you're not sure how to do it, here are a few tips:

- Don't feel you have to be a stand-up comedian to use humor effectively. Anyone wanting to be perceived as the next Bill Cosby will be frustrated. Come to appreciate your own style rather than comparing yourself to professional comedians.
- Be adventurous and give humor a try. Try to add one new humorous story or example every time you speak.
- Learning to use humor is not difficult, and it's one investment on which you'll always get a great return. Once you have an understanding of humor, you'll feel more comfortable using it.
- Get your creative juices flowing by looking all around you for sources of humor. Politics, news, television shows, current movies, sports, best-selling books, the group you are speaking to, and even the people in it are all potential sources of topical humor.
- Read books on humor—anthologies, collections of jokes for speakers, and so on. See what people before you have used in various situations. Almost every industry has some sort of humorous slant, inside jokes, and vocabulary. I once addressed an insurance group as the "people who knew how to fill out a 5500 C form"—something everyone present could relate to.

- The better prepared you are, the more spontaneous you can be. The best way to learn how to come up with something funny on the spur of the moment is to learn how to do this *before* the moment occurs.
- If you have a strong comic sense, that's great. But realize that if you can tell a simple story—and I've never met anyone who couldn't—you will get warm chuckles of empathy and recognition, which are just as encouraging for the speaker as laughter.

Audiences Are Hungry for Humor

In my speech, "The Power of Questions," I ask the audience if they are asking enough questions. "For instance," I say, "do you willingly ask for directions when driving?" That gets a little titter. I follow that with, "Is that a sexist question?" That gets a bigger laugh. Let's face it, neither of those lines is a side-splitter. Yet I get a laugh every time. My theory is that people listen to so many boring speeches, they appreciate even the mildest humor. So even if you make the smallest effort to keep them entertained, you'll have them on your side from the start.

What to Do if You Don't Get a Laugh

Know when humor just isn't appropriate. Nothing falls flatter than a joke with a negative response or none at all. If you think a joke is appropriate and it just doesn't get a laugh, continue with the rest of your speech. I've also used this recovery when a joke I tell meets with silence: "Well, your chairperson shared that joke with me a little while ago; I guess you can see why she wanted to give it away." Once I heard a speaker add the following when a joke fell flat: "I'm like the famous second-story burglar—except I'm a second-story man. Let me try that one more time." I have also heard a speaker point out to an audience that studies have established a strong correlation between laughter and intelligence, and then pause and wait for the laughter.

Things Are Not Always What They Seem: Ad-libs Can Be Planned

According to Michael Iapoce in his book, *A Funny Thing Happened on the Way to the Boardroom*, there are many ad-libs you can have prepared in case you run into an unexpected situation. Practically anything you say will get a laugh when you appear to be ad-libbing.

The 3 Kinds of Humor

Platform speakers tend to use three kinds of humor: original stories from personal experience, borrowed humor, and adapted humor.

Original Stories from Your Personal Experience

Everyone can tell a story, and the stories about you and your foibles are the most humorous. Using humor from your own life brings the people in audience closer to you; they also see and appreciate your ability to poke fun at or make wry comments about yourself. Using stories from your life also diminishes the changes that the audience has heard the story before. You should always be looking for something to trigger a story. In your little black book for gathering speech material should be a humor section for ideas, stories, and incidents you might be able to use at a later date.

We all have so many stories from our lives, things that are also part of a "common experience." Poking fun at ourselves puts audiences at ease, and once you come up with this sort of angle on yourself, you can reuse whatever characteristic you've chosen. One very successful speaker always makes pointed comments about her height—she's well over 6 feet tall. I make fun of being short, and the peculiarities I possess as a native New Yorker. Obviously, effective speakers don't dwell on aspects of themselves, but they use those things deftly, to reveal themselves, to establish rapport, and then move on with an amused audience in tow.

Potential material is everywhere. Once I was looking for an original story I could use to make a point about how we feel powerless when we're out of control. Then I remembered an exchange my husband and I had the last time he drove me to the airport. We had had our usual "calm" discussion about his driving ability. He thinks it's absolutely "smashing"; I, on the other hand, am petrified he might be right. After jumping a divider to avoid hitting an oil truck in front of him, he explained to me calmly, while I tried to recover from what felt like a heart attack, that whenever he's in the vulnerable passenger seat, as I was, he feels the same anxiety I was feeling because he's not in control. Looking back, I realized I had a perfect example of a story that could be told humorously.

I have told this story many times, and it always gets a warm chuckle of recognition, because most people can empathize with the situation: They either are backseat drivers or have one in the family. Whatever story you choose to tell, be sure to practice it many times before your speech. Audiences are everywhere; I try out a lot of my new material with cab drivers.

Borrowed Humor

Secondary sources can add wit and authority to any presentation. When you borrow humor from others you often end up borrowing vivid style as well.

Where do you find borrowed humor? The most important source is the printed page—newspapers, magazines, and books. Humor anthologies, *Reader's Digest, Parade* magazine, and your local newspaper are all sources of humor that you can borrow and use in a variety of situations. But never borrow without giving credit, unless you have really changed and adapted an anecdote to fit your own life.

Adapted Humor

Many speakers remodel jokes to fit their situations. A good story can have many lives, and you can edit it to suit many different audiences. The "lightbulb" jokes that swept the country a few years ago are brief examples of how the punch line of the same joke can vary, depending on who is the target of the humor.

Rules for Selecting the Right Jokes

How do you know if an audience will find a joke funny? You don't. Tad Friend, in a *New Yorker* article (November 11, 2002) called "What's So Funny," writes: "How the brain processes humor remains a mystery. It's easy to make someone smile or cry by electronically stimulating a single region of the brain, but it's astonishingly difficult to make someone laugh." There is no guarantee that what you find funny will tickle your audience as well, but there are ways you can stack the odds in your favor.

Choose material that fits your talent and doesn't depend on your weaknesses. If you're not good at foreign accents, stay away from jokes that require one. Most good speakers don't try to act funny or perform stand-up comedy. They look for humor, not comedy. How can you tell the difference? When you read a story or a joke, ask yourself if it's funny on paper. Comedy often relies on a funny character, a funny accent, or some special delivery to put it across. Humor will be funny on paper.

Humor usually reads easily and is also easy to speak. You can use a comfortable rate of speech. It doesn't require a tongue-twisting or machine-gun delivery and doesn't contain a lot of dialogue. When you find a joke with a lot of alternating dialogue, study it carefully to make sure it's not too complex for a comfortable delivery.

Fit your material to your audience. Humor is very subjective, and the same jokes won't be funny to everyone. Some jokes are devices that let the audience laugh at someone. It's essential that you pick the right target. But the platform speaker has an advantage over the nightclub comic: facing an audience with which they share something in common—the same club, the same company, and so on. Shared characteristics make it easier to pick specific targets that your listeners are willing to laugh at.

Members of an audience enjoy laughing at people who they regard as superior in some way, from sweepstakes winners to the president of the United States. Bosses or authority figures are perfect targets, as are government officials and politicians—anyone who is in charge of things. People also like to laugh at anyone who disturbs their peace and self-esteem: in-laws, supervisors, neighbors, and competitors.

Although audiences also like to laugh at people they regard as inferior, a speaker can be haunted forever by a public insult that he or she thought was a good joke. If you choose to make fun of groups, do it subtly, as one Baptist minister did. Addressing an outdoor conference on a cloudy day, he said, "Well, the weatherman hasn't done us any big favors today. But this weather isn't bad.... It's certainly plenty good enough for Methodists."

There are two important targets to stay away from: sacred cows—people whose accomplishments or reputations make them immune to laughter—and the audience itself. People don't like to laugh at themselves, and audiences are not good sports.

Occasionally, you can get your listeners to laugh at themselves—if you include yourself in the joke. An investment counselor speaking to a group of doctors about stocks and bonds managed this opening: "It's such a pleasure to be able to talk to a bunch of doctors, for a change, without having to take off my clothes." Sometimes I try to really personalize a presentation by asking ahead of time for the names of three people I can gently pick on during my talk. Clear this beforehand to make sure that no one is offended.

The Best Target of All

You are the best target of your jokes. You not only entertain that way but also win all sorts of extra points with your audience. For one thing, who is going to resent your jokes? You're telling the audience you are a good sport. You win over those in your audience when you use yourself as the target of your jokes, and it's a distinct advantage to have them on your side.

Charlie Chaplin once said, "To truly laugh, you must be able to take your pain and play with it." Examples of self-deprecating humor are everywhere. Joan Rivers says she's such a bad housekeeper, she reports a burglary once a year, so the cops can come in and dust for fingerprints.

The more dignified and prestigious the speaker, the better self-mockery works. Some examples: "Here in the business word I'm Chairman of the Board. At home I'm chairman of the storm windows." Senator Stephen Douglas once called Abraham Lincoln a two-faced man; Lincoln said, "I leave it to my audience—if I had another face, do you think I would wear this one?"

Tricks of the Trade

A good storyteller uses a battery of devices to hold you rapt: a smile, a shrug, a cheerful nod, a significant pause, and a rush of energy toward the story's end. But even if you're not a born raconteur, you can carry off a story with confidence. Follow these rules when practicing telling a joke:

1. Don't announce that you are going to tell a joke, oversell the humor to come, or promise the audience "this one will have you rolling in the aisles." Better to take the audience by surprise.

2. Don't apologize even before you begin by saying "I'm not much of a comedienne" or "I'm not sure I can tell this right." It's hard for an audience to recover from a negative introduction like that—even if the joke to come is hilarious.

3. Identify only characters, characteristics, or facts that are going to be essential to the story. If you say, "Sarah Serene, Sunday school teacher," you are cuing your listeners to wait for the point at which her name and occupation pay off. And if you don't, your punch line may be lost in the audience's expectation of something else.

4. Make direct eye contact with your audience during the joke. Look from face to face, and shift your gaze from one part of the room to another. You should have practiced your jokes to the point where you are totally comfortable with them.

5. Have a good time while you're telling your joke—smile and put a bounce in your voice (and your step, if you move around). If you don't enjoy the story, why should your audience?

6. Speak at a brisk pace and eliminate all but the essential words. A good joke is edited down to its pure essence and doesn't distract the audience with superfluous detail.
7. Stick to simple words that move the story along.
8. Time your humor realistically. Don't tell a 3-minute joke in a 7-minute speech.
9. Don't rush the laughter—only inexperienced speakers do this. Enjoy it; don't wait until the laughs die out entirely before proceeding, but don't rush things by cutting them off either.
10. Practice telling the joke in different ways. Always evaluate your reception after a speech and think of ways to shape and improve your humor. Never let it get stale. Sometimes the addition or deletion of a single word makes all the difference.
11. Proceed undiverted to the climax.
12. Deliver a clear, exact punch line.

John F. Kennedy said we must do what we can with humor. Speakers who follow this advice—and who don't overdo the jokes—find humor to be a formidable ally.

Professional Projects: Simple Ways to Add Humor

1. Devise a humorous title for a presentation on the topic of avoiding computer viruses.
2. You have to present a speech on leadership. Develop two humorous items to include in the speech; use newspapers, magazines, or your own experience as your sources.
3. Create a humorous story about your most embarrassing moment, your first date, your worst blind date, or the foibles of your family.

Chapter 18

Stage Managing: Staying One Step Ahead of Murphy's Law

If anything can go wrong, it will, and at the worst possible moment.

—Murphy's Law

It's difficult enough to give a speech; on top of this you must be your own stage manager. Even if you have someone helping you out, you're the one who's ultimately in charge of your speaking situation: how the stage is set up, what equipment you might need, what props you use and where they're placed, etc.

Stage managing is speech insurance: You may not feel you need it, and you may be right; many speeches go smoothly, and all the unseen details fall into place. But that takes extraordinary luck, and any professional speaker knows not to rely on luck.

A prepared speaker controls the speaking environment; he or she *manages* the setting and the room as if it were an extension of the speech itself. And it is. Speakers depend on their environment to get their points across; if audiences are uncomfortable because the room is stifling, or if there aren't enough seats, the words may be brilliant, but the audience will be counting the minutes until departure time. Do your best to control the environment, and you will control how your audience will receive the words you've worked so hard to shape. Proper stage managing can take the place of a certain amount of talent or confidence. This chapter will touch on everything you should see to before approaching the podium.

It's All in the Details

The more public speaking I do, the more I realize how much can go wrong: On a bad day it's mind boggling and enough to prompt you to swear off speaking. As a result, proper stage managing seems overwhelming. There are endless details to worry about. Most speakers make the mistake of approaching this task in parts. For example, if they are using visual aids, they may check the equipment carefully but not focus on which seating arrangement is best for showing slides.

Even seasoned professionals can look bad if they have not checked out everything. A well-known media personality and musician was the featured speaker at a recent conference I attended. Although he should have known better, he broke almost every rule of persuasive speaking. His notes were on lightweight onionskin paper, and the lectern was not wide enough to hold both the read and unread sheets, so there was constant juggling and rattling. After he spoke, he brought his messy notes over to the piano with him, and laid them precariously on top. When he hit the climactic chord, the papers cascaded noisily to the floor. Needless to say, he lost the confidence of the audience. People were actually laughing. A few minutes of thought and planning could have saved the day.

Comprehensive stage managing is best, and that means having a sense of all that you need to check up on. This chapter spells out the many details speakers have to attend to; a thorough checklist is included at the end. Stage managing is an administrative responsibility. A polished, memorable performance, whether in the theater or at a convention, is only the tip of the iceberg. The final, smooth performance is visible, and all the preliminary effort is not, even though the memorable words would not be possible without the stage managing.

George Bernard Shaw once said, "People who get on in this world are the people who get up, look for the circumstances they want, and if they can't find them, make them." A well-managed room is one you set up in the way most advantageous to you.

Obviously you won't be able to control or to change all the circumstances that you face, but you can change many of the basic ones speakers often overlook. That's true even if you are part of a symposium or are sandwiched between other managers during a corporate presentation.

What to Watch out for

Here are the main concerns any speaker needs to address:

Seating and Room Size

Given the purpose of your presentation, what is the best seating arrangement for your audience? Don't be afraid to change the way the chairs were arranged by the person ahead of you; you can call a break to do the reshuffling. If you are specifying seating in advance, be quite clear about what you need.

Seating arrangements also depend on the degree of audience participation. If you are speaking before a large group and limiting participation to a question-and-answer period, *auditorium style,* with its rows facing the speaker, does nicely. *Classroom style* puts three to six people at a long table. *U-shaped arrangements* that let the audience fan out around the speaker are useful for speakers with small audiences who want to encourage participation. Audiences in U-shaped seating can see both the speaker and each other; the speaker doesn't seem too removed and can walk into the audience.

Find out the size of the room in advance. If you have to choose between one that is slightly too small and one that is slightly too large, choose the small room. Try to get people to sit toward the front, and have someone remove empty chairs from the back, keeping a few free for latecomers.

Speaking Order

Speaking order plays an important role. If you are one of several speakers on a program, find out when you're slotted to appear. If you can, try to get the opening spot. You'll be remembered more if you appear first or last, and first is probably best. If you're last you can sometimes suffer if other speakers run over their times and the audience becomes restless.

If you *are* speaking last, and you see the program is running behind schedule, start looking for ways to cut your speech. It is always better to give a speech that is a little short than one that is too long. (And your audience will certainly appreciate you for it.)

Speakers scheduled in the middle of a meeting should try to get a slot after a break, so they can use the time to set up. If you can't and have to appear with virtually no time to set up, try to keep your presentation simple; audiences that have to wait for 10 minutes or longer, while you fiddle, will lack in goodwill.

If you are the only speaker, you have the most flexibility and control possible. Arrive as early as you need to make sure everything is in place. An hour before is usually sufficient, especially in a hotel where the staff is used to last minute changes.

The Stage

Many speakers assume they must speak from an elevated area. Even though I'm barely more than 5 feet tall, I try not to use podiums or lecterns; the height of the former and the barrier created by the latter put distance between the speaker and the audience. Remember, power comes from being close to your audience, not removed from it. But if you are on a podium or behind a lectern, find out the height of the podium, whether the lectern has a light, and, if it does, what size bulb is needed (so you can bring a spare). Again, if you do have a choice, state your preference. I once arrived to give a presentation and found a huge raised platform—exactly what I did not want—simply because I had not specified that I wanted to speak from the floor.

Light and Sound

Although the lighting is often handled by someone else, you still need to think about what kind of lighting your presentation will demand and then to make sure the room can accommodate it. Try to have the brightest light available; avoid fluorescent lighting, which can be depressing.

If you are using slides, locate the controls for the room lights. Does the room have many large windows? Will the daylight make your slides too hard to see? Are shades available?

The microphone is another technical detail you confront as you prepare to speak. You should use a microphone whenever possible, unless you're speaking in a small room where amplified sound would be overwhelming. The microphone allows you to use all the nuances of your voice.

There are many varieties of microphones, and you either need to find out what type of microphone is available to you, or bring your own. Here are some options you may find:

- The stationary microphone, which is often attached to a lecturn or podium. This is the most limiting of all microphones, because it means you can't walk around the stage.
- The Standing Microphone: This is a the kind of microphone that is atop an adjustable pole; it is usually situated center stage. Make

sure you adjust it to the right height for you; the previous speaker may have adjusted it to match his or her height, and that could leave you stretching or crouching. The best position for most speakers is at chin height, about 6 inches away, which allows for a comfortable, conversational style. You can usually take the microphone off the stand and walk around with it, but you must be careful of the cord. It's easy to get it tangled around your feet or caught on furniture around the stage.

- The lavaliere or clip-on microphone: This is the best choice for speakers today. Some older models still have cords attached; avoid this if at all possible. A wireless clip on microphone is your best choice because it gives you freedom to move around the stage and even into the audience, should you so desire. But be vigilant about remembering to turn the microphone off when you go to the bathroom or when you're having a private conversation. Many professional speakers travel with their own cordless mike. It's a good choice, but women need to wear a business suit with strong pockets, because part of the apparatus has to be carried on you.

Once you begin to speak, don't touch the microphone. If it squeals you may be accidentally touching it; take your hand away and it should stop. If you get a loud popping sound from the mike, adjust it so that you are speaking into it at an angle instead of straight on.

Whatever mike you choose, practice with it first. If you plan on having mikes in the audiences, work with the person who will be circulating, and check out those mikes, too. Always try to get to the room ahead of time, so you can check the lighting, try out all the microphones, and test the sound levels.

Keeping Track of Time

It's important for you, and for your audience, that you keep track of how long you've been speaking. If you have half an hour for your speech, don't assume it's okay if you run over by 10 or 15 minutes, especially if you're speaking at a seminar or conference where there are many speakers, and sessions have been carefully planned and scheduled.

Bring a timer with you if possible, and place it somewhere you can see it but the audience can't. This is a much better option than a watch. You need to check your timing throughout your presentation; if you check your watch every few minutes, the audience will get the impression that you can't wait to get to the end. Some speakers like to take off the watch and use it as a timer, but because I have a colleague who left a brand new Rolex at his last speaking engagement, I don't recommend removing the watch from your wrist. You can always ask someone to signal when you have five minutes, and then one minute, left. Be sure that person is not forgetful.

Check Those Audiovisuals

Every piece of equipment comes with a series of things to be checked:

- ☑ Overall condition.
- ☑ Threading of film.
- ☑ Switch locations.
- ☑ Spare bulbs.
- ☑ Spare cords and cord length.
- ☑ Order of slides or transparencies.
- ☑ Condition and location of screen.
- ☑ Pens and spare sheets for overhead transparencies.

Props

Other visual aids have their own vital parts: chalk and erasers for the blackboard, the right number of handouts, and easel for the flip chart. Go through your presentation step by step ahead of time; note everything you need to have. A trash basket? This is usually missing from meeting rooms. Tape for putting a visual aid on the wall? Who will set up and remove props if you don't? Mentally pack the suitcase you need for a successful speech days in advance. Of course, your needs will vary depending on the type of presentation. Always be flexible and always have an alternate plan.

Spare Parts

The less you leave to chance, the better. Some speakers bring an extra set of their note cards in addition to the obligatory spare bulbs, extensions cords, markers, and so on. The ultimate spare part—one every speaker needs—is a backup plan, in case, after all your advance preparation, the slide projector still decides to die as you approach it.

Comfort

A comfortable audience is a receptive one. Professional speakers also attend to the following details, which make for a contented crowd:

- Setting water pitchers and glasses on tables.
- Knowing where the thermostat is and keeping the room at a comfortable temperature. A room will heat up as people fill it; keep the temperature a little on the cool side. Nothing encourages mass sleeping like an overheated room after lunch.
- Telling people where restrooms and phones are located. If yours is a more formal presentation, hopefully the introducer or the emcée will have shared all these important details.

Assistance

In many cases, hotel personnel will be assisting with your presentation. Carry at least three phone numbers of people to call in an emergency: your main hotel contact, a backup person, and a third person or office in case the first two aren't around when you suddenly need them.

Distractions

Few speakers walk into a room that is perfectly designed for their presentation; more often they encounter distractions that are a function of the room's frequent use. Things to watch out for include:

- *Dirty ashtrays and glasses.* Make sure items used by the group before you have been cleared away. This is true for meetings as well.
- *Visual aids left up on the walls.* I once arrived to give a presentation in a room where the previous speaker had covered the walls with vivid examples of direct mail campaigns. The schedule was tight, and I didn't have time to remove everything. Now I always find out who is speaking before me and whether they are using visual aids. With the permission of the person running the meeting, I try to schedule a short break to remove materials.
- *Loud neighbors.* If you are renting a room in a hotel, try to find out who will be in the rooms adjacent to yours. One corporate training session I gave was held in half of a room; a group telling jokes and laughing met in the other half, with only a room divider separating the two groups. It was very distracting. Of course, it's not always possible to control who meets where, but you can at least ask and make your preferences and needs known early on.

Communicate Your Wishes

I always send the organization sponsoring my speech a complete list of my requirements—audiovisual and otherwise. Be as specific as possible; if you think you are spelling out something too much, do it anyway. Never assume. I once asked for a room to be set up "classroom style," because I was conducting a training session. But when I arrived there were no tables for people to write on, even though I had specified they would be necessary. Luckily, I had arrived an hour early and was able to find some tables. Always allow yourself extra time to correct crisis situations.

Careful stage managing is vital before any important meeting or discussion you are involved in. For example, if you are meeting with your boss to discuss your department's strategy for the next year, you will want to time the meeting right and hold it in a place where interruptions and distractions will be minimal.

Check and double-check all details and make copies of the checklists at the end of this chapter. Don't let the details of stage managing throw you; in reality, knowing you have addressed them makes you appear much more professional and at ease—qualities that you can't help but communicate to your audience. And once you have managed your surroundings, you will be in a much better position to manage the questions your audience sends your way at the end of your presentation.

For those speakers who have to travel to make presentations, I have also have included a transportation checklist. The last checklist, the Postprogram Summary, will be of help to professional speakers and those of you who make frequent presentations to the public.

Professional Projects: Careful Stage Managing

1. Develop your own list of details to check and double-check before your next presentation.
2. The next time you attend a meeting, imagine you were stage managing it. What would you do differently? What can you learn from how the meeting is organized?

Stage Managing Checklist:

1. Do I have the phone number of an expert or immediately available helper? ______
2. Have I tested all the equipment and visual aids in advance? ______
3. Do I know where all switches are, such as, the switch for the overhead projector? ______
4. What materials do I need up front?

Water	______	Table	______
Lectern	______	Chair	______
Pointer	______	Markers	______
Microphone	______	Computer	______

5. Have I checked the requirement for:

Lighting	______	Heat	______
Air conditioning	______		

6. What equipment am I using? Is everything working and clean? Are there spare parts?

a. Projector

Lenses, attachments	______	Remote control	______
Stand	______	Location of screen	______
Size of screen	______		

b. Easels (flip charts)

Type	______	Clamp	______
Paper size	______		

c. Chalkboard

Size	______	Location	______
Erasers	______		

d. Video camera and monitor

Location	______	Operation instructions	______
Color	______	Tape size (1/2" or 3/4")	______

e. Microphone

Type ______

Location of audience microphone(s) ______

f. Computer

Outlet (if necessary) ______ Program disk (if necessary) ______

7. Is the room set up exactly as I need it and as I requested, for example, classroom, theater, U-shaped? ________
8. Do audience members have name cards (if necessary)? ________
9. Is my timer or timepiece clearly visible? ________
10. Have I accounted for breaks? ________
11. Do I know where the restrooms and telephones are? ________
12. Do I need to follow any special protocol? ________

Stage Managing: Personal Checklist

1. Do I have my timer? ________
2. Male and female: Am I zipped, polished? ________

   Female: Do I have an extra pair of stockings? ________
3. Do I have my

   Glasses? ________ Pointer? ________
4. Do I have all my accessories?

   Notes ________ Visuals ________

   Markers ________ Extra copy of my introduction________

   Extra items as necessary:

   Paper clips ________ Scotch tape ________

   Masking tape ________ Tape recorder or CD player ________

   Other: ____

   ____
5. Is there anything else I know I will need?

   ____

   ____

   ____

   ____

   ____

Transportation Checklist:

Travel date ____________________

Leave office ____________________

Means of travel ____________________

Time, flight number ____________________

Arrival time ____________________

Ground transportation ____________________

Pickup arrangements

Who ____________________

When ____________________

Where ____________________

Directions to hotel or meeting facility

____

____

Distance from airport (time and miles)

____

Shipment of materials and equipment

Method ____________________

Date shipped ____________________

Shipping contact ____________________

Date of arrival ____________________

Other ______________________________

____

____

Postprogram Checklist:

This form is especially helpful for speakers who give frequent presentations outside of their own organizations.

Date of program ____________________

Contact's name ____________________

Organization's name ____________________

Department or division name ____________________

Organization address:

- Street ____________________
- City ____________________
- State and Zip ____________________
- Phone Number ____________________
- E-mail address ____________________

Type of meeting ____________________

Title of my presentation ____________________

- Subtitle ____________________

Number of people at meeting ____________________

Type of people ____________________

Room setup ____________________

Quality of facility ____________________

Quality of equipment ____________________

Quality of ventilation, heat, air conditioning ____________________

Quality of lighting ____________________

Clothes I wore ____________________

Other comments ____________________

____

____

Things for me to do after the program

Read evaluation cards ____________

Pick follow-up materials ____________

Sort out my materials ____________

Clean out job folder ____________

Save two sets of handouts ____________

Send invoice if appropriate ____________

Write thank-yous to: ____________

____

Key people from the meeting:

Introduced by ____________

Other speakers ____________

VIPs ____________

____

____

Memorable people ____________

____

____

____

Miscellaneous information:

____

____

____

____

____

____

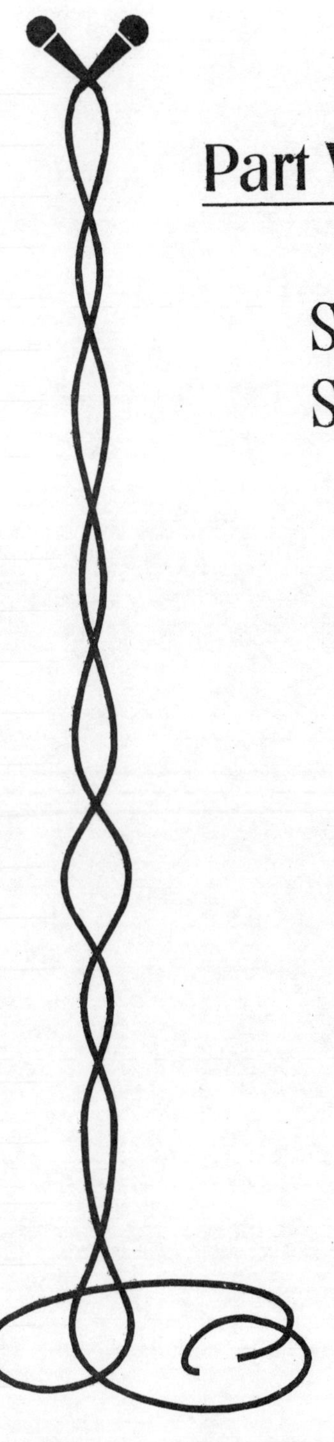

Part V

Special Speaking Situations

Chapter 19

How to Handle the Media Like a Pro

Consider the press. Treat it with tact and courtesy. It will accept much from you if you are clever enough to win it to your side.... Coax it, charm it, interest it, stimulate it, shock it now and then if you must, make it laugh, make it cry, but above all...never, never bore the living hell out of it.

—Noel Coward

Although a question-and-answer session with an audience inspires a fair share of fear, that fear pales when compared with the anxiety caused by facing the media. Yet business speakers are increasingly faced with—and increasingly surprised by—press interest in what they have to say. It's quite possible that the media may want to interview you after you have delivered an important speech. Take these interviews with the press or television reporters seriously. To make a good impression in an interview, you must prepare as carefully as you did when writing your speech.

Unless you're a celebrity, your personality is likely to have little to do with the media's interest. They're after a news story, and if you want to satisfy them *and* give a good impression, you have to give them that story. Because they are going to write or create a story no matter what you say, you should make it one you want told. And that's where the preparation comes in.

Know Your Objectives Ahead of Time

Before you meet the media, you must decide what your objectives are. What are the main points you want to get across to your interviewers? When you wake up in the morning and read the newspaper, exactly what kind of story about your topic or your company do you want to see?

No matter how well prepared you are, the story is not going to be told entirely from your perspective. And even if your wishes are granted, your story may be presented in a way that alters the public's perception of you in ways you had not planned. Here's an example: A visiting bishop came to a large city to deliver a speech at a banquet. Because he wanted to use some of the same stories at a meeting he was attending the next day, he asked reporters present at the banquet not to print the stories in their accounts of his talk. One newspaper reporter, commenting on the speech, concluded his article by writing: "and the bishop told a lot of stories that cannot be published."

What lesson can you learn from the bishop? If you're talking to the press, make sure you pick out the main points you want to get across and that the interviewer picks them up and isn't sidetracked by a colorful aspect of your talk that you are trying to downplay. For example, if you're being interviewed about a new product, decide ahead of time what product benefits you want to get across. Make those benefits crystal clear in your mind and focus on them throughout your interview.

Don't allow yourself to be sidetracked from your objectives, no matter how dogged the interviewer is. When I was on tour for my book *Smart Questions: The Essential Strategy for Successful Managers,* one interviewer kept harping on the fact that she thought questions were manipulative tools. Every time she brought up this point of view, I responded by saying, "Let me show you how you can use questions in a positive way..." and would proceed to give her examples. I never fell into the trap of explaining how questions could be manipulative: I kept going back to my objective—to show how questions could be used constructively.

Make sure your points will be of interest to the public at large. Newspapers, television, and radio are public forums, and reporters know their news stories must relate to current public interests.

Pre-interview Essentials

Preparation is even more important when facing an interview than it is when you have to give a speech. Although it's possible to toss off an impromptu speech that isn't half bad, it's extremely difficult to go into an interview unprepared and avoid saying something you will regret later. Here are some of the basics to which professional spokespeople always attend before going "live":

- Watch or listen to the shows on which you're going to appear. Get to know the interviewer's style, the length of the segments, and the mix of guests.

- Think of the questions you might face ahead of time—both supportive and antagonistic. Practice your answers to both types.
- Create a list of appropriate questions and send it, along with whatever supporting materials might be necessary, to the interviewer well ahead of time. And always bring an extra set with you. But be prepared for a session in which the interviewer has not read anything you sent. Not all interviewers will be well prepared, but you should always be.

Fine Points

Certain people make great guests and others just seem to fizzle. The successful ones tend to have learned well the following rules of interviewing:

1. Be enthusiastic. Bring some passion for your subject to the interview; you're there for a reason, and it's to communicate. Without some passion and conviction on your part, you'll bore the interviewer and the audience as well.
2. Don't give yes or no answers. This is one time when you should not be succinct. Answers need to be amplified for the sake of the interviewer, who is trying to create an interesting show or article. Also, you won't even begin to get your objective across if you depend on the interviewer to ask the perfect question; sometimes you have to lead him or her to that question by amplifying a point from a previous one.
3. Personalize your language; pretend you are speaking to a friend, and avoid technical words or other jargon. Make the interview an extended conversation, not a stiff recitation of facts.
4. Don't bring facts about your competitors or other extraneous information into the conversation. Most interviews are brief, and you should stick to your own story as best you can.
5. Use *you*. You are there because presumably you have information deemed to be of interest to the general public. Let them know it. Involve them by using the word *you* as often as possible.
6. If the interviewer makes an error or says something you feel is incorrect or not true, correct it right away so misconceptions don't linger. If you don't correct a misstatement or charge that you feel is untrue, it is tantamount to agreement, so state your disagreement pleasantly and immediately.

7. Always say *something,* no matter how tough the question. The infamous "No comment" is equivalent to a guilty plea.

8. Write a thank-you note afterward. It is a gracious touch most guests ignore and can pave the way to a return visit.

Three types of media interviews prevail today: television, radio, and print (newspapers and magazines). Each has fine points that go beyond the basics given above.

Techniques for Different Media

Television

Do's and Don'ts for Communicating With Confidence on Television

1. Get to the studio early to familiarize yourself and get comfortable.
2. You will usually be brought first to make-up (find out in advance if make-up will be supplied).
3. From make-up you will be escorted either to the "green room" (waiting room) or escorted directly onto the set.
4. During this period, drink room temperature water—not coffee—and do deep breathing.
5. When seated on the set, let the crew place your microphone on you.
6. Make any requests you have through the floor director who will relay questions or requests to the control room.
7. Ask the floor director where you should look. If you are the guest, you will probably focus solely on the interviewer.
8. Ask the floor director which is your close-up camera and what the other cameras are for.
9. Try to project warmth and animation in your face and in your tone.
10. Don't psyche yourself out by thinking of all those viewers.
11. Think of the studio interview as an engaging dialogue shared by one viewer at home.
12. You could be on camera at all times so watch what you do.
13. Try not to look at yourself in the monitor. It can destroy your concentration. Ask the floor director if the monitor can be turned away—out of your range of vision.

When the communication is at one location and you are at another location speaking to the television camera:

14. Look directly into the camera lens, not at the TV monitor or around the room.
15. Imagine that the camera lens is the eyes of the interviewer. Adopt a low-key, personable tone.
16. Keep looking into the lens even when other guests are speaking.
17. If there are other guests on the air, speak directly to them—not through the interviewer.
18. Speak as if you were both talking to each other in the same room—don't yell.
19. Animate your face to project a personable manner.
20. Try to project a relaxed informal "dialogue" tone.
21. Make sure the earpiece is snugly fitted. If it falls out, put it back in smoothly and continue.
22. Don't look away from the camera while the question is asked or another guest is commenting.
23. If you can't hear the question, politely ask that it be repeated.

Verbal and Non-verbal Communication for Television

Verbal communication:

- Pace yourself. Too fast or too slow will frustrate the viewers. Vary the pace to keep it interesting.
- Watch your inflection. Varying the emphasis you place on words helps to draw attention to key concepts.
- Don't be afraid to pause. Pausing before or after a key word emphasizes the importance of that word.
- Use a confident tone. Confidence is communicated through a relaxed, measured speaking style, with a friendly tone. Speak as if you are engaged in an animated, friendly dialogue.
- Choose your words carefully. Clear, everyday language is essential to understanding. Avoid jargon, bureaucratese, or a highly technical vocabulary. Don't bore the audience with run-on sentences.

- Keep your energy high. Ultimately it is the energy that you project about the subject that the viewers or listeners remember. Don't let the volume peter out at the end of sentences.
- Communicate to one person in the audience.
- Don't think of an impersonal "mass" audience.
- Communicate energy, warmth, and friendliness in word choice.
- Be polite but assertive.
- Keep sentences brief.
- Avoid "uh," "um," and "okay."

Focus on projecting that you are:	**Stay away from sounding:**
Modest	Smug, arrogant
Reasonable, open	Hostile, defensive
Relaxed, friendly	Uptight
Positive	Negative
Confident	Trying too hard to please

Non-verbal communication:

- An animated face connects your feelings with words; raise your eyebrows; open up your face.
- Project a balance between low-key thoughtfulness and energy for what you are saying.
- Communicate warmth through facial expression and through open body language.
- Maintain direct eye contact with the interviewer, but don't stare with a fixed gaze.
- Smile when appropriate.
- Don't distract with needless gestures.

Posture:

- Don't hunch your shoulders; sit on your jacket.
- Sit with your upper torso straight; don't lean to one side.
- Keep your feet either flat on the floor, or cross your legs at the knee—towards the interviewer, away from the camera.
- Rest your elbows lightly on the arms of your chair—don't lean on one arm or put one arm back.
- Don't tilt your head to one side—it communicates uncertainty or weakness—keep your head straight.

Dress and appearance for men:

- Avoid three piece suits. They look stuffy and overly formal.
- Don't wear black suits; they project a lack of trust.
- Avoid extremes of color, pattern, or style. Conservative styles in the median range of colors—greys and blues in particular—enhance your image. Navy blue is the most flattering color (except for men who are very fair or light-skinned; in that case, wear charcoal grey.)
- Stay away from printed, closely striped, or short-sleeved shirts.
- Wear either a white or pale-blue shirt.
- Wear a tie that has a strong color to it, such as burgundy, to reflect color in your face. Make sure the tie is straight and touches your belt buckle.
- If you wear a beard or mustache, make sure it is well-groomed and doesn't cover your upper lip. Because a beard or mustache restricts the range of facial expression, you will have to compensate even more with facial animation. If you are bald or have a receding hairline, you will need powder to avoid glare.

Dress and appearance for women:

- Extremes are out.
- Avoid short skirts, flashy outfits, and revealing necklines.
- Also avoid an overly severe or colorless outfit, which may project coldness.

- Strong colors project confidence: for example, royal blue, red (not too bright), emerald green and, these days, black is also fine.
- Wear a jacket and skirt/pant combination or a well-tailored dress. Avoid casual dresses.
- Keep jewelry to a minimum.
- Avoid pure white blouses (unless worn with a jacket) and closely patterned stripes and prints that can create havoc with the camera lens.
- Keep hair off your face.

Dress and appearance for everyone:

- Clothing can reinforce your message and tone and project self-confidence.
- If you must wear glasses, do so—preferably non-reflective lenses. If you need to wear glasses, avoid the half-frame style, or ones that block the view of your eyes.

Camera Smarts

- While it may be tempting to look at the camera, face the interviewer at all times.
- Things happen fast on TV; a half-hour on radio or an hour with a newspaper reporter becomes four minutes on the screen. Try to make your points as quickly as possible, and realize it's an inherently more superficial medium. Don't repeat the question; that only wastes time. Instead, clarify or restate it if you need to, then give a short concise reply.
- Be sure you get your main point across at least once, no matter how far afield the interviewer tries to lead you. After all, you are there to deliver your message. Be sure it gets out.
- You may be asked to deliver a short presentation on television (as opposed to participating in an interview). In that case, it's likely that you'll be reading your script from a TelePrompTer, the device used by TV talent (such as newscasters), which enables you to read a script while looking directly at the camera lens. In fact, newer models often display the text of the speech directly on the camera lens itself.

Here are some tips and techniques to follow if you find yourself reading from a TelePrompTer:

1. The text scrolls down as you read. Remember that you are in control of the speed. If you slow down, the TelePrompTer operator will slow down to match your pace, and if you speed up, he or she will do the same. Newer models are voice activated (as opposed to hand operated) and are programmed to stay ahead of the speaker, but even these models vary the speed according to your voice.

2. Picture someone you know standing behind the prompter. That way, even though you'll be looking directly into the camera, you can still "connect" with your audience.

3. Concentrate on the message, not the words. Pause normally, stop at periods, and practice vocal variation.

4. Take advantage of the fact that you have your script in front of you. Ask for the words you want to emphasize to be italicized or capitalized. If you are including foreign names or words that are difficult to pronounce, ask to have them spelled out phonetically. Stage directions (such as "pause" or "smile") can also be inserted into a TelePrompTer script.

5. It's okay to ad-lib—a bit. You can change words and short phrases with no problems. But don't go so far off the script that the TelePrompTer operator gets lost.

6. Practice, practice, practice. Read your presentation aloud over and over before you have to do it on camera. Ask the director for rehearsal time using the actual studio TelePrompTer (especially if you've never done it before). Practice gesturing and changing your facial expressions as you read. Don't be afraid to pause or move your eyes, head, shoulders, and hands. You want to look as natural as possible—as if you were telling a story, not reading a script.

We've all seen newscasts where the anchor stops talking in the middle of a sentence; it's easy to figure out that the TelePrompTer has stalled or stopped working. Always remember that you're dealing with technology—which means that it's wise to be prepared for any possibility. In 1999, President Clinton began to give his annual State of the Union address to Congress and to millions of television viewers by reading it off the TelePrompTer. As soon as he began, he realized that it was his 1998 State of the Union address that appeared before him.

Luckily, Clinton, quick-thinking and thoroughly prepared, kept right on talking. He ad-libbed the beginning of his address until a technician realized what was going on and corrected the situation. No one watching could tell that anything had gone wrong.

You, too, must be prepared for any technical difficulties that might arise—that means knowing your speech well enough that you could keep going no matter what might happen to the TelePrompTer.

Radio

- Because your voice has to carry a radio interview and, therefore, takes on an exaggerated importance, it's a good idea to practice answering your questions into a tape recorder with a friend serving as your interrogator. Play it back and listen to your voice objectively. Do you sound defensive? Are you speaking too fast to be heard clearly? Work on your flaws before airtime.
- Many radio interviews are now done by phone tie-ins. These interviews can be conducted with you in any location; you just call the station. Be sure to get as many alternate numbers as possible, in case the number you call is busy or not working. Find out in what order you should call the numbers.
- Try to get on a program that reaches the audience you are trying to reach. For example, if you want to reach a business audience, avoid midday programs, but because many people work at home, it's important to be flexible. Ask questions in advance to find out as much as possible about the audience.

Newspapers and Magazines

- Read the newspaper or magazine before the interview to get a feel for the editorial style and readership.
- Realize that there is no such thing as "off the record." Don't say anything you wouldn't want to see in print, and don't answer any questions you don't understand. Get the reporter to clarify first.
- Try to arrange an opportunity to meet the reporter beforehand to establish rapport.

How to Stay Cool Under Fire

In most situations, the press is satisfied to get the story you want to tell. Sometimes, however, speakers are controversial, and a press conference becomes an opportunity for reporters to open fire. Here are some proven ways to stand your ground if attacked by those in search of a lively story:

1. If your credibility is challenged, don't get shaky or defensive. Stick up for yourself and reiterate or reinforce your expertise and authority.

2. If an interviewer asks you potentially lethal questions, answer in a *positive* manner and defuse the situation. Recently the president of a new race track was challenged because he was presenting a race with a multimillion-dollar purse on the same day as the Preakness. The media were on him like flies, accusing him of using his wealth to ruin the gentlemanly tradition of the sport. The president was a clever and experienced media person. Instead of responding to the notion that he was destroying racing tradition, he talked about all the wonderful things his track was doing for racing and for the public.

   As any politician will tell you, reporters' questions aren't always traps; you can turn them into opportunities. You don't necessarily have to answer the question that was asked; you can turn the question around. You can even ignore it completely and talk about something else, though you should be prepared for attempts to get you back on track. Whatever you do, don't allow yourself to be baited by the questioner, and don't react by losing your temper: Displays of anger never look good the next day in the morning newspaper.

   Listen to the media pros being interviewed on "Nightline" or other "Meet the Press"-type shows. They respond momentarily to the question, then immediately go forward and talk about what *they* want to talk about.

3. If your interviewer says something that you don't agree with, don't let it go. Correct the impression right away, because silence signals your agreement.

For most people, a media interview is not treacherous. If you are clear about the points you want to get across, and make sure you have a direct way to say them, you'll be home free.

Professional Projects: Handle the Media like a Pro

1. You are the spokesperson for a food company that is in the news because it has been accused of adding unhealthy preservatives to its products. You are asked: "When will your company show more concern for the public and stop tampering with our food?" How will you answer this question?

2. Watch programs such as *Meet the Press*, *Nightline*, and *Crossfire*. Note two excellent examples of handling questions and two answers that could have been improved. Be sure to write out how you would have answered them.

Chapter 20

How to Be an Outstanding Audio- or Videoconference Leader

Electric communication will never be a substitute for the face of someone who with their soul encourages another person to be brave and true.

—Charles Dickens

Samuel Morse transmitted the first electrical telegraph message in 1844; however, he wasn't the first to try innovative ways to communicate over long distances. Records show that in the fourth century B.C., for example, messages were "transported" by a line of men shouting to each other and passing the message down the line. Smoke signals and mirrors reflecting the sunlight could also be considered early forms of sending messages over long distances to more than one person at a time.

Although the technology has advanced tremendously, the problem remains the same—finding ways to communicate with others who are located in different parts of the building, the town, or the world. Today, the solution often comes in the form of *teleconferencing*: the holding of a conference among people remote from one another by means of telecommunication devices (such as telephones, video cameras, and computer terminals).

Today, the need for long-distance communication is greater than ever. Because of the Internet and other advancements, more and more companies do business across the country and around the world, and the need to stay in touch with their own employees at distant locations, or with far-away customers and vendors is greater than ever. The threats of war around the world as well as economic hardships have forced many businesspeople to cut way back on their travel time and expenses. Fortunately, however, the tools used to make long-distance communication possible are improving constantly.

According to an article titled "Conference Call Volume Growing at Rapid Rate" by Rebecca Kumar in the *Bergen County Record* (September 12, 2002), teleconferencing has seen tremendous growth in recent years, with an increase of more than 40 percent in call volume since 1997—and that volume was expected to grow by another 50 percent in 2002.

Audioconferencing

Sometimes terms can be confusing. The term *teleconferencing* used to refer only to what is also called conference calling—when several people are able to speak to each other at the same time via telephone. Today, teleconferencing includes any medium that allows several people to communicate at once. In order to distinguish the media, this section is now being called *audioconferencing*, which means that there is no visual communication included.

The Important Differences Between Face-to-Face and Teleconferencing

In a perfect world, all meetings would be face-to-face. The whole point of communication is to make connections; it's much easier to connect with a live person than with a disembodied voice. There can be no eye contact over the telephone, and the eyes, as you know, are the windows to the soul. There's no better way to tell what a person is feeling than by looking into his or her eyes. When this is not possible, you have to rely on your listening skills to get as much information as you can from the other person's words, tone, and vocal inflections.

The Added Importance of Your Voice

We get visual clues from people all the time, and we give them as well, whether we know it or not. If those visual clues are not available (which is the case in audioconferencing), we have to rely solely on our voice to convey our meaning and messages to the other parties. In Chapter 8, we learned that how we look forms 55 percent of people's initial perceptions of each other. When that is taken away, we have to fill in that huge space using only how we sound and what we say.

Therefore, practicing the voice techniques in Chapter 8 is more important than ever. Practice your vocal variety and your diction. Tape record yourself, play it back, and make sure that you can understand every word clearly and distinctly. Leave voice messages for friends and family and ask them to evaluate your clarity and articulation.

Look for ways to be sure your voice is commanding. If you have a breathy voice, breathe more carefully (and from the diaphragm) so that your voice sounds firm and you're not breathing directly into the telephone or microphone. Watch the sounds that are easily distorted over the telephone, especially at the ends of words. For example, I have to be especially careful when telling people my name over the telephone, and put the emphasis in Leeds on the DS, so that it comes out LeeDZ. Otherwise people think I'm saying "Lees."

If you're leading a conference, you want to be sure that your voice is welcoming and warm. At the same time, it has to have authority. You want to use good articulation, and you want to sound sharp. You don't want to drop sounds—it's much more powerful to say "going to" than "gonna."

Practice building a stronger, more resonant, more authoritative voice because when you're on the phone, your voice is your entire image; it's the only perception people will have of you.

Distractions and How to Deal With Them

When you're doing a telephone conference call, there will always be distractions. People may be sitting at their desks sending and receiving e-mail while they're talking, they may be sending hand signals to officemates, they may even be wolfing down a Tai chicken wrap and a latté while they're participating in a teleconference. You have no control over those things.

There are also many different kinds of audioconferences. There are audioconferences between two or three people that are very much involved in an issue. Distractions are usually not a problem in this setting. There are audioconferences that are held weekly with staff members all over the world who have to keep in touch and give reports on what they're doing. Some people, who are not as interested in reports about A or B, may lose interest until it's their turn to make a report. Then there is the large audioconference (50 people or more), where people come and go as needed.

There are some things you can do to keep distractions to a minimum. Have an important person as one of your participants. That way people are anxious to be heard—to make an impression on the "boss." Let people know that their contributions are valuable. Call on individuals by name. Ask people to summarize from time to time so everyone can stay on track. One of the best ways is to make sure that only people who really need to be involved are taking part, and schedule people for when their areas of interest are going to be discussed. If people sense that you're making an effort to appreciate their time, they will be less distracted.

Techniques for Keeping People Involved

The best way to keep people involved is to ask interesting, engaging questions (this is a whole other subject that I covered thoroughly in my book *The 7 Powers of Questions*). Instead of asking, "What did you think about such and such?" ask, "Mary, what did you think about the relationship between A and B?" Ask specific questions of specific people. Then people will know that you're going to do that. Ask thought-provoking questions. For example, I recently took a trip to Cuba. Instead of simply asking people there, "What do you think about Cuba," I asked, "As Fidel Castro goes around this country, what do you think he feels are his biggest disappointments?" That's a question that got people to think. Try not to ask closed-ended questions that begin with *who, what, when*, and *where*.

How to Use the Equipment

If you are using the phone to communicate to a large number of people (or more than two, at least), then sound quality is the key. Conference calls on low-quality speakerphones can ruin an otherwise well-planned meeting. Communication will suffer because whole words and phrases will be "swallowed up" by the equipment, leaving listeners wondering what they've missed. And you must be sure that if you're calling among numerous locations, that all callers can hear each other clearly.

Whatever equipment you're using, contact the manufacturer or distributor. They have booklets or brochures on how to make the best use of the equipment. Many of them also have helpful materials on how to run a successful teleconference.

Tips for Leading an Audioconferencing Meeting

If you are asked to lead an audioconference meeting, you are responsible for making it both effective and efficient. Here are some tips to help you make that happen:

- Be ready early. The better you have prepared, the better the meeting will go.
- Start the meeting on time. Everyone's time is valuable. If people are late, they will catch up.
- Make sure your meeting has a clear, stated purpose.

- Communicate to the group all "ground rules" you have established. Can they interrupt with questions? If so, how should they do it? Will there be a question-and-answer session at the end of the presentation (or at the end of each, if there is more than one)?
- Briefly review the agenda at the beginning of the meeting.
- Set a time limit for each agenda item, and abide by your schedule. Let people know that a segment is ending by saying something like, "We have five minutes left, so we can take one more question on this topic...."
- Address issues that affect the total community—don't discuss anything that can be discussed outside of the conference call.
- Speak and act naturally.
- It's easy for people to get bored or distracted when they are on speakerphone. If there has been a long presentation or monologue, be sure to follow it with something that will reenergize the group. This is a good time for a question-and-answer session, or an activity that allows everyone to participate.
- Ask participants to identify themselves when speaking, even after you've introduced everyone. It can be difficult to identify people just by their voices, especially if the equipment is not quite up to par. Also, ask people not to use acronyms or jargon unless they're absolutely sure everyone listening will know what they mean.
- If the microphones are sensitive, let participants know that rustling papers or fidgeting in their seats will be distracting to other people. Don't expect everyone to sit completely still, but ask them to be aware of making unnecessary noise.
- Make sure that you are not focusing attention during the meeting on one site or person more than others.
- Summarize the meeting before ending.
- If appropriate, plan for the next meeting.
- End the meeting on time.
- Follow up the meeting with written notes or minutes by mail or e-mail, and send these to people who need the information, but could not attend the conference.

Many of these points apply to videoconferencing as well.

Questioning Techniques to Gain Involvement and Control Results (Audio- and Videoconferencing)

- Phrase your question clearly and concisely.
- Ask questions that require participants to draw on their own experience.
- Ask questions that encourage the participants to explain their own viewpoints.
- Direct questions and comments to specific individuals or locations.
- Word your question so it is clear whether it is intended for the whole group or for a specific participant.
- Try to begin your questions with *what, why,* and *how*. Or, use other, more descriptive words such as *list*, *prioritize*, *explain* or *describe*.
- Ask questions that cannot be answered in one word.

Questioning Techniques for Teleconference Success

There are many ways to use questions to keep your audioconference interesting, flowing, effective, and informative. Here are some of them:

To open a discussion	To keep discussion to the point
To bring out reactions to films and other media	To direct attention to another phase of the subject
To bring out opinions and attitudes	To uncover causes or relationships
To suggest an action, idea, or decision	To achieve a conclusion or agreement
To get information	To test ideas
To call attention to a point, an idea, a fact, a problem, or a situation	To bring out reactions to a point made by a conferee
To develop new ideas	To summarize or end a discussion

Keep Your Conference in Control

Here are some techniques for keeping the distractions to a minimum, and helping participants stay focused and on track:

Conferee talks too much	Interrupt tactfully with a question or summarizing statement. When the talker pauses, rephrase one of his or her statements and pass on to another question. Seat this participant in your "blind spot" right next to you and ignore some of his or her comments. Allow the group to cut this participant off, which they probably will if the talking persists.
Conferee doesn't participate	When asking a question, make eye contact with this participant. Phrase questions in a way to stimulate this particular conferee's participation. Ask a direct question of this conferee.
Conferees engage in side conversations	Stop talking and wait for side conversation to end. Stand behind the conferees who are talking. Change the seating arrangement. Ask a direct question of one of the talkers.
One conferee adamantly disagrees with the group on a particular point.	Let the group handle this participant. Change the subject. Have the participant summarize the position he or she disagrees with. If all else fails, talk with this participant after the conference.

Videoconferencing

At the 1969 World's Fair, one of the most popular exhibits was the AT&T Pavilion. That's because visitors could use what was then called the "Picturephone," an astounding invention that allowed you to simultaneously speak with and see someone who was using a Picturephone at the other side of the Fair. It was a glimpse into a future only the people at Bell Labs had imagined.

Today, of course, the ability to videoconference is being used by businesses every day around the world. Because the camera is tougher than an audience of thousands, it is essential for anyone utilizing the wonders of videoconferencing to develop the skills necessary to seem natural, confident, and authoritative—yet accessible. As you can see from watching politicians, this is not an easy task. However, there are ways to minimize the glitches and maximize the effectiveness of this growing meeting medium.

There are a variety of reasons for choosing videoconferencing:

- Holding meetings in companies with multiple locations.
- Holding meetings for various companies in multiple locations.
- Holding meetings for team projects, when team members are working independently.
- Holding annual board meetings.
- Introducing new employees in companies with multiple locations.
- Introducing new products to employees and/or customers in multiple locations.
- Training staff in multiple locations.

Videoconferencing versus Face-to-Face

Videoconference is more like an in-person meeting than audioconferencing because you can see people's faces, expressions, gestures, and movements. But there are still a number of differences, as you can see in the chart on page 231.

Seeing Is Believing: Visual Aids for Videoconferencing

Visual aids are ideal for television or video, to emphasize your message or to clarify important information. Some examples include:

- 35 mm slides (check the dimensions required with the producer).
- Videotaped illustrations (check for format requirements).
- Photographs: must have a matte or dull finish, should be mounted on a pastel-colored graphic card usually in a 4 x 3 ratio (width to height). Again, check with producer (if appropriate) for the right dimensions, or do a test-run in front of a camera.
- Flip charts.
- Poster-sized graphics.
- Maps/models/physical objects.

Videoconferencing versus Face-to-Face

Videoconferencing	Face-to-Face Meetings
You can easily hold meetings with people who are far away from the meeting site.	People who are far away will miss the meeting, or it will be costly to bring them to the site.
You can often accommodate more people by using a number of sites.	Meeting space may be limited.
There is much more set-up and preparation time needed.	Set-up is usually minimal.
Videoconferencing is never spontaneous.	A face-to-face meeting can be spur of the moment.
Distractions are more noticeable; people coming and going are more disruptive.	It's easier to "slip in" or out without causing distraction.
More technical glitches are likely to occur.	Unless special equipment is being used, no technology is involved.
In most cases, once the camera(s) is in place, it isn't moved, which means you are always in view.	You face less personal scrutiny.
People tend to behave differently on-camera.	People are more at ease in a familiar meeting situation.
You can only see what the camera is focused on.	You can see everything that's in the room.

Pointers for Preparing Presentation Materials:

- To be most effective, visual aids must be: clear, simple, and bold.
- The more directive you are in using your visual aids, the more the audience will follow you.
- Transitions before and after a visual aid must be interesting, varied, and directive.
- You must also vary your visual aids. Don't follow a pattern.
- Each visual is a mini-presentation and, as such, requires an opening and a closing.

How to Hold Visual Aids for the Camera

- If in the studio, find out in advance which will be your close-up camera.
- Don't reveal your aid until you are ready to use it; give the director a few seconds to react before moving the aid so that the camera operator can get into position to shoot it.
- Hold or place your aid so that it is clearly visible to the cameras. Hold it steady; tilt it slightly forward to avoid glare from the lights.
- If holding the aid, make sure it doesn't hide your face.
- Talk to the interviewer or camera, not to the aid.
- When you are finished with it, slowly put it aside so that the camera operators have time to react.
- Keep the graphic simple; viewers cannot easily grasp and assimilate too much detail in a short period of time.

Videoconferencing is an effective tool when you want to disseminate information to people who are at different locations, and you want them to see each other's faces and expressions. If you have to work as a long-distance team, it's easier to work together when you can attach names to faces. This is especially important during the early phases of a project, when it's important to build relationships. It's also effective when all team members need to see and discuss the same data, presentations, or visual images.

Professional Projects: Expand Your Meeting Possibilities

1. At the next audio- and videoconference you attend, make a list of the things that worked and the things that didn't.
2. Contact professional companies who run teleconferencing and try to get as many how-to's as you can from them on how to run an audioconference and/or a videoconference.
3. Check with people within your company who do these on a regular basis. Find out the best things you can do to run a better meeting and to be a better participant.

Chapter 21

How to Read a Speech or Script Effectively, No Matter Who Wrote It

It is not all books that are as dull as their readers.

—Henry David Thoreau

For every time you may have to give an actual speech, there may be dozens of business situations in which you have to *read* key words—your own script or prose inherited from others. Think of the following scenarios:

- Your boss gets a promotion to the London office and leaves you to give his presentation to the executive committee.
- You have a fine speech writer on staff and feel compelled to use her services.
- You must read accurate and precise instructions to your staff in a way that ensures everyone gets the right information simultaneously.
- Reading speeches is the established custom where you work, and trendsetters get nowhere in your company.
- You just don't fully accept all that I've said about the advantages of extemporaneous speaking and simply feel more confident reading from a script.

Think about all the boring speeches you have been forced to listen to. Most scripts that are read are boring, and because my premise is that, as a speaker, you should *never be boring*, I find it difficult to recommend reading a speech. But for all those times when you have to or want to read, there are steps you can take to make a speech that is read as lively, interesting, and entertaining as one that is given from notes—starting with a concerted effort not to be boring. The lively reading approach isn't easy, but mastering it is well worth the effort.

Reading Doesn't Mean Easy

Don't make the mistake of thinking that having every word in front of you means you can practice less. As an actress, I gave many performances without scripts, but I also performed in several productions from visible scripts—where we stood in front of lecterns and *read* our parts. We spent just as much time in rehearsal with productions when we read from scripts as we did with traditional productions when we memorized. It is just as hard to read and be outstanding as it is to memorize and shine.

If you are extraordinarily fortunate and have a speech writer who knows your style and is a good writer, you can get by with one or two practices. But that person is rare, and a talented speech writer is usually expensive too. In most cases, you will have to tinker with the words yourself.

How to Make the Written Word Interesting and Compelling—Even if It Isn't Yours

The material you need to read can take on many forms. For example, it can be a straight speech or a list of compiled data or regulations. It can be very straightforward and not prone to embellishment: You may have to read a 20-minute report to the board on safety rules and regulations in your department. Of all the techniques to make your information interesting, practice is the most important. Don't expect to just pick up the information, read it, and bowl over your audience. Reading aloud is a skill in itself.

Beyond sheer practice is belief. You must believe in your message and really want to communicate it to your group. Any audience will be turned off by a reluctant reader who can't wait to finish. At a recent function, I actually heard the speaker, a well-known entertainer say, "I'm going to read my few words and then we can get the hell out of here." Signs alerting your audience to the fact that you would rather be elsewhere don't have to be this overt; an inadvertent sigh can communicate the same message.

4 Easy-to-Follow Steps to Make Any Reading More Interesting

1. Familiarize Yourself With the Material

The purpose of what you are reading must be totally clear to you. Write out the purpose in simple sentences. This is essential if you are working with a professional writer, and he or she doesn't know your ultimate objective. Your purpose should be prominent in your subconscious and conscious thoughts at all times. It helps you to stay centered and gets your message through.

Read the material several times. Check pronunciations of any difficult words or names. The last name of Hana Mandlikova, the tennis player, could be pronounced MandLIK'ova or MandliKO'va. Which pronunciation is right? It's the job of the speaker to find out.

Separate the whole script into logical parts. Examine each part for its content and intention. Study the words that are being used and the feelings, attitudes, and emotions beneath them. If the writer has used an expression such as "deep in the city," is that meant to evoke feelings of excitement and activity, or gloom and despair?

Then pay attention to your verbal transitions. Are they clear? Are you going to add any physical transitions of your own? Does the script build toward a conclusion, and if so, how is this accomplished? What can you do to complement the writing? (For example, if you were using Julius Caesar's inspiring words, "I came, I saw, I conquered," you might want to raise your arm at the conclusion.)

To increase your overall familiarity with what you are reading, practice as much as you can. Work with the material at least a day before you give your talk, and try to allow a week to prepare in case there is additional information you need.

2. Personalize Your Message

Once you are familiar with the material, you will need to personalize it, both for yourself and your audience. Make it yours; eliminate any expressions or words that don't sound like you. If you are giving a motivational speech to your department and you seldom use words of more than three syllables, don't call people lackadaisical or ethereal (even if they are). Look for places where you can inject a personal story, or at least start with one. Very often, the best place to personalize will be at the beginning. But don't make the mistake of telling a warm personal story and then totally switching gears into an impersonal, read speech. A speech needs to be personalized throughout.

Try to use personal pronouns. Don't say "Employees will resist change if it is not presented in a favorable light." Make sure you say *your* employees or *our* employees or just *you* if you are addressing your employees directly. People listening to you read should also feel as if you are talking to them. Much of the power of our great presidents was directly related to their ability to personalize their speeches. Franklin Delano Roosevelt could personalize so well that on the eve of his death, a young soldier said, "I felt as if he knew me, and I felt as if he liked me." Professor Larry J. Sabato, a political science professor at the University of Virginia, once said about President Clinton, "He pierces you with his eyes. He knows your emotions. He cares about you. Personally. It may be totally phony, or it may not be, but he really seems to love you. It may be the rhetorical equivalent of cotton candy, but it works." You want your audience to feel the same way about you.

3. Wielding Emphasis Well

Using emphasis is the greatest antidote for relieving boredom. Emphasize your important points and de-emphasize what is not crucial. In doing so, you add variety, that delightful and necessary ingredient. Without vocal variety, no matter how potent your speech is on paper, it will sound dull and boring coming out of your mouth.

Great actors and speakers know the secrets of emphasis, which are easy to emulate. One is physical: You can easily make marks telling yourself what to emphasize right on your script; integrating them into your vocal delivery takes listening and practice. You need to become aware of your own vocal patterns so you can make changes in pitch, rhythm, and volume. It takes effort to be on; it's not easy to keep an audience with you. But the people in your audience will love you for not boring them. Even more important, they will listen and learn if you keep their attention. Remember that if you don't have their attention, you're not communicating.

How to Add Emphasis and Meaning to Your Script

First go through your script and mark all the thought/breath groups. These are the places where you'll need to pause to take a breath or to move on to a new idea. Don't follow the written punctuation. Here's an example of a paragraph with written punctuation followed by the same paragraph with thought/breath group punctuation.

No one can understand America with his brains. It is too big, too puzzling. It tempts, and it deceives. But many an illiterate immigrant has felt the true America in his pulse before he ever crossed the Atlantic. The descendant of the Pilgrims still remains ignorant of our national life if he does not respond to its glorious zest, its throbbing energy, its forward urge, its uncomprehending belief in the future, its sense of the fresh and mighty world just beyond today's horizon. Whitman's "Pioneers, O Pioneers" is one of the truest of American poems because it beats with the pulse of this onward movement, because it is full of this laughing and conquering fellowship and undefeated faith.

No one can understand America with his brains/ It is too big/ too puzzling/ It tempts/ and it deceives/ But many an illiterate immigrant has felt the true America in his pulse/ before he ever crossed the Atlantic/ The descendant of the Pilgrims still remains ignorant of our national life/ if he does not respond to its glorious zest/ its throbbing energy/its forward urge/ its uncomprehending belief in the future/ its sense of the fresh and mighty world just beyond today's horizon/ Whitman's "Pioneers, O Pioneers" is one of the truest of American poems/because it beats with the pulse of this onward movement/ because it is full of this laughing and conquering fellowship and undefeated faith/

(Reprinted from Bliss Perry, "The American Mind" in *First Principles of Speech Training*.)

Then underline the words that carry meaning, the ones that will require emphasis. You should also de-emphasize all the other words. Here is the same paragraph with word emphasis added:

<u>No one</u> can <u>understand America</u> with his <u>brains</u>/ It is <u>too big</u>/ <u>too puzzling</u>/ It <u>tempts</u>/ and it <u>deceives</u>/ But many an <u>illiterate immigrant</u> has <u>felt</u> the <u>true America</u> in his <u>pulses</u>/ before he ever <u>crossed</u> the <u>Atlantic</u>/ The <u>descendant</u> of the <u>Pilgrims still remains ignorant</u> of <u>our national life</u>/ if he does not <u>respond</u> to its <u>glorious zest</u>/ its <u>throbbing energy</u>/ its <u>forward urge</u>/ its <u>uncomprehending belief in the future</u>/ its sense of the <u>fresh and mighty world just beyond to-day's horizon</u>/ <u>Whitman's "Pioneers, O Pioneers"</u> is one of the <u>truest</u> of <u>American poems</u>/ because it <u>beats</u> with the <u>pulse</u> of this <u>onward movement</u>/ because it is <u>full</u> of this <u>laughing</u> and <u>conquering fellowship</u> and <u>undefeated faith</u>/

In Chapter 8, I discussed how to achieve variety through emphasis in detail, but let's summarize briefly here. To gain emphasis you can:

- Add force or volume.
- Change your pitch, intonation, and inflection.
- Vary your pace.
- Alter your rhythm.
- Vary your attitude.

Listening to yourself is so crucial because you actually hear yourself change tone, pitch, volume, and so on. Many scripts that are read are uninteresting because readers follow this pattern: They start a sentence on a high pitch with great volume and then fade out as the sentence concludes. Like any pattern, this speaking style soon becomes monotonous. But you can add variety by changing the pattern. Be unpredictable. Pause before an important point; take off your glasses and look around at your audience. Reduce your volume before an important point instead of getting louder. Allow your creativity to emerge. Be dramatic. You may feel silly, but you'll keep your audience with you. People resent being bored. Whatever you do to prevent monotony will be secretly—and overtly—appreciated.

4. Harmonize Your Script and Your Reading

Look at those in your audience and simply *talk* to them: An effective speech should be an extended conversation. Even a written speech must sound warm and caring when read. Use the word *you.* Look for ways to bring the members of your audience into your script, to get them to join in with you. Instead of phrases such as "this next point is…" try "as we move together into this next area…."

Connect with your audience through your words, gestures, eyes, and language. Even though you are behind a lectern and on a podium, find places in your script where you can reach out or emphasize a point with gestures. (You can write these places in the margins as reminders.) Direct yourself when to pause, look up, or connect with your eyes. One of the greatest dangers in reading a speech is that you lose eye contact. That's another reason why practice is so important. Don't allow your eyes to become glued to the script. Spend extra time looking at your audience.

With written language, you can refer back or reread. When you are making a speech, your audience doesn't have that luxury. All they have are your words, in the present moment.

- Because written language and conversational language are different, adopt a conversational style: Use contractions, shorter sentences, common words, and the active voice. You can see the difference yourself between the two passages below:
  - The essential element, noticeably absent, from this assembled congregation, was a cohesiveness, which immediately materialized when the charismatic leader approached the platform.
  - We weren't working together. We lacked a team spirit. But as soon as Tom took over, we joined forces and rallied behind him. And we're still with him.

  One style is dull and removed; the other is vivid simply because it describes actual people's actions.
- Use short, simple sentences. Break up compound sentences.
  - Wrong way: The test results, after elimination of spurious data and normalization of the remainder, with application of standard statistical techniques, were positive.
  - Better way: We took the test data, threw out the bad points, and normalized the rest. To analyze the results we used standard statistical methods. The results, we were delighted to see, were positive.
- Good spoken English may mean writing ungrammatically.
  - Wrong way: There were several days about which she could not account.
  - Better way: There were a few days she couldn't account for.
- Stay away from using jargon, "tech speak," or acronyms.
- Watch your word order.
  - If you say, "James Madison, Alexander Hamilton, George Washington, Thomas Jefferson, James Monroe, and Aaron Burr—they all wore wigs," you don't say why the names are being mentioned until the end. Better to put it up front.
- Make your transitions clear and easy to spot.
  - Example: The three main problems are: 1, 2, 3.

- Avoid generalities when using adjectives and adverbs. People can't imagine generalities.
  - Wrong way: He did a good job.
  - Better way: He submitted his work without one grammatical error.
- Plant your facts: Build suspense by using rhetorical questions.
  - Example: What are the real results of their innovative research?
- Don't be afraid to make powerful, single words statements or phrases such as, "Unbelievable!" or "Outstanding!"
- Always read your speech out loud, to "hear" it, as you're writing it. If you stumble over a long sentence or one that does not flow well, change it.
- Repeat, emphasize, capsulize, query.
  - Example: Let me say that again. We are spending 1 billion—'B' not 'M'—for foreign oil.
- Really relate to your audience and personalize your message.

Hints for Easier Reading

Because reading a script is a physical activity, here is a checklist of steps that make the physical process easier.

- Use heavy paper—no less than 20-pound; 60-pound is better.
- Be sure you have a lectern wide enough for sliding the pages to the other side as you read them. (Do not staple them together.)
- Be sure all the pages are numbered.
- Never end a page in the middle of a sentence or thought group.
- Use only one side of the page.
- Leave a wide margin for directions to yourself.
- Double- or triple-space.
- Use a typeface that is easy to read.
- Use a large, bold font.
- Mark your script for thought/breath groups and emphasis, and put in all your self-directions on the wide right-hand margins.

If you follow these steps and make sure you familiarize, personalize, emphasize, and harmonize, you will become one of those rare speakers who not only present well but make the written word come alive. And the next chapter will show you how to use that ability in meetings, those frequent forums where the written word plays such a key role.

Professional Projects: Become an Interesting Reader

1. Select an editorial from your local paper and prepare it for oral reading. Practice by recording your reading and then play it back and critique yourself.
2. Find a narrative poem and prepare it for oral reading; then follow the steps for the first project.
3. If you have children, choose a lively bedtime story such as Dr. Seuss's *Sam I Am*, and practice reading it with as much vocal variety as possible. Children love repetition, so practice until you are really good with it.

Chapter 22

Ongoing Advancement: Use Meetings to Polish Your Public-Speaking Skills

We are a meeting society—a world made up of small groups that come together to share information, plan, and solve problems.

—Michael Doyle and David Straus

People I train always ask me, "How can I practice my public speaking more, if I only give a speech every six months?" Like any skill, public speaking needs to be practiced often. The answer lies in meetings. Studies have shown that up to 80 percent of executives' time is spent in meetings. Yet many people ignore the chance that meetings present to hone their speaking skills and strengthen their reputations as powerful and persuasive speakers. Even small meetings provide important forums to the speaker who knows how to run one properly, because each meeting is an opportunity to give a speech—however brief.

Because most meetings in companies *aren't* well run, meetings have developed a bad reputation as time wasters. This poor impression just makes for more of an opportunity for you; if you can do a good job running meetings, you really stand out.

What to Do Before, During, and After

To run a meeting well, you have to attend to the business of the meeting—before, during, and after the meeting. The "before" stage involves the preparation any good speech demands: What are your objectives, your purpose? What results do you hope for? How does your audience affect those objectives? You'll also need to decide how long the meeting will be, who should be there, and where to hold it. Then send out an agenda you plan to stick to; an advance agenda shows that you are organized and capable and plan to lead the meeting well.

During the meeting, you use the tools of a speaker's trade: openings, transitions, closings. The meetings people complain about usually lack discipline; people talk on and on to a degree they would never think of if they were speaking before a large audience as part of a formal program. Treat your meeting audience with the same respect and formality you would give to a large audience: Plan ahead; be succinct, vivid, and knowledgeable.

Any successful meeting demands follow-up. Send out a post-meeting summary that includes the title of the meeting, the date, the name of the person who ran it, and who was present. Summarize conclusions the group reached, commitments people made, and what future action the group will take.

The 4 Major Types of Meetings

Most meetings fall into one of four categories:

1. Report- and information-oriented.
2. Decision-making and problem-solving.
3. Creative and brainstorming.
4. Training and skill-building.

You need to decide which type your meeting will be at the outset. If you can choose the format, consider what you want your audience to come away with. If you have to operate within a set format, you can still shape the outcome by knowing the ins and outs of each meeting type.

1. *Report- and Information-oriented.* This kind of meeting requires the most advance preparation. Leadership is very important, because these meetings easily become boring and tend to be filled with too much information. If more than one person will be speaking, try to review the other presentations beforehand, to see if they can be pared down. This preplanning will reflect well on you. Some conferences that overload on information use small discussion groups, which allow people time to digest and sort out information.

The most formally structured of the four types, report- and information-oriented meetings give you plenty of opportunity to shine with an interesting opening, a lively introduction for each speaker, smooth transitions that carry the theme throughout the meeting, and a strong conclusion. What you say and how you say it can leave people thinking they just attended a very well-constructed meeting.

If you are giving a report at one of these meetings rather than leading it, all the rules of persuasive presentations apply. Your report is your chance to stand out from the others. Make it a memorable one.

2. *Decision-making and Problem-solving.* These meetings are tricky because all their aspects demand a display of leadership from the chairperson: where people are sitting, who gets the floor, how long the meeting lasts, and so on. You should make succinct summaries of progress during the meeting. Don't let people get off track, and watch the time carefully.

   Stick to the agenda, which should be clear-cut so people can do valuable thinking beforehand. But don't make the agenda so clear-cut that people are locked into a decision before the meeting even begins. You don't want people coming in with their minds made up. I've experimented with my training sessions; when I ask people to make individual decisions before a meeting, they take twice as long to come up with a consensus as when they arrive with an open mind.

   Because this is a "results" meeting, the challenge to you is to move things along and get the group to make the decision or solve the problem. If you can reach that successful point, the results can reflect very well on you.

3. *Creative and Brainstorming.* These meetings tend to be free-flowing and minimize your leadership role. But you can still exercise leadership by establishing the right atmosphere—one in which people feel free to come up with new slogans, ways to save money, and so on. Try to be nonjudgmental. I once sat in on a meeting where management wanted to brainstorm ideas for cutting down on staff errors. The first person brave enough to speak up said the company used too many different temporary workers, who weren't familiar with procedures and never had a chance to learn how to do things right. The executive running the meeting cut the staff member off and said aloud, "You are absolutely wrong." Needless to say, no one else contributed after that.

   These meetings work best if everyone has a high level of energy. Avoid scheduling them after lunch.

4. *Training and Skill-building.* Really prepare for these meetings in advance. You'll need to make them long enough so that people will be able to really get involved. Save time for the practicing that the members of your audience will need to reinforce what they are learning.

   In these meetings, you're really more of a facilitator, so let other people get actively involved. Your audience will learn by doing, not by just viewing and listening. The more they are involved—the more questions they ask and the more give-and-take there is—the better your reputation will be. These gatherings also give you lots of room for powerful summing up; don't be afraid to shine as you impart your final words.

In all four types of meetings, keep the continued attention of your audience by bridging all your topics with transitions and by summarizing frequently.

Here are guidelines for running successful group meetings:

- Start on time.
- State the meeting's purpose clearly.
- Use a title and try to make it—and the meeting—interesting. (Call a presentation designed to train people how to fill out new forms "Don't Be Written Off, Write It Down" instead of "Filling Out This Year's Forms.")
- Be positive.
- Keep the meeting going; guide it along.
- Remain impartial if people start to bicker with each other. Stress cooperation, not conflict. But if real conflict erupts, bring it out into the open, especially during decision-making and problem-solving meetings.
- Don't play favorites.
- Use humor where you can.
- If someone starts to dominate, it's your responsibility to bring that person under control.
- Ask direct questions if you need to. Make them clear and non-threatening and record the answers.

- Have the person taking minutes read back what people have agreed to do. Discuss decisions, acknowledge differences or problems that surfaced, and sum up what will be done in the future. This person should be an active part of the group, not a secretary.
- Wind up with a motivational conclusion. This is your chance to show your style and to tie everything together. Don't let people run off early.
- End on time.

Fine-Tuning the One-on-One Meeting

A quick talk with a colleague or the boss may not seem like a "meeting," but you should treat it like one nonetheless. Even a telephone call puts demands on your ability to organize your thoughts and get your points across. No matter how brief, one-on-one meetings are chances to communicate, and to do it well. Here are some tips:

- Start on time.
- Have a clear purpose.
- Devise a good opening.
- Be positive.
- Listen well.
- Summarize your key points at the end.

How to Introduce Others With Aplomb

Meetings where someone is presenting a report and company get-togethers are just two of the many opportunities executives have to introduce people. These introductions are often done hastily, clumsily, and with something less than grace. Yet they are prime opportunities to make people take notice of your own public-speaking abilities.

Introductions have two purposes: to warm up the audience for the speaker and to help put the speaker at ease, both of which make the speaker's job easier. But the rewards of good introductions go both ways: They provide the introducer with a perfect opportunity to be gracious and charming—in public. Here's a checklist to consult before you deliver your next introduction.

☑ Find out what you need to know about the audience. If you can, ask the speaker beforehand what he or she feels would be the most pertinent things to pass on to this audience.

☑ Get all the background on the speaker you might need: special training, positions held, schooling, books or articles published, affiliations, anything particularly relevant to the group being addressed.

☑ Construct your introduction just like a miniature speech, complete with an introduction, body, transitions, and a conclusion.

☑ Stay away from a joke-filled introduction, unless the speaker is giving a humorous speech or you know the audience well.

☑ Try to memorize as much of the opening as you can; it sounds better than if you read it. You want to seem conversational, and reading instills a formality that you must displace.

☑ Pause long enough to get attention before you begin. Then speak with energy, enthusiasm, and warmth. Remember it's your job to get the audience *interested* in what's to come.

☑ Make sure you pronounce the speaker's name correctly.

☑ Insert a personal remark about how you met the speaker; it makes him or her seem more accessible to the audience.

☑ End with a nice touch like "Please join me in welcoming…"; lead the applause. Speakers welcome a warm beginning.

Because meetings are so important I have included a checklist and several forms at the end of this chapter.

Running a meeting automatically puts you in a position of power. Don't wait for the next big speech or presentation; use that position to practice your speaking skills on a weekly—even daily—basis. Recognize that "meetings" occur all the time, whether they are formal and planned or a chance encounter in the hallway. Taking advantage of all your chances to hone your speaking skills is the first step to being your own coach, which is the key to ongoing training and success as a speaker.

Meeting Checklist

You can use this checklist to evaluate yourself as a meeting leader and to review the presentations of others.

Preparation

1. Were the room and the seating appropriate? ____________
2. Were the visual aids supportive and visible? ____________
3. How were the handouts and support materials handled?
____
4. Was the agenda distributed in advance? ____________
5. Were the right people there? ____________
6. Were name cards, smoking sections, breaks, and so on accounted for?
____

Conducting the Meeting

1. Was the purpose clear? ____________
2. Did I or the facilitator keep the meeting on track?
____
3. Was I or the facilitator in control but not monopolizing?
____
4. How were interruptions and distractions handled?
____
5. Was maximum involvement and participation encouraged?
____
6. Was the group and the group process fully utilized?
____
7. Were all the key issues, key commitments, and future actions carefully noted by the recorder or minutes-taker?
____

8. Were the presentations interesting, pertinent, and well coordinated with the rest of the meeting?

___

9. Was the timing appropriate to the meeting priorities?

___

Concluding the Meeting

1. Were there sufficient summaries?

___

2. Did the minutes-taker have time to "feedback" key commitments?

___

3. If this was a decision-making meeting, was that decision made? Why or why not?

___

___

___

4. Were all future actions and assignments clear? ___
5. Was an evaluation form distributed? ___
6. Was there a clear summary and memorable closing remarks?

___

Follow-up

1. Thank you notes sent? ___
2. Any necessary follow-up or commitment? ___
3. Distribution of results (don't let meeting participants be the last to know). ___
4. Announcement of the next meeting. ___

Meeting Evaluation Form

You can get valuable feedback on your meeting style by asking attendees to fill out this form after a meeting.

I want to keep improving our meetings. Please take a moment to fill out this form. Thank you for your help.

1. Did you feel adequately prepared for the meeting?

___

2. Was the meeting run effectively?

___

3. Could the agenda have been improved?

___

4. Was the group process fully utilized?

___

5. Was the timing appropriate?

___

6. Were you clear on future actions and commitments?

___

7. On a scale of 1 to 10, how would you rate this meeting?

1	2	3	4	5	6	7	8	9	10
Poor			Fair			Good			Excellent

8. Any other suggestions for improvement?

___

___

___

___

___

Training Meeting Evaluation Form

1. The major benefits I derived from this session were:

___

___

___

2. The changes I'll make and actions I'll take as a result of this session are:

___

___

___

3. What is your overall evaluation of the workshop trainer?
   ( ) Excellent ( ) Good ( ) Satisfactory ( ) Unsatisfactory
4. What is your overall evaluation of this workshop?
   ( ) Excellent ( ) Good ( ) Satisfactory ( ) Unsatisfactory
5. What sections of this program were most helpful? Why?

___

___

___

6. What sections were least helpful? Why?

___

___

___

7. Other suggestions for program improvement.

___

___

Professional Projects: Improve Your Meetings

1. You have been asked to chair a year-end department progress meeting. List the steps you will take to assure a timely and interesting session.
2. You have to run a brainstorming session on how to solve the turn-over problem. Who would you have at such a session? Develop an agenda and a time table for such a meeting.
3. Observe for a month the meetings you attend paying attention to leadership, organization, participation, and all the plusses and minuses. Use this to improve the next meeting you run.
4. Lucky you! You have been chosen to introduce your company president at an employee-orientation program. Write out a powerful introduction, which will make both you and your president look good.

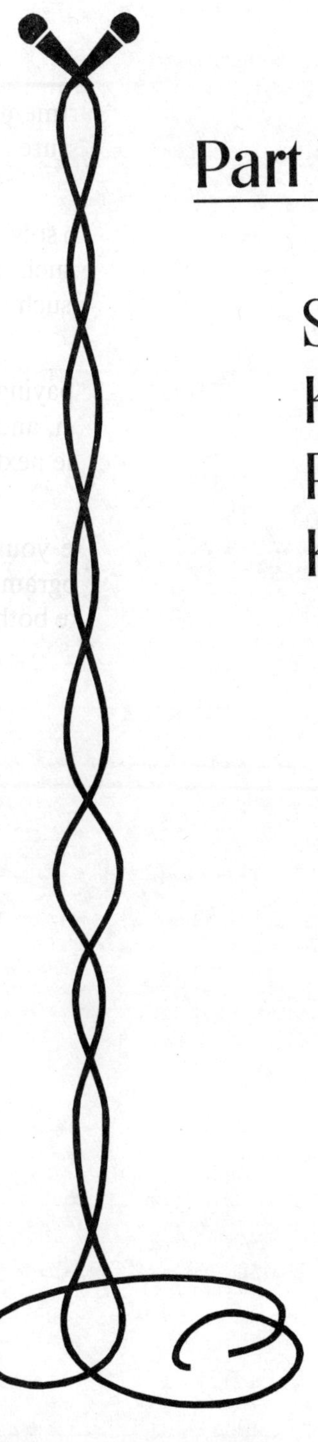

Part VI

Success Is Turning Knowledge Into Positive Action. Keep Growing!

Chapter 23

How to Be Your Own Coach

'0 wud some Pow'r the giftie gie us
To See ourselves as others see us!

—Robert Burns

This book has given you specific skills on how to become a more powerful speaker. But it would not be complete without some way to evaluate your progress, which can be a strangely neglected task. I once attended a gathering of professional speakers. A speech trainer was there to critique those who wanted to be evaluated. Only 10 percent of the speakers wanted this kind of feedback, and I was amazed. Getting criticism is the only way to improve as a speaker, and rarely do speakers get the chance to be judged objectively.

Professionals such as Luciano Pavarotti, Renee Flemming, the Williams Sisters, and Tiger Wood wouldn't dream of advancing through the ranks without some sort of equally professional coaching assistance. So they call upon coaches to give them the criticism and support that lead to improvement.

Speakers—especially the occasional corporate ones—have no such luxury and usually just rely on audience reaction before moving on to the next presentation, which may be months away. But speakers get power only through feedback and criticism. You can be an effective critic for yourself, but only if you go about it constructively. Getting reactions is the first step in becoming your own coach, and this chapter will show you how. You can use the forms at the end to evaluate yourself and others, or you can give other forms to people so that they can evaluate your performance.

Steps to Self-Criticism—Not Self-Destruction

In the public-speaking training courses I give, people look at video tapes of their speeches. When it comes time to give and get feedback, people are twice as hard on themselves as they are on other course members. When I ask what they think are their strengths and weaknesses, they list a long series of weaknesses right off the bat and are often unsure of any strengths.

For self-criticism to work, you have to be gentle with yourself and learn from feedback: If people say you were good, why not believe them? Coaching is criticism, but it is also developing your confidence by ignoring your insecurities and accepting positive comments. You have to be able to pick out critically the *good* things about your performance, the things you improved since the last speech. Be gentle with yourself and make self-evaluation an uplifting, not a negative, experience. Here are five ways to improve:

1. *Evaluate yourself.* Record every speech you give and evaluate each one for presentation style, content, voice, and speech. If you have access to a video camera, you can also assess your gestures, mannerisms, and overall body language. Make a list of the things you did well and improved since your last talk, and list the things you still want to work on. Remember: Be gentle, not brutal.

2. *Have someone else evaluate you.* It could be a colleague, your boss, or a friend, depending on the situation. Ask them to be honest and to write down their reactions as you speak. You can use this technique in rehearsals and in the actual presentation.

3. *Provide evaluation forms after each presentation.* Pay attention to the evaluations, even if they are painful. Listen to criticism, adapt if it's appropriate, and you will be stronger the next time around. Once I was told my visual aids did not look professional; after that I had them done by a graphic artist and felt much more confident about the entire presentation.

4. *Evaluate other speakers.* At the end of this chapter is a form listing some of the criteria speakers are judged by. Use it when you attend presentations, and you'll get a much better sense of where you, too, need improving. You'll also become more aware

of exactly where and how other speakers score points, because the form breaks down a speech into its parts and makes evaluation a step-by-step process.

5. *Practice speaking as often as possible.* You don't have to wait for corporate presentations to hone your skills. Join a local Toastmasters chapter; volunteer to give speeches to local groups. The only way to reap the benefits of your coaching and to continue to grow is through more speaking.

Keep practicing at meetings and get evaluations there too. At the end of each presentation, large or small, ask yourself what you did well and what you need to improve. Before any presentation, single out one or two things you are going to work on and improve, and note them on confidence cards. Practice those improvements over and over; it takes at least seven dry runs before these changes become a comfortable part of your delivery. Realize you only improve a little at a time—it does not happen all at once.

Self-Coaching Objectives

Coaching has one main objective—to improve every time you speak—that you achieve through a series of smaller ones:

- Get feedback from other people.
- Be kind to yourself. Try to be truly objective about your performance, which means finding both good and bad aspects.
- Don't concentrate only on your weaknesses; keep remembering your strengths.
- Don't try to solve too many problems at one time.
- Remember that there are major and minor problems. For example, holding a marker during an entire presentation is a minor problem and easily corrected, whereas having too much information in your presentation is major and may take some work to fix.
- Work to correct one delivery technique at a time. For example, if you say "uh" a lot, get rid of that habit before working on others.
- Content-related faults such as not having a good opening and lacking sufficient transitions can be worked on simultaneously.

- Practice self-evaluation regularly; realize it is an ongoing process.
- Don't expect too much.
- Prioritize the things that are really wrong.
- Focus on the six major speaking faults and the trouble spots.
- Don't ask your most critical colleagues to criticize you (nor your most supportive).
- Build yourself up by thinking of how much you have improved.
- *Listen* to that feedback; if someone compliments you, believe it. That's how self-confidence and positive energy develop.

The only way to grow as a speaker is to keep coaching yourself. Professionals use coaches because excellence is a process; you learn as you go along, you learn from your experience. Because coaching pinpoints both strengths and weaknesses, professional speakers find coaching to be a very important part of the path to speaking with power.

You learn powerful public speaking by having to speak; you also learn it by listening carefully to others. Use the form on page 259 when you hear people speak, and it will help you quickly pinpoint common strengths and weaknesses. You can also adapt it for use as a handout after you speak.

Professional Projects: Be Your Own Coach

1. Watch a well-known preacher on television and use a speaker evaluation form to critique him or her.
2. Make a five-minute motivational talk at your next staff meeting. Pass out evaluation forms after the presentation. Then make a list of the major and minor points you need to improve and an action plan for how you are going to do it.

Overall Speaker Evaluation Form

1. Overcoming the 6 Major Speaking Faults

a. Was the purpose clearly stated?

_____Yes _____Needs improvement _____No

b. How was the talk organized?
Was there a clear pattern of organization?

_____Yes _____Needs improvement _____No

c. Was there too much information to take in?

_____Yes _____Needs improvement _____No

d. Was there support for the information?

_____Yes _____Needs improvement _____No

What support was used? (for example, stories and analogies)

____

e. Was the voice clear, varied, and interesting?

_____Yes _____Needs improvement _____No

f. Did the presentation help solve the audience's problems and meet its needs?

_____Yes _____Needs improvement _____No

2. The Trouble Spots

A. The Opening

a. Did the speaker appear confident and purposeful before starting to speak?

_____Yes _____Needs improvement _____No

b. Did the speaker get the audience's attention?

_____Yes _____Needs improvement _____No

c. Did the speaker direct the audience?

_____Yes _____Needs improvement _____No

d. Did the speaker reveal himself or herself?

_____Yes _____Needs improvement _____No

B. Transitions

a. Were transitions clear?

_____Yes _____Needs improvement _____No

C. Conclusion

a. Did the speaker summarize key points?

____Yes ____Needs improvement ____No

b. Was the conclusion strong and memorable?

____Yes ____Needs improvement ____No

D. Handling Questions

a. Did the speaker maintain control?

____Yes ____Needs improvement ____No

E. Visual Aids and Handouts

a. Were materials well prepared?

____Yes ____Needs improvement ____No

b. Were they visible?

____Yes ____Needs improvement ____No

3. The Fine Points

A. Powerful and Persuasive Language

a. Did the speaker use colorful examples?

____Yes ____Needs improvement ____No

b. Did the speaker avoid passive language?

____Yes ____Needs improvement ____No

c. Did the speaker use benefit statements and emotional appeals to persuade?

____Yes ____Needs improvement ____No

B. Overall Body Language

a. Preparation: Did the speaker make good use of visual aids, notes, room setup, and so on?

____Yes ____Needs improvement ____No

b. Were the speaker's gestures, mannerisms, and posture confident?

____Yes ____Needs improvement ____No

c. Did the speaker smile and make eye contact with the audience?

____Yes ____Needs improvement ____No

4. Summary

A. Did the speaker accomplish his or her purpose?

_____Yes _______Needs improvement _____No

B. On a scale of 1 to 10, was the presentation helpful, interesting, and persuasive?

1	2	3	4	5	6	7	8	9	10
No				Somewhat					Yes

5. Suggestions for improvement

(If you're evaluating yourself after you speak, you could add the following questions.)

A. How pleased was I with this presentation?

1	2	3	4	5	6	7	8	9	10
Not very									Extremely

B. What can I do to improve?

6 Major Faults

1. ____________________
2. ____________________
3. ____________________
4. ____________________
5. ____________________
6. ____________________

Other Areas

1. ____________________
2. ____________________
3. ____________________
4. ____________________
5. ____________________
6. ____________________

You can use this form with a variety of audiences to get feedback about your presentations. Vary it according to the type of presentation.

Simple Evaluation Form

1. How valuable were the ideas, information, and concepts to you?

1	2	3	4	5	6	7	8	9	10
Not at all			Slightly			Fairly			Highly

2. How effective was my presentation of the material?

1	2	3	4	5	6	7	8	9	10
Not at all			Slightly			Fairly			Highly

3. Compared to other meetings covering a similar subject, how would you rate today's program?

1	2	3	4	5	6	7	8	9	10
Poor			Fair			Good			Excellent

4. What idea was most valuable to you?

____

____

____

____

____

5. How can I improve?

____

____

____

____

____

____

____

Chapter 24

Delivering With Style: Individually or With a Team

Charm is that extra quality that defies description.

—Alfred Lunt

Enthusiasm Can Make the Difference

My botany professor created my lifelong love of plants because he was so enthusiastic about his course from the very first day. On that first morning he literally jumped up and down and said, "Ladies and gentlemen, guess what I have here?" Shivering with excitement he handed us a leaf, saying, "It's a *living thing.*" That kind of attitude is contagious; the best speakers are genuinely excited about their topics. They have passion and aren't afraid to let it show. They know they cannot be neutral or apathetic if their mission is to persuade.

Whether you're facing an audience, active questioners, your boss, or a potential customer, it is your lot that your words tell only part of the story; the rest lies in *how* it's told. No matter how powerful or persuasive your words, your delivery will make or break your speech. Body language makes an initial impression with your audience, but it's your own style of delivery that will continue to shape those impressions. I still remember that botany professor because the way he presented plants was passionate. Look around and listen, and I think you will find it's the passionate speakers who are the powerful ones.

Use enthusiasm throughout your speech. With your opening words, show enthusiasm for both your subject and audience. Let your audience know you are delighted to talk with them.

Real enthusiasm leads to vivid presentations and makes your speech sound fresh to each audience, no matter how many times you have given it before. And you should take advantage of every actor's secret—make each time you speak about something seem like the first time.

Build on Your Strengths

Just as we all have unique ways of walking, dressing, and talking, we also have a unique style of delivery. Videotape yourself giving a speech and look at how you delivered it. Look at four television interviewers with essentially the same job and see the huge differences in style: Oprah Winfrey, Barbara Walters, Charlie Rose, and Larry King all shape their shows around their personal styles.

The key to developing that style is to recognize your strengths and build on them. If you are a born raconteur, incorporate stories in your speeches. If you keep your friends amused and attentive with lively facial expressions and hand gestures, don't cut them out of your speech. Too much style can be distracting, and some speakers mistake it for substance. I am a very animated speaker and am aware that I sometimes have to tone down my gestures and movements. But for the most part, if you take advantage of your own natural style, it will enhance your relationship with your audience.

Establish Rapport

Somewhere in the opening of your speech you need to let your audience know who you are; each speaker does this in a unique way. Your audience already knows something from your appearance and your introduction, but you need to let down your guard and reveal something personal about yourself. It can be in the form of an anecdote, a humorous story, and so on. But it should be something they can empathize with. President Kennedy once endeared himself to the French people when he made a speech in Paris after Mrs. Kennedy had made quite a splash there. He opened by saying, "I'm the gentleman who accompanied Mrs. Kennedy to Paris."

By putting your experience into the context of your talk, you personalize it; by sharing that experience with the members of your audience, you interest them in yourself, which will leave them that much more attuned to your words.

The 4 Delivery Methods

Even though your confidence will grow as you get through your speech, the way it is received will hinge on the method you use to deliver it. There are four ways to deliver a speech: you can memorize it, read it, give an impromptu speech, or speak extemporaneously.

Memorization

Delivering a word-for-word memorized speech is very difficult, and I don't advise novice speakers to do it. Memorizing puts too much pressure on you, and unless you're an exceptionally fine deliverer, it will *sound* memorized. In many companies, people who memorize are much touted and I agree that it is impressive. However, in the final analysis, if a speaker is interesting and thought provoking, the audience doesn't mind if notes are used.

Professional speakers often memorize their speeches because they frequently use the same speech. Yet for each new audience they make cuts or additions and customize the speech. Only a very fine speaker can do the same speech over and over again and make it seem fresh each time. So unless you're a very proficient actor—or a politician whose every word will be analyzed in tomorrow's newspaper—don't memorize your speech. "He who speaks as though he were reciting," said Quintilian, "forfeits the whole charm of what he has written."

Reading

Reading a written speech has similar pitfalls. Unless your writing is superb and you are a true prose stylist, it's usually a mistake to read verbatim. Presidents of the United States are a notable exception, and they tend to have very good writers on staff. I once heard Jane Trahey, a gifted writer, make a keynote speech. Even though she read the speech, she made it work because her remarkable writing carried her delivery.

But most of us are not exceptional writers, and we stiffen up when we have to write something down. Lacking the confidence professional writers exhibit in their prose style, our written language becomes stilted. Compare a newspaper headline to the way you would relay news to a friend. In conversation we tend to be more natural, using shorter sentences, more colorful language, contractions, and slang. We're more informal and more interesting, which is exactly how a speech should be.

Another drawback of reading is that when you read your speech, you're communicating with the text instead of the audience. Novice speakers often believe that if they memorize their speeches by reading them over and over word for word; they'll be able to stand up and deliver the speech verbatim without reading. It's a great idea, but it just doesn't work. And if you practice by reading from a written manuscript, you will become so wedded to the paper that it is virtually impossible to break away from it. You also lose most of the expressiveness and engaging body language that make speeches work in the first place.

If you feel that you must read your speech, begin by talking it into a tape recorder; then type it up and read from that script—at least then the speech will sound like spoken language.

Impromptu

If you've become known as a speaker, people will sometimes ask you to stand up and give a talk on the spur of the moment. (And this can happen no matter what your status as a speaker is.) Bishop Fulton Sheen went so far as to say, "I never resort to a prepared script. Anyone who does not have it in his head to do 30 minutes of impromptu talk is not entitled to be heard."

Once you've had some experience speaking, you'll probably do a good job with an impromptu speech. Its elements are a condensed version of any prepared speech of general communication. The more you plan, prepare, and polish your formal presentations, the more persuasive you will be in all your communications.

- Know your main point.
- Know your purpose.
- Work in a couple of good examples.
- Try for a memorable conclusion.
- Be sure to make a circle (relate your conclusion back to your opening). People always find this very impressive.

If you are known in a certain field, it's always a good idea to have a few brief speeches under your belt that you can deliver impromptu.

Extemporaneous

If you shouldn't memorize your speech, and you shouldn't read it, and you don't want to speak off the top of your head unless you absolutely have to, what *is* the best kind of delivery? The fourth kind—the extemporaneous speech—is the one that works best for almost every speaker. It means being very well prepared, but not having every word set. From the beginning, practice using notes, but never a typed script. The idea of practicing is not to memorize your speech but to become thoroughly familiar with the expression and flow of ideas. Don't memorize; familiarize. You can also prepare by reciting your speech into a tape recorder, using your outline to guide you. Again, talking keeps your speech fresh and helps you avoid the traps of written words.

Rehearse aloud, on your feet, at least six times. Edit your notes after each playback of the tape recorder. The more you rehearse, the better your speech will be. Those who knew Abraham Lincoln well said that the effectiveness of his talks was in direct proportion to the amount of time he spent rehearsing them aloud and on his feet.

Even when speaking extemporaneously, you should memorize certain key elements of your talk: the opening; the transition from the opening that takes you to your first point; every important transition that follows; and the conclusion.

Memorizing these parts ensures that you will know how to get from point to point and will help you maintain eye contact at all important moments.

When you speak extemporaneously, you incorporate techniques from the other kinds of deliveries. You end up committing certain parts to memory; you occasionally read a note from your note cards; and you may even throw in an off-the-cuff, impromptu remark. Because your delivery style is flexible, the speech can evolve, and you will still be comfortable and in control because you know where you're going and how you're going to get there.

"Confidence Cards": Aids to a Smooth Delivery

Many presentations with excellent content are less effective because the speaker uses notes that are either too skimpy or that contain every word of the speech. Properly used, note cards become what I call *confidence cards*: They add to a smooth delivery by helping speakers get from one main point to the next. Acting as cues, they contain your speech outline, notes to yourself, stories you will need to tell, key points and phrases, and reminders where to use your visual aids—anything and everything that will help you. And they save speakers from their greatest fear: forgetting what they're going to say next.

These cards—whether 3 x 5 inches or 4 x 6 inches—are easy to hold, don't rattle or shake the way larger papers do, and give an air of professionalism and preparation to your presentation. They are extensions of your own style because they only outline your speech, forcing you to talk in your own words. They also give you something to do with your hands. But you still need to practice your speech many times using the cards, or else you'll tend to go over the time limit or get off track.

Remember the following key points when using confidence cards:

- Write so that you can see your information easily.
- Make only short, key statements that will trigger your memory.
- Number the cards once you have them all, to protect yourself from chaos if they fall off the lectern. Also, you may need to shorten your speech at the last minute, and you can do that by simply removing a few cards. If they are numbered you know just where you are at all times. To help you make last-minute decisions, try color-coding the ones you can eliminate if you need to.
- Never read from the card. Glance at your notes and then speak to the audience to retain eye contact.
- Note on the cards which visual aids you are using to develop the key points.

As you go through your note cards in your practice sessions, write little reminders on them: where you want to pause, where you want to smile, and so on. If you have trouble remembering to look around at the whole audience, you can use a card to remind yourself to take in all sides of the room. Confidence cards make excellent security blankets; don't hesitate to rely on them.

Confidence cards don't have to be actual cards. I've seen excellent speakers use a clip board. When I'm conducting workshops, I use a loose-leaf notebook that holds my script, which I place on a table in front of me and refer to from time to time. The purpose is to give you that confident edge and to help keep you on track.

How to Tailor Your Presentation by Size and Space

Many of us speak in such varied situations—to the decision-maker, one-on-one, in a boardroom to a decision-making group, and often to large audiences at company or industry conferences. Every time you present to a large, medium, or small group, you must alter your presentation to fit the number of people and the size of the room. While most of the techniques and concepts covered in this book apply to all forms of speaking in all situations, there are some differences between speaking one-on-one, in a boardroom, and to thousands.

We'll take each speaking situation—large group, boardroom, and one-on-one, and analyze it in relation to preparation, stage managing, delivery, and visual aids.

Preparation

Recently, I observed a physician running a meeting for 25 in a hotel conference facility. Arriving late, she had little time to prepare or check the equipment or her microphone.

Microphones are very sensitive to other amplifiers. The attending audiovisual technician never turned off the wall speakers that were permanently positioned around the room. Every time she moved—even a step—the resulting feedback was so horrible that she was forced to speak without the mike. This diminished her impact vocally, for she had a soft breathy voice. She also appeared less prepared, thus further reducing her credibility.

Little things make a huge difference when presenting. Poor lighting, microphone feedback, and not having the proper markers can all have disastrous effects. All three speaking situations require preparation. The secret to being well prepared is to create a checklist, and ask questions.

- **Large Group:** If using a TelePrompTer, you must follow it word for word—no ad-libbing allowed. Have your speech completely written out in a conversational style. Use contractions and short sentences. When I work with my clients, this is the most difficult part. Most speechwriters, even experienced ones, write for the eye, not for the ear. Use strong language and repetition for effect, and have a clear, organized pattern. Utilize rhetorical questions to keep your audience's attention, such as, *"What are the real results of their innovative research?"* If you're not using a TelePrompTer, there's no need to write out the speech. But it must still be well prepared.

- **Boardroom:** Provide an intro for the meeting chairman (if there is one), so he or she can introduce you. You should always write your own introduction, but it is better to have someone else deliver it: your boss, the host, or a colleague. Find out how the meeting is structured. What's the protocol for questions? Who are the decision-makers and thought-leaders? Prepare for difficult questions and interruptions. Practice staying in control.

DIVISIONS FOR LONG NARROW ROOM

1 (LEFT BACK)	2 (RIGHT BACK)
3 (LEFT FRONT)	4 (RIGHT FRONT)

YOU

DIVISIONS FOR WIDE ROOM

1 (LEFT BACK)	2 (CENTER BACK)	3 (RIGHT BACK)
4 (LEFT FRONT)	5 (CENTER FRONT)	6 (RIGHT FRONT)

YOU

- **One-on-One:** Your success here depends on how well you organize your time, and the clarity and specificity of your purpose. I have found that people do not put much thought into preparing for less formal meetings, when they think they can "wing it."

Stage Managing

- **Large Group:** You usually have less control over the environment when you're speaking in front of a large group. Make friends with the meeting planner, and he or she will help you. Ask lots of questions. Will the room be or wide or long? If you have a choice, go for horizontal seating: The sight lines are better. Lighting is essential. Do everything you can to not dim the lights. Use your LCD (liquid crystal display), computer, and any visual aids you deem appropriate. If you have to turn off the lights, be sure you have them turned back on periodically. Go early to your presentation area, or get a floor plan. The more you know about the setting, the space, and the lighting, the better. Know what's going to happen before and after you speak. Will you be speaking behind a lectern or on a podium? You can never ask too many questions. Have tissues, water, and a timer handy. Do not look at your watch. Make a complete checklist.

- **Boardroom:** Find out in advance as many details as possible. Stand: you have greater impact. Find out how many people will be attending the presentation. Where will they be seated? Will they be wearing nametags? How will you identify each person there? Figure out the most beneficial placement for your visuals. Try to get an agenda, so you fully understand the flow of the meeting, and where you fit in.

- **One-on-One:** Find out the setting for your presentation. There are many possibilities: office, small conference room, or restaurant. Pick the most advantageous setting for you. If you will be in an office, it's a good idea to use a desk for visual aids. Try using a desktop flipchart. If you need an outlet, find out in advance where one is located. If you need to do any projecting, be sure you have a clear white surface available.

Delivery

- **Large Group:** Be aware of your visual impact; when communicating, your eyes are your most important feature. Use broad gestures and strong movement. Mentally divide room into sections, and try to cover all areas equally.

  Get comfortable with covering the space on the stage. A microphone gives you a wonderful opportunity to use both the highs and lows of your voice. However, watch the tendency to sigh. Look for places to add vocal emphasis, and vary your pace. Move more quickly over less important information.

- **Boardroom:** Curtail the broadness of your gestures to suit the smaller size of the room. If you don't have to cope with a large conference, a U is the best seating arrangement for this type of presentation, but be sure to "work the U." I recently observed a woman running her first major meeting and she had the room U shaped, but never really walked into the U. Using space efficiently is a wonderful way to demonstrate your confidence. If the seating setup is stationary, try to move around the large boardroom table, stopping to make key points. Establish eye contact with each person there. Use actual and rhetorical questions to help vary your voice.

- **One-on-One:** Eye contact must be constant while using normal conversational gestures. Ask the right questions and listen. Don't spend too much time in chitchat. If you are at a restaurant, you will probably chat longer. But don't wait for dessert to get to the real business! Watch annoying vocal patterns ("Uh," "Okay," "You know," "So," and "Ah"). Bad habits are often magnified in less formal settings.

Visual Aids

- **Large Room:** Always have an alternate plan. Pay great attention to lighting, especially if you will be using an LCD, or computer. When using a slide or LCD projector, the more powerful the projector, the stronger the image, and there is less need to lower the lights. Try to be in a room where the lights are controlled and there are none directly above the screen. This reduces the need for light dimming. Remember: Attention decreases in direct relation to intensity of light. Use bright colors, not dark, when creating visuals.

- **Boardroom:** Try for multimedia—use computer-driven slides, *plus* flipcharts. Many of my clients have become fans of my two-flipchart strategy. I advise them to use two, with at least 10 feet or more between them. Flipcharts are the least problematic, most interactive, and encourage horizontal (side-to-side) movement. Horizontal movement engenders more interest than vertical (forwards-and-backwards) movement.
- **One-on-One:** In this setting, brochures and product descriptions work best. Computers or desktop flipcharts can be used in an office. Be flexible and use what is available. If the office boasts a flip chart, use it!

Team Presentations

There may come a time when you are asked to give a presentation along with several other people. The advantages of team presentations are endless. Not only do you have the brains of many people, you also have the talents. If one person falls short in a certain area of presenting (for example, he isn't able to deliver financial reports and be engaging at the same time), another can pick up. But that doesn't lessen each individual's responsibility to the team. A team presentation can be quite a time commitment, but it is imperative to the success of the presentation that the group meet regularly to plan, to perfect, and to rehearse vigorously.

The Plan's the Thing

Without planning thoroughly, the group members will lose direction quickly. Without planning, it is easy to wind up with four separate presentations, rather than a strong cohesive one. When the group is together for planning, to ensure maximum success, these are the points to cover:

- **Purpose:** Each person should be made aware of what the purpose of the team presentation is. It is important that they all be clear on why they are working together. This goes for the people who are assisting you behind the scenes.
- **Delegate Roles:** The group should assess each member's abilities, strengths, weaknesses, and background. You would not want a serious, monotone speaker to deliver the rousing and memorable conclusion to

a speech—the more energetic member of the crew should do that. Nor do you want the creative team member to be delivering the technical information.

- **Define Individual Purposes:** Each team member, now assigned a different role, must develop (with the group) his purpose and how that contributes to the overall purpose.
- **Map out a Logical Agenda:** It is time to decide who goes when and for how long. Keep in mind your audience, the group's time restraints, which part is most important, and what needs to be said.
- **How to Cover Introductions**: You have a few options as to how you can introduce the speakers. You can introduce everyone at the beginning of the entire presentation. You can also wait until each presenter is about to begin his part of the presentation. Another way to handle the introductions is to briefly introduce everyone in the beginning and then do a more in-depth introduction as each person begins his section. Introducing a speaker right before his speech serves as a good transition between speakers. "Here is Joan Smith. She will enhance the points Jack made and how they apply specifically to your situation. She is highly qualified to do this because she was a client of ours and knows how this applies across the board" serves both as an introduction and a transition.
- **Visual Aids:** All visual aids—for each person on the team—should look like they were designed by the same person. It is not good to have catchy, computerized visual aids for one person and hand-drawn transparencies for another. Be consistent! The most efficient way to accomplish this is to have one person designing all of the visual aids. This person can be a support staff member, or a team member, who is especially deft at graphics. The visual aids should have the same design and purpose, as the material allows. Go back to the chapter on visual aids and revisit the key points to make visual aids an integral part of your presentation, and not a distraction.
- **How to Handle Questions and Interruptions:** It is good to maintain a consistency throughout the team presentation. A team captain should be in charge of the questioning procedure. He or she should field questions appropriately. Your group can accept questions all at once at the very end of the entire presentation, or they can accept questions at the end of each individual presentation. A more challenging

option is to handle questions as they arise at any time during the presentation—this may be more desirable for a proposal presentation. The same applies for handouts and other interruptions—decide beforehand when and how handouts will be distributed and by whom. Also, are the audience members free to come and go as they please (this may be unavoidable in a client's busy office), or would you rather have them not be getting up and down during the presentation?

➤ **Plan Transitions:** Transitions can make or break a team presentation. The audience should be able to easily follow the presentation and make the connection between each speaker and how he is contributing to the team presentation. Comfortable and impactive transitions ("or passing the baton") make the difference between a so-so presentation and an outstanding one.

Regular group meetings are a must and they should happen well in advance of the actual presentation. Team members should come to these meetings prepared to give a report on their progress; inform the group on the outline for their parts and any numbers, stories, or examples they will be using; and state how they will start and end their section. Each part should flow easily and subtly into the next section and these meetings are a time to make sure they do.

Rehearse, Run Through, and Repeat

Pay special attention to the introduction and conclusion of the entire presentation, not to mention the transitions between each section. Practice not only presenting the talk, but also the standing and moving. Team members don't want to be bumbling and bumping into one another—that looks neither professional nor organized. Audiences appreciate not only good verbal transitions, but they also appreciate good physical transitions. The more time you spend rearranging visual aids, microphones, and walking around one another, the more you are losing your audience's attention.

The entire team should be "onstage" throughout the presentation. Every team member must contribute and be supportive if the team is going to be a winner. If your listeners see one person presenting his section and his team members are off to the side not paying attention, they won't see this group as a team. Support each other at all times.

Test your presentation in front of an audience of coworkers and colleagues—as long as they are not connected in any way to your presentation. They must also be a group of people who will not feel hesitant about offering constructive criticism. Before you rehearse your presentation in front of them, ask them to write down their expectations of the talk. Afterwards, have an evaluation form on hand for them to fill out. Make sure it covers whether their expectations were met, what the purpose of the presentation was from their perspective, and if there was any information they thought was excessive or left out. Mention team members individually. Ask questions such as, "Were the transitions smooth?" "Did you understand who was speaking and why?" "Did you understand the purpose of each presentation?" Videotape the presentation and play it back, so you can see how you are perceived and fix any trouble spots.

The Telling Aspects of the Technical Details

It's not just what you say, it's what you *use* to say it. Visual aids are part of any speaker's style; if they aren't cohesive, they will reflect badly on you. Even the type of microphone you use will affect your delivery. A cordless mike allows you to move around and is a good choice for restless speakers. People whose delivery style is stationary will want a mike they can hold onto. As I said earlier, if you wish to appear intimate, speak softly and close to the mike. How you use the mike can become part of your unique style.

Be Powerful—Be Yourself

A good delivery does justice to the points you've gathered and to the speech you've worked hard to shape. It comes with practice and a lot of planning and from trusting and relying on your individual style. Don't try to adopt someone else's style; your audience will sense something is amiss, and you won't feel comfortable. If you be yourself and be enthusiastic, you will be well on your way to a stylish delivery, ready to use your delivery skills on a daily basis, starting with meetings.

Professional Projects: Focus on Style

1. If someone were to observe you, how would they define your style as a communicator?
2. What are your main strengths as a presenter?
3. Watch different newscasters for a week and define their delivery styles.

Chapter 25

Your Final Source of Speaking Power

Be skillful in speech, that you may be strong.

—Merikare (2135–2040 B.C.)

The most important thing I can tell you about how to become an outstanding public speaker is this: Analyze your strengths and build on them. If you're lively and energetic, build those qualities into your speech. If you feel comfortable asking questions or taking questions from the audience, do that. If you tend to be serious and more deadpan, look for humor or stories that emphasize or even make fun of that quality. If you're sincere, go with that.

In my speech training courses, if I give a group of 10 students an assignment to sell me a pencil, they'll come up with 10 entirely different solutions—that's how unique we all are. We're unique in the way we move, use gestures, interpret information, tell stories, and use timing. Even our voices differ. Give a speech and play it back, listening to how *you* sound. Analyze your strengths and look for ways to build on them: They make you unique. Use the PowerSpeak forms to evaluate other speakers and yourself; note what you need to work on.

Once you combine your strengths with an awareness of the six major speaking faults and a devotion to the credo "Never Be Boring," you are ready to build your career and your self-confidence through strong, effective communication.

This book has provided the basics for powerful speaking; the rest is up to you. Good luck, and enjoy yourself as you progress.

Bibliography

Adler, Bill. *The Robert F. Kennedy Wit.* New York: Berkley Publishing Group, 1968.

Allen, Woody. *Getting Even.* New York: Warner Books, 1972.

———. *Without Feathers.* New York: Warner Books, 1976.

———. *Side Effects.* New York: Ballantine Books, 1981.

Avery, Elizabeth, Jane Dorsey, and Vera A. Sickels. *First Principles of Speech Training.* New York: Appleton-Century-Crofts, Inc., 1928.

Bartlett, John. *Bartlett's Familiar Quotations.* 15th ed. Boston: Little, Brown & Co., 1980.

Boettinger, Henry M. *Moving Mountains or The Art of Letting Others See Things Your Way.* New York: Collier Books, 1969.

Boiler, Paul F., Jr. *Presidential Anecdotes.* New York: Penguin Books, 1982.

Brandreth, Gyles. *The Biggest Tongue Twister Book in the World.* New York: Sterling Publishing Co., Inc., 1981.

Braude, Jacob M. *Braude's Treasury of Wit & Humor.* Englewood Cliffs, N.J.: Prentice-Hall, Inc., 1964.

———. *Braude's Handbook of Stories for Toastmasters and Speakers.* Englewood Cliffs, N.J.: Prentice-Hall, Inc., 1975.

Bremer, Roslyn. *How to Write a Speech—One That Talks.* New York: Kodama Arts,1980.

Bristol, Claude M. *The Magic of Believing.* New York: Pocket Books, 1975.

Cohl, H. Aaron. *The Friars Club Encyclopaedia of Jokes: 2000 One-Liners, Straight Lines, Stories, Gags, Roasts, Ribs and Put Downs.* New York: Black Dog & Leventhal Publishing, 1997.

Copeland, Lewis and Lawrence W. Lamm, eds. *The World's Great Speeches.* New York: Dover Publications, 1973.

Crosbie, John S. *Crosbie's Dictionary of Riddles.* New York: Harmony Books, 1980.

Fast, Julius. *Body Language.* New York: Pocket Books, 1971.

Greene, Mel. *The Greatest Joke Book Ever.* New York: Avon Books, 1999.

Herman, Lewis, and Marguerite Shalett Herman. *Foreign Dialects.* New York: Theatre Arts Books, 1943.

———. *American Dialects.* New York: Theatre Arts Books, 1947.

Herndon, Booten, ed. *The Humor of J.F.K.* Greenwich, Conn.: Fawcett Gold Medal, 1964.

Humes, James C. *Podium Humor.* New York: Perennial Library, 1975.

———. *Speaker's Treasury of Anecdotes About the Famous.* New York: Barnes & Noble Books, 1985.

Jones, Daniel. *Everyman's English Pronouncing Dictionary.* Edited by A. C. Gimson. New York: E. P. Dutton & Co., Inc., 1967.

Kenyon, John S. and Thomas A. Knott. *A Pronouncing Dictionary of American English.* Springfield, Mass.: G. & C. Merriam Co., 1953.

Laird, Charlton. *The Miracle of Language.* New York: Fawcett Publications, Inc., 1957.

Lee, Irving. *The Language of Wisdom and Folly.* New York: Harper & Brothers, 1949.

Leeds, Dorothy. *Smart Questions: The Essential Strategy for Successful Managers.* New York: Berkley Publishing, 1987.

———.*The 7 Powers of Questions: Secrets to Successful Communication in Life and Work.* New York: Perigree Books, 2000.

Lewis, Norman. *Better English.* New York: Dell Publishing Co., Inc., 1961.

———.*Correct Spelling Made Easy.* New York: Dell Publishing Co., Inc., 1963.

Leiberman, Gerald F. *3,500 Good Jokes for Speakers.* Garden City, N.Y.: Doubleday & Co., Inc., 1975.

Livo, Norma J. and Sandra A. Rietz. *Storytelling: Process and Practice.* Littleton, Colo.: Libraries Unlimited, 1986.

Macauley, Thomas. *History of England: Volume I.* London: D. Appleton and Company, 1880.

Mager, N. H., S. K. Mager, and P. S. Mager, eds, and comps. *Power Writing, Power Speaking.* New York: William Morrow & Co., 1978.

Martin, Dick. *The Executive's Guide to Handling a Press Interview.* New York: Pilot Books, 1977.

Morris, Desmond. *The Naked Ape.* New York: Dell Publishing Co., Inc.

———. *Manwatching: A Field Guide to Human Behavior.* New York: Harry N. Abrams Publishers, 1977.

Morris, Desmond, Peter Collet, Peter Marsh, and Marie O'Shaugnessy. *Gestures.* Briarcliff Manor, N.Y.: Stein & Day, 1979.

Morris, John O. *Make Yourself Clear!* New York: McGraw-Hill, 1972.

Moscovitch, Rosalie. *What's In A Word.* Boston: Houghton Mifflin Co., 1985.

Nichols, William, ed. *The Best of Words to Live By.* New York: Essandess Special Editions, 1967.

Nierenberg, Gerald I., and Henry H. Calero. *How to Read a Person Like a Book.* New York: Pocket Books, 1971.

———.*Meta-Talk.* New York: Pocket Books, 1974.

Novak, William, and Moshe Waldoks. *The Big Book of Jewish Humor.* New York: Harper & Row Publishers, 1981.

Peale, Norman Vincent. *The Power of Positive Thinking.* Englewood Cliffs, N.J. : Prentice-Hall, Inc., 1952.

Pendleton, Winston K. *Complete Speaker's Galaxy of Funny Stories, Jokes and Anecdotes.* West Nyack. N.Y.: Parker Publishing Co., Inc., 1981.

Phillips, Leroy. *Peter Piper's Practical Principles of Plain and Perfect Pronunciation.* New York: Dover Publications, Inc., 1970.

Postman, Neil. *Crazy Talk, Stupid Talk.* New York: Delta Books, 1976.

Prochnow, Herbert V. *1,497 Jokes, Stories and Anecdotes: A Speaker's Handbook.* New York: Stealing Publishing Co., Inc., 1985.

Ritt, Thomas C., Jr. *Roget's International Thesaurus.* 4th ed. New York: Harper & Row Publishers, 1977.

Safran, Louis A. *2000 Insults for All Occasions.* New York: Pocket Books, 1967.

Seuss, Dr. *Green Eggs and Ham.* New York: Random House, Inc., 1960.

Skinner, Edith Warman. *Speak with Distinction.* New Brunswick, N.J., 1965.

Starr, Douglas P. *How to Handle Speechwriting Assignments.* New York: Pilot Books, 1978.

Strunk, William, Jr., and E. B. White. *The Elements of Style.* 2d ed. New York: Macmillan Publishing Co., Inc., 1972.

Weintraub, Joseph. The *Wit and Wisdom of Mae West.* New York: Perigree Books/G.P. Putnam's Sons, 1967.

Welsh, James J. *The Speech Writing Guide—Professional Techniques for Regular and Occasional Speakers.* New York: John Wiley & Sons, Inc., 1968.

White, E. B., and K. S. White, eds. *A Subtreasury of American Humor.* New York: Random House, Inc., 1941.

Wilde, Larry. *The Official Politician's Joke Book.* New York: Bantam Books, 1984.

Williams, Pat. *Winning One Liners: 3,400 Hilarious Laugh Lines to Tickle Your Funny Bone and Spice Up Your Speeches.* Deefield, Fla.: Heath Communications, 2002.

Zinsser, William. *On Writing Well.* 2d. ed. New York: Harper & Row Publishers, 1980.

Index

C

D

E

F

O

P

About the Author

As one of America's most sought-after speakers and workshop leaders, Dorothy Leeds counts among her clients numerous *Fortune* 500 companies including Pfizer, Verizon, IBM, and Conde Nast. She is listed in *Dun's Business Month* as one of the top 10 motivational speakers in the country.

Dorothy is the author of 12 books on communication, including *The 7 Powers of Questions: Secrets to Successful Communication in Work and in Life* and *Smart Questions: The Essential Strategy for Successful Managers.*

Because of her expertise and her experience as a media personality and film critic for MSNBC, she's a frequent guest on programs such as the *Nightly Business Report*, *Good Morning America*, and *Today*. She has written for and/or been featured in articles in such publications as the *New York Times,* the *Daily News*, *USA Today*, *Cosmopolitan*, *Forbes*, and *Business Week*.

Her pursuit of the perfect job has led to her five diverse careers, from Broadway actress to advertising executive to knitwear designer. A fitness and travel enthusiast, her commitment to positive energy in work and life has helped her overcome cancer and depression. She holds a Masters Degree from Columbia University and is listed in *Who's Who in the East*. Married, the mother of two children, and the grandmother of three, Dorothy is a native New Yorker and lives in Manhattan.

Speeches, Seminars and Presentations

"Success is turning knowledge into positive action."

Dorothy Leeds's presentations—delivered with dynamic, theatrical learning techniques—will help you manage better, communicate more effectively, and improve your image and relationships. More important, they will help you to take your knowledge and use it.

If you want to know more about Dorothy Leeds's speeches, seminars, and audiocassette programs, please call or write to:

Dorothy Leeds, President
Organizational Technologies Inc., Suite 10A
800 West End Avenue
New York, NY 10025
(212) 864-2424

If you would like an electronic adventure, visit Ms. Leeds's Website at *www.dorothyleeds.com* or e-mail her at dleeds@dorothyleeds.com.

Her keynote speeches include:

- "The Power of Questions: Lead, Succeed, and Activate Change"
- The PowerSpeak Show
- "Women's Unique Strengths"

Her new one-woman show, entertainment with heart, humor, and a message, is "Mom, I Almost Made It!"

Her workshops include:

- "PowerSpeak: The Complete Guide to Persuasive Public Speaking and Presenting"
- "Smart Questions + Smart Listening = Dialogue Selling"
- "Smart Questions: An Essential Strategy for Successful Managers"
- "How to be An Outstanding Facilitator"
- "PowerWriting: How to Get Your Message Across with Ease and Authority"
- "Assertiveness Training for Women in Business (and Men, Too!)"

Her audiocassette programs are:

- "Smart Questions: The Key to Sales Success" (six cassettes with comprehensive workbook) $95.00 for the set.
- "PowerSpeak: The Complete Guide to Persuasive Public Speaking and Presenting" (six cassettes with comprehensive workbook) $95.00 for the set.
- "Marketing Yourself: The Ultimate Job Seeker's Guide" (six cassettes with comprehensive workbook) $95.00 for the set.